Groundwaters 2021

AN ANNUAL PUBLICATION BY AMATEUR & PROFESSIONAL WRITERS FOR LOCAL READERS

"Bubbling up in our own good time"

D1733613

Editors & Publishing Team:

Pat Edwards, Managing Editor
Jennifer Chambers, Promotions &
Co-Editor

The Groundwaters Annual Anthology

FICTION • NON-FICTION • ESSAYS • POETRY • ARTWORK • PHOTOGRAPHY

Deadline Each Year - **AUGUST 15**

Submission Guidelines

1. Email submissions are preferred. Copy text into the body of an email message or MS-Word or Word-Perfect file attachments, please; no headers, footers, or in-line graphics. Use tabs or justifications---NOT indents or centering using the space bar. If you can't send it electronically, save your submission to a thumbdrive and mail. **Handwritten entries are strongly discouraged.**

2. Include a phone number or email address with each submission as well as an updated biography. You may use a pseudonym, but all work must be your own.

3. Submission limit is suggested for 2,500 words for each piece of prose, but that may be increased according to need. Submit as many stories and poems as you want, but we will use only those we can and others that pass review will be kept in a pending file for future issues.

4. Please be respectful to all. Read some of *Groundwaters'* back issues to understand its audience and speak from the heart. We try to maintain a family-friendly format and every age is welcome. Featured authors and artists are representative of all ages and levels of experience.

We do not accept political or religious opinion pieces that try to sway the readers to a particular point of view and/or assume that the reader agrees with those beliefs. We ask our submitters to limit the use of profanity to only what the story requires. No explicit sexual content or unnecessary violence will be accepted. The editors reserve the right to edit the unacceptable if it is to be published.

5. Include a short biography about yourself and your submission to share with our readers. Each contributor has a webpage on our site (http://www.groundwaterspublishing.com/Contributors.htm) and readers can learn more about you there. Please check your page often and send us the updates (i.e. new photos, biographies, newly-released books, awards, etc. as often as you wish.

6. Original works are protected under the copyright of *Groundwaters* Publishing, LLC, and may not be reproduced without permission of the author or artist. They remain the property of the author/artist. *Groundwaters* does not retain any rights to them.

7. Edits may be made in submitted material due to grammatical errors, punctuation, confusing phrasing and space constraints. Whenever possible, the material and content will not be altered and any major edits will be brought to the author's attention in advance of publication.

8. Contributing authors and poets will be offered a 40% discount from the retail price of all books they wish to purchase for their own use or to sell. Contact us for information on how to obtain your discount for on-line orders.

Contact info:

Email: contact@groundwaterspublishing.com or paedwards42@yahoo.com

Mail: *Groundwaters* Publishing, LLC

P.O. Box 50, Lorane, OR 97451
http://groundwaterspublishing.com

Greetings from Pat Edwards...

I begin this intro with some hesitation, because once I write out these next words, I will be committed.

This, the 7th annual edition of our *Groundwaters* anthology, will be my last. It's not that I don't love doing the intricate work involved in fitting so many pieces and elements together into one cohesive book—I do love it. But, I'm finding that it's taking me longer and with the advancing years, I find that I'm not able to design, multi-task or figure things out nearly as well as I used to. I don't want to reach that point where the quality of my work begins to noticeably ebb, because my goal has always been to showcase the work of our authors and poets in the best way possible.

I wish I could have used all of the stories and poems that were submitted this year, but 200 pages is as large as I wanted it to get. We have been able to give almost all of our contributors a place to shine. You'll find work from established, published authors to those who will be seeing their work in print for the very first time. That's the way all of us who have published *Groundwaters* have intended it to be. Each of the pieces included represent the voice of someone who deserves to be heard.

This year, because I've struggled a bit with fitting all of the pieces of this giant jigsaw puzzle together neatly, I have gone back into our archives and selected some of my favorite "just the right size" poems we published in the *Groundwaters* magazine to fill white spaces that remained. While I was searching for them, I pulled out a few others that I wanted to share with you, too. They are the ones showing the volume and issue numbers on them below the poets' bylines.

Anyone who knows me, knows how important "family" is to me. In the literary journals, we included a well-used children's section called "Bubbling Up." We haven't used it in the anthologies, but this year, Millie Graves and Jen Chambers sent us submissions and drawings from their young family members and they are included. You will find them alongside Millie's and Jen's pieces. And, while searching through our archives, I came across some poems that my daughter and granddaughter wrote while they were in high school... a long time ago... and they, too, are represented.

I have not included any of my stories or writings in this issue. For a number of years, I have written a weekly column for two local weekly newspapers, *The Fern Ridge-Tribune News and The Creswell Chronicle.* Those weekly columns are all I've had the time and energy to write this year. Rather than taking up space by including one or two of them in this anthology, I welcome you to browse them on my personal website at http://allthingslorane.com.

Thanks to all of you who have contributed your work through the years and those who have told me how much you enjoy reading *Groundwaters*. That's all of the payment I've ever needed or wanted for my labor of love, and the friendships I've made are dear to my heart.

God bless each of you with love.

Greetings from Jen Chambers...

I feel a bit like writing this introduction for 2021 is a repeat of my intro for 2020. We've all been inside. We're all trying to navigate a new way, a better way, maybe a permanent way. There is a big difference, though: this year, we're not afraid to hope.

Change is hard, even at the best of times. The last two years have been a series of changes, right? Or to put it more aptly, stops and starts, will we/won't we's, and how are we supposed to do this again... and again.

I feel like 2020 was where I lost my way a bit. I don't know about you, but because I have a rare autoimmune disease, every decision during the early pandemic was terrifying. It felt like every time I went outside, or my family left our home, we were in danger of bringing the virus back and making me very, very sick. I'm not afraid to tell you that it was more than a little dark. There were months when I only left the house to go for a walk or to the grocery store during the special early hours. It felt like it would never end.

My place is not to tell you what choice to make with your health. At the same time, I understand that not everyone has that privilege, or wants to make that choice. But for me, and I would guess a lot of people like me, getting the vaccine was like a life preserver thrown from a boat. I feel incredibly grateful to live in a place where I have access to the vaccines.

Let me tell you a story. When I was twelve, I started to show symptoms that made no sense. After we got home from the lake one day, I couldn't see; one eye was blood red and to me it looked like I was gazing out through a scab (sorry for the visual). I turned out to have a disease called Uveitis, an inflammation of the eye, generally common to the elderly and those with diabetes, neither of which fit me, and it was just the beginning of a series of odd symptoms. It turned out, over twenty years of searching, my disease is so rare that only six other people in the world have it, the researchers believe. I was able to manage my symptoms thanks to a special space-age medicine, and it has greatly improved my life.

The reason I'm telling you this is that this summer, I got to meet the man who made my medicine. This rock star doctor knew me! I'm "Patient X." For real. The best part is knowing that my problems made a difference for others. He has gone on to help hundreds of other patients and is working towards helping them with their diseases. I'm happy that I could be a tiny part of making things better for other people, part of a community searching for answers and a narrative to navigate life.

Our *Groundwaters* family is similar. We all have different talents, different needs, different perspectives. All of us work together to make this book each year and hope that what we make resonates with others. We never know when something we have done can help another person in some way. I'm so glad that you are all on this journey with us. Thank you for being part of our helping community.

Table of Contents

CARTOONS, PHOTOGRAPHY & ILLUSTRATIONS

I Dream a World

I dream a world
where our sisters
and brothers across
the globe can feel, can see,
can empathize with one another.

I dream a world

that has no starvation,
no famine,
and when these things exist
others can learn to go without
so that a belly can be full elsewhere,
a life can be saved, and cherished

I dream a world
where when immigrants
come knocking on the door,
folks can envision the horrors
they are escaping.
That we have some
sense of what these families
have seen and witnessed.
That we feel the collective
pain they have endured,
and empathize, as we would
want others to empathize
with our own trials
and traumas.

I dream a world
based on shared resources
not the capitalist society we live in
so clearly benefiting the few,
the one or two,
so brazenly
guilty
and full
at
the
tip top
of our
species.

I dream a world
where woman does not
pack lunch for a man

and man does not
pack lunch for a woman
but they both pack their
lunches for themselves.
I dream a world truly equal.

I dream a world
where children are more
familiar with flora and fauna,
than Belle and Madonna.

I dream a world
where when one falls,
others do not kick them.

I dream a world
where mothers and fathers
take responsibility for their
offspring…sheltering them
from harm, gore and neglect.

I dream a world
that cares for its ecosystems
by replenishing them
with buffalo,
and quenching them
by refusing to bottle
city water and then reselling it
to its people labelled
"Mountain Spring."

I dream a world
where big box store
demolition is a favorite
pastime.

I dream a world
where Native American
culture is restored and revered,
guiding us to walking lighter
on this shared earth.
I dream a world
that is a collective,
and land that is sacred,
and life that is equally as
valued as the next one.

I dream a world
where we are utilizing all
our senses, sight, sound,
taste, touch to understand
each other, to create harmony
together, in our own little tribes
and families, with a clear understanding
of the challenges facing those less fortunate
in, on the periphery, or outside our own circles.

I dream a world
where we understand
that every choice
has a butterfly effect.

I dream a world
where less
is enough.

I dream a world
where minimalism
is magnified.

I dream a world
(not an earth)
that is ours
for the taking
that is ours
for the making.

I dream of
a different
world...

   a better one

~ Terah Van Dusen

Agnostic

I am agnostic
I admit it...
at least when it is daylight and my
mind is clear from last night's meanderings
I know that I don't know
I doubt that I can ever know
a shrug of the shoulders
nothing more
what I can weigh and measure
I can know and replicate
what I see is what I see
what I hear and smell
I hear and smell
I know nothing of beginnings and endings
and whether there is a master hand
or a loving God at work
I don't know
I have no evidence
and what I see often prompts my skepticism
but just as I know nothing of any grand plan
at times this world can be wondrous enough
to warrant one
I suppose there could be one
maybe it is even likely there is one
but I don't know that
I can wonder all day long
I can experiment and test
I can reason and argue
I can attempt to prove or refute
until I become exhausted
But then the twilight begins to settle
the edges soften
and I can sink into my chair
to write my poems
leaving behind the rules of evidence
the keen observations of linearity
of cause and effect
and become a shadow pantheist
writing from my heart
of the wonder
of the mysteries
and of the smell of new puppies

~ Marv Himmel

How to Lighten Up

Laugh more.
Play.
Go barefoot.
Love a dog.   Smile.
Listen to quiet.   Find a friend.
Watch bugs.   Imagine something good.
Sit in the sunshine.   Be yourself.
                         Take a nap...

~ Judy Hays-Eberts
Groundwaters, Vol 5 Iss 4 (2009)

Miss Octavia
By Randall Luce

Miss Octavia McVay: her hands were the color of dark chocolate, her fingers spread across the cream-colored keys. Hands and keys together—they were beautiful.

When Elon came for his first lesson, the first thing Miss Octavia did, was she had Elon stretch his hands out on the keyboard. "You see that," she said. "You see how wide they span? You were born to play this instrument. Look at mine."

She splayed her fingers across the keys. Elon wanted to touch them, but he didn't dare. What he did do was to reach back to his back pocket where his book was, and place his fingers there.

They sat side-by-side on her piano bench. To their right was the one window in her parlor. She would play a chord and hold her hand still as the sound faded. Elon could study her hand, it's placement on the keys, with the sound of the music all around it. Then he would play the chord himself. The keys glowed in the warm light of the afternoon, copper turning to rose. He would look at her head silhouetted in the glowing light. Her graying hair smelled like rosemary, her breath like mint.

Through the years he practiced on her piano. She would be in the kitchen or out of the house when he did. And all the while, sitting there, he could feel the book in his back pocket. But sometimes he'd forget because the music filled him so.

One afternoon, while he was playing back his lesson, playing each note flawlessly and briskly, she put her hand on his and said, "That's fine, Elon, that's perfect. You know all the notes and you know how to play them. You can do that better than any student I've ever had. But now you need to take the next step. You're the first student I've had to take it and I doubt if I'll ever have another. Because, Elon, now you need to learn how to *play,* and that's like starting over.

"Here, close your eyes," she told him, "and place your fingers on the keys. Now, just play. Keep your eyes closed. You won't need any sheet music. You don't just want to play the notes; you want to play *this piano.* You'll learn its very span. And you'll learn to play *yourself.*

"But you must remember this—this will be your life-long calling. To play jazz—anything, but especially jazz—you need to tell a story, your story, and that story will never be finished until the day you die."

Miss Octavia put Elon's hands aside. "Here, listen to me."

Then she told him stories from her life. And while she talked, she played 'Go Tell It on the Mountain' that first time—softly, slowly at first; the notes and chords clothing her voice.

"Your listening now," she told him, "is as important as your exercises. If you listen to my story and my playing, you'll see how they fit together. You'll come to understand how to play beyond the notes. You're so young now, Elon, your story's just beginning. So, for now, you just listen to mine."

"When I was a child, we lived on a farm we owned free and clear. Not many colored folks can say that. My daddy and uncle inherited that land from my grandfather, and we had our own mules and harnesses and plows. We had our own gin—we even had our own school and church. Not many colored folks could ever say that. We were one of the first families, white or colored, to settle in here, and clear our land and farm it, and that was all on account of my grandfather, who was born a slave, over near the Pearl, here in Mississippi. But I'll tell you about him later.

"We didn't have a piano in our house. Nobody did. Our piano was in the church that was built by my uncle and my father out of the brush arbor built by my grandfather. One day, after the service, I walked up to that piano and pressed my finger on a key. Then four fingers. And then I laid my hand cross-ways on the keys. My mother shushed me away, but that was it for me. That sound. I could make that sound. I can remember exactly how long ago that was. I was five years old. Right that day, that very day, that was it for me.

"But it was years before I got up the gumption. Then, I'd sneak out at night, through my bedroom window after the family was asleep, and go into the church and light a candle and teach myself to play. They wouldn't have forbidden me to play. My Aunt Beulah—she was my father's brother's wife—she would've taught me. But, touching that key and hearing that sound—that touched my soul so deep—I didn't want anybody between me and that piano. I wanted to hear it by myself, alone, and explore its every sound. Of course, that was foolishness. I'd have learned so much faster from my Aunt Beulah. But that was just me! I was ignorant and head-strong, and I don't regret for a minute what I did—or how I did it. Every minute it took, it was all necessary for me.

"That first night, I was determined to come away with something. I played single notes, very slowly, and listened carefully to each one—how it would sound and fade. Then I tried to peck out a tune. Fits and starts, fits and starts, but I did it. And every note—oh, I savored every sound; 'Abide With Me,' that was the song." She played it now, with a stately rhythm.

"That night, I don't know how long it took me to learn it. I made myself play it four times in a row without a mistake before I let myself go back to bed.

"It got so I'd be playing almost every night. I'd pick out some notes 'til I found the ones that fit a song I knew. A song we sang in church. I didn't know any others.

"On the nights with moonlight, I'd open the shutters. I could see well enough in the moonlight. It was pearly gray. I'd listen to how the notes sounded in the night, with no day-time sounds and no singing, just the dark and the wind and the walls and the pews—they were high-backed benches of yellow polished wood, but everything was pewter dark in the moonlight. And the church smelled so new: the polish on the woodwork, the flowers beside the pulpit—and how the notes sounded in the night was new, and my hands were new, and the way I felt, so open and daring. Sometimes I shivered. There was no time passing. I had… no skin.

"It'd been some weeks then, when I turned and saw my Aunt Beulah sitting in the back pew. She came up to me. I was so scared.

"She said to me, 'You play good.'

"I nodded my head. 'Yes, ma'am.'

"She sat down beside me. 'Do you know "Wasn't That A Mighty Day"?'

"'No ma'am.'

"'Here, put your hands right here.' She placed my fingers on the keyboard, and put her fingers over mine.

"'Now sing it. Sing it softly.'"

Wasn't that a mighty day
When Jesus Christ was born?

"We sang it together—

Star shown in the East
Star shown in the East,
When Jesus Christ was born.

"She showed me every note and all the chords.

"She asked me, 'Could I teach you how to play?'

"I told her, 'Yes, ma'am.'

"I was trembling. But not just from fear—it was the importance of it all. She squeezed me tight.

"I looked up at her face, its color in the lamplight. I asked her, 'Could we come at night?'

"She looked at me a while and then she laughed—a smiling, light and pleasant laugh. She rubbed my head. 'Of course. Of course we can.'

"Six weeks later, Aunt Beulah had it all arranged. The whole family took their places in church, but instead of Aunt Beulah at the piano, I sat there. Nobody knew yet. I played the whole service. My father was beaming. Uncle Paul called it a miracle."

Elon's lessons were always in the afternoon, but after he grew, he remembered Miss Octavia in a small, warm light—a candle's flicker or a kerosene-lamp's glow. In his memories, everything took place at night. That was because her stories sounded like nighttime stories. He pictured her as a child, with her siblings and her parents, her aunt and uncle and cousins, all gathered in a circle tight, their dark faces shining in the lamplight's glow, all cheek bones and foreheads and noses, and behind them the

blackest night. Her Uncle Paul told them their family stories. And decades later, Miss Octavia sat at her piano and played, and told them in her turn.

She told him, "Elon, this is our Genesis story...

"My Grandfather McVay was a slave... Mister Joseph McVay. He and all the slaves, left the plantation when the Yankees came. They didn't tell their white folks. First light came and they were gone—right before the Yankees came. They hid in the woods until the Yankees left, and then they combed through the rubble and the ash—where the big house used to be. Some of the women snatched the missus' dresses and searched in vain for jewels. Most went straight for the kitchen. They and the men—the men searched the barn and stables—they couldn't find a thing. Those Yankees took almost everything. Not a morsel of food, not a plow or an animal was left.

"My grandfather found an empty box of fine-grained, polished wood, lined with red velvet. Its hinges were busted. The Yankees must've broken it. Grandfather knew about this box. He didn't care about what'd been inside. This box was what he'd hoped to find. So, he studied those hinges. He could fix this box. And he could carry it inside a coat without its showing. Because he'd never again—never—be a slave.

"Of course, he needed a coat to carry it in. He searched and finally found one, old and worn, but Grandfather didn't care. Then, like so many of the slaves, he searched out the Yankee army. He would've fought if he had the chance. Never again a slave. All the stories he told his children about his life, he never once told about his slave days. His life, he said, began the day he claimed that box.

"I never saw it. Sometimes I'd wonder, did it ever exist? But it was the emblem of our family. My grandfather came from Carthage, by the Pearl. After Freedom he rambled all over that country. There was no work he wouldn't do or couldn't do. After every job, when he was paid, he'd put his money in that box—whatever he could save. He preferred paper money—it muffled the sounds the coins made when he'd carry that box around. That box was his secret.

"And he was stubborn. Uncle Paul told us Grandfather never considered himself free, even after the war and Emancipation and him with his box, because he still had to work for white folks. But never for very long—they were short-term jobs, just what was necessary, and he'd be on his way.

"Everywhere he traveled he'd study the land. As soon as he saw what it was he'd be gone. He didn't stop until he came west into this Delta, into the wilderness. He came here looking for virgin land.

"Grandfather had married my grandmother by then—Miriam Massey McVay—and she gave him two boys: my Uncle Paul, the eldest, and my father, John Matthew McVay. They ran the family after Grandfather died. There was no decision made without their first discussing it. And their word was law. But it was Uncle Paul who told us our grandfather's stories, because he was the oldest, the highest, of the two. He'd tell these stories over and over because they were the stories that fit us into life. They explained the purpose of our living together as a family and why each of us had to take life head-on and hard, so that our family's work that came before us wouldn't be in vain.

"Grandfather owned a horse and a mule—that was pretty high up for our people back then. He'd saved the money for them in his box—and he and his family walked and rode this Delta country, traversing the Indian trails and fording the creeks, and they saw the devastation that the War had done. It was a wild country. Most of it had never been settled. But the parts the whites had settled, before the War—Mother Nature took all that back. My uncle told us about abandoned plantations, the fences down and rotting, the fields up in weeds and brush and saplings, the master's cabin with no door and the vines up through its floor-boards, and the smaller cabins, the kitchen and the slave shacks, made of smaller logs and daubed instead of chinked. There were no big, white-painted houses like in Vicksburg and Natchez—it was mostly cabins and shacks, vacant and wind-blown, but my grandfather never once bedded his family down there, in one of those places for a nighttime's shelter. There was no telling if this land was owned or not anymore, and no telling what would happen should any white man come across my family squatting there, where they didn't belong. So, they slept outside, and my grandfather stayed up half the night, and then my grandmother, and then my uncle and my father.

"But my grandfather took one liberty... he'd take a stick and whittle himself a point and drive it into the soil, as far as he could force it, to measure how deep the soil was and to see how black and sweet it was. And it was very sweet. He would taste it. My grandfather was an expert on that land. He knew just how far from the rivers that sweet loam ran before the soil turned to clay, and he finally found a spot with that sweet loam soil, but far enough from the river, and wooded so it'd have to be cleared—that way, no white man would likely want it—and that's where he bought his first piece of land, in 1882, and he was one of the first settlers, white or colored there—he was a true pioneer, a first father of that land.

"He bought it with the money he saved in that box. From the very beginning that's what it was for."

Miss Octavia chuckled. She stopped playing.

"He couldn't read or write. But he taught himself to count."

(To be continued on page 112...)

Saying Goodbye Takes a Lifetime

Saying goodbye takes a lifetime really.
People don't mention that... but it's true.
All the stages, the mental journeys from year to year.
The ebb and flow of it,
Pictures, the anniversaries, the memories.
Some days, we are strong enough to face them,
Some days... not.

Some days, the ache it brings is not welcome.
Other days, the familiar things do comfort us.
We gather them around us as a child does a favorite blanket.

I remember studying grief with a friend–
The stages, the transitions, the types of loss.
Each of us deciding which phase we were currently in.

We had experienced:
Anticipatory grief of terminal illness,
"Normal" grief after a death,
Ambiguous grief when you somehow lose someone who is still alive.
If you've been there with ambiguous grief, you get it.
If you haven't, you don't.
Consider dementia, addiction, MIA, mental illness, a child
Taken away and location unknown. This is the slippery slope
Of ambiguous grief.

Did it help us to discuss? Yes. But I didn't know the process would
Wind through my life, branching into new paths over time.
The loss morphs, changes shapes, reappears in unexpected places.
A sound, a scent, a time of day, when people-watching,
Or when written words sometimes pierce.
These twinges surprised me.

I write this for my friends who are on the path today.
Or on the path again.
I see you there.
You are not invisible, I see you.
I hear your laughter, and also your deep cries.
We don't ever walk away from it,
But we can walk *beside* each other.
And, if that helps, I'm here.

~ *Kathryn Fisher*

The Music Lesson
By William Crutchfield

There she was again, hurrying along the boulevard at mid-morning, wearing that distinctive long coat. It was jet black and utterly stylish, almost too much so for the middle of the morning. I had seen her several times before, in nearly the same locale, always with the long black coat, and always with the finely tailored Italian boots accenting her long lithe frame. I couldn't refrain from watching her as she made her way slowly down the sidewalk. She struck me as out of place here in the business district—more like she belonged on a Gucci runway or a Louis Vuitton photo shoot. Too much glamour for this early in the day, especially here, I thought. Her long auburn hair was spun into a single long braid—a French Weave I think they are called.

She wore sensible, horned-rim glasses; the tortoise-shell color frames highlighting her attractive features, but also suggesting a professional, no-nonsense individual. I couldn't tell if they were worn primarily for her vision or for her image. In any regard, they suited her well. She was very, very attractive in an athletic, academic sort of way.

I recalled seeing her recently, purposefully striding through the downtown district, past the law offices and professional suites. Usually she was heading out towards the nearby college campus, making her way past the banks and the trendy arts enclaves filled with galleries, cafes, and music venues. She usually carried an oversized artists' portfolio, a briefcase or sometimes, an instrument case.

This morning I noticed she had both the portfolio and the instrument case. It looked to be a violin or mandolin case of some sort. With the corners of her coat, she was shielding it from the light rain that had just begun to fall. I wondered what the contents of her portfolio might reveal about her; sheet music perhaps, charcoal sketches or architect renderings? The music case bolstered my theory of a string instrument—antique and elegant, and burnished with years of passionate use. The briefcase would no doubt be filled with classical music scores, and the portfolio stuffed with works in progress.

My windshield wipers moved sluggishly back and forth, doing more to smear and streak the glass than clean it. Mildly annoyed, I peered through the streaks as the traffic inched ahead through the busy downtown boulevard. There was a center divider, festooned with planter boxes, evergreen shrubs, and several fancy wooden benches bordering the intersection. Surely, she wouldn't be stopping to sit on the bench, as the rain was now really coming down. I turned the volume down on the car radio, concentrating on her as she skipped across the gathering puddles.

She made her way halfway across the meridian and paused, looking both directions, while tucking the case inside her long coat. She adjusted her coat, brushing off her case and portfolio.

As I approached the crosswalk, I tentatively rolled down the window and offered her a ride. "Excuse me miss, may I offer you a lift? I'm not going far, but it looks like it's really starting to come down. You're liable to get soaked out there."

She glanced up at the sky, scanned the intersection, and gave my vehicle a quick but discerning once-over. Deciding my offer was respectably safe; she nodded 'yes,' her eyebrows raised in a demure gesture of appreciation.

"Thanks so much, this is very nice of you," she said, settling into the front passenger seat. "I'm just heading over to the music academy for a rehearsal and I'm already behind schedule, and now the weather, so I appreciate it."

She seemed a little nervous, and began whisking the moisture off the portfolio in long, determined strokes, parallel to the grain of its worn leather. Apologizing for the water dripping on the seats, she adjusted her glasses, but her eyes never left my hands on the steering wheel. In a lame attempt to put her at ease, I assured her that "chivalry's not actually dead, it's just resting!" She didn't immediately respond like I thought she would, so I continued my hackneyed spiel. "...you know, always ready to rescue a damsel in distress... be prepared... like a Boy Scout." I immediately felt like a sophomore at prom night, saying stupid things to fill an awkward silence.

"Sorry, bad humor," I said, hoping she would see past my awkwardness. Trying to cover for it, I nodded towards the violin case, "So you play? Violin or...? Classical stuff no doubt?"

I searched my brain for another reference, some other genre, and taking liberties based on her appearance, I joked, "I don't imagine you playin those plain ol' fiddle tunes, like bluegrass or that Cajun jambalaya stuff?"

She smiled and shook her head almost imperceptibly. "No, you're right, I'm second chair violin at the Academy, but I did study viola, as well as cello. I love all the strings, but violin is my instrument of choice—at least this year. The music inspires me in some indescribable way. It takes me out of myself."

"Ah yes," I nodded, "Vivaldi, the Four Seasons, Paganini and what's his name? That older guy, Perelman," I interjected, trying to sound semi-learned.

"All the masters—especially Vivaldi," I had quickly exhausted my classical repertoire in one ridiculously ignorant breath.

She steadied the case in her lap, and brushing off the wet surface as she conceded, "Yeah, I was classically trained and, of course, I still practice a lot. I'm still learning."

I silently interrupted her in my thoughts, congratulating myself on at least one of my guesses.

"But actually, I do favor the more contemporary stuff. I'm into the post-modern players—the jazz/fusion dudes. That's what does it for me—the electrified, intense stuff; music from the..." she hesitated, surveying the traffic jam ahead,

"...you know, the cosmic realm—like Jean Luc Ponty, or Niculescu, or that Dave Matthews' guy, Boyd what's 'is name?" She answered her own question, "Tinsley! Boyd Tinsley. He's unreal! He has that dead-on vibe, sorta like an otherworldly Mahavishnu sound."

I barely knew who she was referring to. "Yeah, I always wanted to study music. but never had the patience—sorta like math with notes, and I don't get math."

She laughed slightly, becoming animated and a little restless at this point. She set about adjusting the portfolios' position, pulling it from under the seat and leaning it against the door panel. It appeared to be overflowing, stuffed full. I imagined it crammed with important renderings, or complicated arrangements. She opened it up and shuffled a few pages. She pulled out a couple, glancing at them briefly. She folded them in half and set them on the console, tapping them gently.

"Ahh, actually it's not that hard," she remarked, "you just have to start with a few simple chords, then move on. It's all about practice—training your hands to go where they should go."

She closed the portfolio and then picked up the instrument case positioning it on her lap. Peeking out from one corner, there appeared to be towel or cloak of some kind of fabric crammed inside. It was hard to tell.

Concealing my lack of familiarity with the players she mentioned, I nodded in agreement, "Yeah, those dudes are the bomb, especially Dave Matthews." That I didn't know Matthews was a bandleader not the violinist didn't seem to faze her in the least. That, or else she wasn't even listening. 'Hip' and 'with it,' I wasn't.

She began absently flipping the gold latches on the case, open and closed, open and closed, and the traffic inched ahead, at barely a crawl. Sensing perhaps she was about to show me the instrument, I asked what I thought was the next obvious question, "So, do you play a Stradivarius?" again feeling foolish at uttering such a cliché. It was the only name I knew.

"Oh God no," she shaking her head in dismay.

"This one is unique, a very special instrument—an heirloom I guess, from my grandmother's side. It was designed and built in the 1880's—a Knilling Bucharest-C, model 9." She nodded and raised an eyebrow as if I should recognize it.

"Made in Poland?" My ignorance was sinking my ship. "I didn't know they were renown for violins?"

"Yeah, she answered, as she scanned the sidewalk and traffic ahead, "somewhere in Europe; Verona, or Germany, or somewhere." She seemed distracted, and I thought it odd she wouldn't know its precise origin.

She refocused and in an irritated tone, added; "I wouldn't trade it for all the Strads in the world."

I nodded, faking appreciation. I wouldn't know a Bucharest if it bit me in the ass.

As she began to open the case, she looked up, as if startled, and gestured out the window towards the curb. The traffic was now stalled, and the wipers seemed to annoy her.

"Hey, stop here, pull in here," she said, eyeing a stately-looking building across the street. I pulled aside, and as she offered apologies, she slowly opened her door and the violin case at the same time.

The case was lined with deep purple velvet, the elegant color of a Crown Royale pouch, with brilliant gold bunting hemming its edges. A matching velour polishing cloth lay lengthwise inside, smelling of bow resin and hardwood wax.

With a smooth practiced hand she quickly drew back the cloth revealing a black matte Beretta—all business. It looked like a nine millimeter. It was nestled in the folds of the velour, and it was the real deal—definitely not a musical instrument of any vintage.

With utter nonchalance, she picked up the weapon and pointed it directly at my chest. She eased the portfolio out the door and calmly said, "I'm sorry to have troubled you, but please put your wallet and watch on the dashboard. Just lay 'em down and slide 'em over to me very slowly. Drop the car keys outside your window—Now!"

I could hardly believe what was happening. As I began to fish out my wallet, she flicked the pistol up and down towards my face cautioning me to 'move slow and steady.'

"No trouble—and you won't get hurt, ok? Slide your stuff over nice and slow, drop the keys, and put both hands back on the wheel."

All I could feel was the seatbelt gripping my waist, and tightening across my chest. Despite the cool rain, I began sweating and the windows suddenly fogged up.

Gesturing with the gun towards the window. "Keys outside the window. Please don't be stupid, we're almost done."

Following her orders, my hands trembled as I placed them back on the steering wheel. She gathered my things and placed them inside the case, snapping it shut. She slid out the door and, standing at the curb, still brandishing the pistol she discreetly concealed the gun under her coat, and gathered up the portfolio and case all in one swift motion.

She gently pushed the door closed. She didn't slam it, just closed it with a solid click. Opening her coat just a pinch, she checked the traffic and leveled the barrel at me again.

"Now wait till I'm out of sight before you move—please—cause I'm pretty good with this... practice, you know?"

With that, she backed off the curb, pulled the coat close around her and, moving back from the car door, quietly said, "Sorry to have put you out, and we were having such a nice conversation."

She stood up, assessed the traffic, and leaned back down to window level, shaking her head. With a question mark in her voice, she scolded me.

"Vivaldi? Really? Come on, Vivaldi? The Four Seasons? You must be kidding? Vivaldi sucks."

She stood up again, and stepping across the street, she shook the water from her beautiful braid, tossing it behind her. Moving in between the cars, she slowly disappeared down the crowded boulevard, dodging the puddles as she went.

The Tracer of Lost Women
By Olivia Taylor-Young

Way back when I was very young and radio was in its heyday, I remember listening to "Mr. Keen – Tracer of Lost Persons"... a program whose plotline was wholly explained in its title. Today, as someone who lectures about many facets of Women's History, I often feel like Mr. Keen's modern day counterpart.

In fields that range from science to art to investigative journalism, accomplished women too often fit the category of 'gone missing.' This isn't because they fail to exist, but because their achievements have been routinely dismissed as having no value, wrongly credited to male colleagues, been the victim of workplace sabotage or simply written out of history.

Across the years, some of the write-outs and oversights were unconscious results of traditional stereotypes. Others were downright deliberate. In either case, belatedly acknowledging the accomplishments of past and present women—and the identity of the women themselves—will not undo gross injustices, but it will help to set the record straight.

Perhaps the story of Matilda Jocelyn Gage is the perfect place-setter. Ms. Gage was a 19th Century abolitionist, suffragist and sociologist whose writings helped shape the times in which she lived. What she'd truly aspired to be, however, was a physician, but the times in which she lived also deemed females too fragile for scientific thought and banned them from attending medical school.

Today, Matilda Joselyn Gage holds the title of 'the first known woman in America to publish a study of women in science.' Yet *Woman as an Inventor*, the 1883 treatise that earned her that title, was barely acknowledged in her lifetime... and remained tucked away in relative obscurity for over a century.

No wonder! In an era that dubbed mechanical, mathematic, inventive or scientific aptitude unfeminine and beyond the scope of most women's reach, *Woman as an Inventor* cited dozens of female-originated inventions. Among them were the aquarium by naturalist Jeanne Villepreux Power, the deep-sea telescope by Sarah Mather, the production of marble from limestone by sculptress Harriet Hosmer, and other innovative ideas like the baby carriage, the gimlet point screw and a volcanic furnace for smelting ore. Also included in *Woman as an Inventor* were details of how Eli Whitney received step-by-step instructions for building the cotton gin from Revolutionary War widow Catherine Littlefield Greene.

Fast-forward to the 1990s. Prepping for a ground-breaking seminar about female scientists whose discoveries were wrongly credited to men, Cornell science historian Margaret Rossiter happened across a reference to Matilda Joselyn Gage. Tucked away in a little known book about overlooked women intellectuals, the narrative pointed out how *Woman as an Inventor* revealed how men routinely usurped the credit for their female colleagues' achievements. It also showed how such lack of recognition discouraged women from further using their creative talents and/or prevented them from reaping financial benefits. Quoting Ms. Gage herself, "The more a woman worked, the more the men around her profited and the less credit she got." Thus, in memory of her sister science historian who gave early voice to this systemic erasure, Professor Rossiter invented the phrase, "The Matilda Effect."

As it turns out, Matilda's effect has many faces and regularly appears in many places. Austrian born scientist Lise Meitner helped unearth the physical characters of nuclear fission in 1939... and her male partner was awarded the Nobel Prize five years later.

In the 1950s, Chien Shiung Wu proved identical nuclear particles do not always act alike. The discovery's well-deserved Nobel Prize went to her two male colleagues.

Radio Astronomer Joslyn Bell Burnell discovered pulsars in the 1970s. In 2021, a retrospective article about her headlined, "She Changed Astronomy Forever. Her Male Supervisor Won The Nobel Prize For It."

I guess waiting half a century for recognition is better than never.

Another well-kept woman-secret concerns the earliest stages of the Mercury space program. NASA's doctor in charge of astronaut physical training strongly suggested female's smaller and lighter body types made them well-suited for the cramped conditions of space flight. Yet in spite of a fit and ready cadre of American women, the agency nixed his recommendation and an early female astronaut program never got off the ground. It probably didn't help that the first American to orbit the Earth actively campaigned against having female colleagues. "It's a matter of our social order." John Glenn insisted. "Men go off to fight the wars and women stay at home."

Steeped in such thinking, it would take more than two decades from the time Alan Shepard became the second man and first American to fly in space before Sally Ride became the first American female to do the same. It also took nearly two decades from the time Ed White became the first American man to walk in space before Kathryn D. Sullivan became the first American woman to follow in his footsteps. And yes, each of those 'firsts' were met with great celebration... as well they should. Firsts pay homage to innovation and reassure the world of unremitting progress. Yet whenever we commemorate a female first, Matilda oversees a long line of women whose work and talents have been belittled and/or sandbagged along the way.

Nowhere is this more evident than in the many fields of science. Williamina Fleming was among the foremost astronomers of the late 19th and early 20th centuries. Discoverer of the Horsehead Nebula in Orion, she was responsible for many other astronomical finds and for developing various methods to classify stars. Yet when a series of circa 1906 newspaper articles featured her as a woman beating the odds in a male-dominated field, they took great pains to reassure readers that the "unique lady astronomer" loved housework, could cook tasty meals with the best of them and, "The strain of intellectual and scientific pursuits has not destroyed that other side—the purely feminine side—of her life."

Sadly, that hogwash cannot be excused as just a product of its times. Seven decades later, while the media besieged Joslyn Bell Burnell's male supervisor with questions about pulsars' details, they besieged the discovering astronomer herself with questions about make-up, hairstyles and the kind of wedding dress she would be likely to choose.

Those earlier newspaper stories also zeroed in on the fact Ms. Fleming had once been a maid in the home of Edward Pickering, Director of the Harvard College Observatory. One hundred plus years later, a 2021 magazine article even noted it was the maid story that, "helped endear her in the hearts of early 20th century Americans and again later in the 21st century through a stage play about the lives of women astronomers, *Silent Sky.*"

Talk about Matilda on steroids! Talk about identity theft! And talk about being written out of history! Not only did that emphasis downplay Ms. Fleming's accomplishments, *Silent Sky* is based on the life of a totally different scientist.

Henrietta Swan Leavitt's 1908 Cepheid variables' discovery enabled astronomers to measure the size of the universe. It was an incredibly significant accomplishment; and it is her—not Williamina Fleming's—story that *Silent Sky* is based upon. As one reviewer wrote: "...In this exquisite blend of science, history, family ties, and fragile love, a passionate young woman must map her own passage through a society determined to keep a woman in her place... If you like stories about underdogs and unsung heroes, you'll love *Silent Sky*."

Underdogs and unsung heroes is an all too accurate description of women in science. And emphasizing the Matilda Effect one more time, when Ms. Leavitt's discovery was originally published, it was under the name of Edward Pickering.

On the other hand, Williamina Fleming published her early findings under her initials, W.P. Fleming, to both ensure her work would be recognized as her own, and to prevent it from being undermined by gender bias. Regarding the maid story, she was 21 years old and expecting their first child when she and her husband emigrated to the United States from Scotland. But when they docked in Boston, apparently Mr. Fleming stepped off of the ship, onto a train... and disappeared from Williamina's life.

Pregnant and alone in a strange country, as luck would have it—or perhaps it was written in the stars—she was hired on as a maid in Edward Pickering's home. Considering scarcity of employment opportunities for women at that time; and that alternatives would likely have meant the sweatshop textile mills in nearby Lowell or Lawrence, a housemaid's position was not undesirable... even for women who weren't in dire straits. That was especially true if the employer was wealthy and/or a person of prestige; and the Director of Harvard's Observatory certainly fell into the second category.

His young housemaid's quick mind and sharp intellect apparently impressed Professor Pickering enough that he offered her part-time clerical work at the observatory. The same characteristics quickly got her promoted to permanent staff. But despite the media's emphasis on that story, Williamina Fleming was not Eliza Doolittle and Edward Pickering was not Henry Higgins... And the narrative should never have been that a professor magically transformed his lowly housemaid into an astronomer; but that a brilliant, resilient woman overcame adversity and ended up making significant contributions both to science and the world.

In the meantime, Edward Pickering was attempting to bring industry-inspired efficiency to exploring the sky. Substituting cameras for the human eye at the operator's end of a telescope, by night his astronomers photographed stars and nebulae; and by day, a group of specially-trained women dubbed 'computers' inspected and analyzed those images to measure and catalog their brightness.

Why the computers were all female is a story of its own. Pickering's male assistants considered those day jobs repetitive drudgery and wanted no part of them. On the other hand, college-educated women from around the country actively sought the positions and some even volunteered to work without pay just to have Harvard on their resume. Thus the Director resigned himself to staffing his 'computer' force with women only. Predictably, the situation became fodder for innuendo; and throughout the scientific community, Harvard's computers became known as "Pickering's Harem."

Another Matilda manifestation... *If you can't discredit women's work and don't want to do it yourself, you might as well turn the whole thing into an off-color joke.* What cannot be denied, however, is that, across time, many women within that so-called harem made groundbreaking discoveries in astronomy and astrophysics.

It should also be noted that while Pickering was praised for having recruited over eighty women scientists to work at Harvard during his tenure, he was definitely a product of his times. Sincerely considering himself to be kind, decent and ultimately fair, he nevertheless firmly believed it was natural and correct to pay those women substantially less than their male counterparts.

In spite of it all, Ms. Fleming became the first American woman elected to honorary membership in England's Royal Astronomical Society. A member of Astronomical and Astrophysical Societies in France and the United States, she was also awarded the Guadalupe Almendaro Medal by the Astronomical Society of Mexico; appointed an honorary fellow at numerous American colleges; and, posthumously, a crater on the moon became her namesake. In fact, the Fleming Lunar Crater is jointly named after Williamina and the discoverer of Penicillin, Alexander Fleming.

The Veil Nebula, which spans about six miles the diameter of the full Moon and the length of whose wisp corresponds to about thirty light years is also named Fleming's Triangular Wisp… in honor of the woman who discovered it. Dare I say 'Pretty good for a girl?'

Williamina Fleming became an inspiration to American women at a time when their prospects were limited and even their right to vote was a long way off. Today, she's an inspiration to scientists around the globe. But it shouldn't have taken decades and even a century for such acknowledgment.

Also today, Dava Sobel's book, *The Glass Universe: How the Ladies of the Harvard Observatory Took Measure of the Stars* gives long overdue recognition to that remarkable group of women once known as human computers. And it is high time… just as it's now high time we take the wraps off the rich histories of all women of science, technology, invention and medicine… and every other field of endeavor.

Matilda deserves a gold watch, a big party, a generous pension and to be permanently sent into retirement.

Elusive Atonement
By Janice Strupp

For the first time in her life she knew herself and it was good. With her newfound knowledge came the revelation of the suffering she had caused others. It pained her to think of it.

Now, she remembered everything. Every wrong she had visited upon another, every slight, every willful, self-serving act she had committed. If only she could somehow make those she had wronged know how sorry, nay, how very ashamed she was at how she had treated them. She owed an apology to many people. A prostrate apology to some.

She knew she would never be able to fulfill this profound need. She prayed that somehow the people she would never see again knew of her sincere remorse. For the disappointments she had caused, the hurt, the sorrow, the wrenching betrayal of an innocent trust. Remorse for the unrelenting selfishness that had caused others to suffer. She knew there was no way to make up for it or to forgive herself for it.

She had given so little, yet had expected others to give all.

Sunset Over Montauk

The evening sun over Montauk
Bookends to a day spent chasing the sun
Shops, vineyards and squares
Quaint in their charms

Being by the sea
The air and mist splashing around
Sun, sea and sand meet
Together in joyful movement
As the sun sets on the beach

There's only one thought in my mind,

Sheer Bliss!

~ Oswald Perez

Stereophonic Alarm

Only at 4:00 a.m. do you notice
that the little white alarm clock on your bathroom windowsill
makes a steady, audible, rhythmic Tic... and then... Toc
Tic to the right, and toc to the left

It's a stereophonic symphony of time
Tic is the lower sound, an alto; while Toc is the mezzo soprano
Together they indifferently proclaim that time is moving forward,
one confident 'tic' and one certain 'toc' at a time

That clock came from a place where time now seems not to move.
No one can go out or continue with the business of daily life.
Martinsicuro, like all places in Italy, lives in a forced standstill,
a dread-filled shutdown, due to a deadly and unexpected invader.

They call it Corona, or more precisely Covid-19,
a silent and invisible interloper, an assassin
ravaging the people of Italy, and those in all the world

Questa sera there will be no baci and abbracci among friends in real time
no walking arm in arm, or strolling gently toward a peaceful crowd
of quiet revelers, eating pizza a taglio and gelati

But that was of another time, before this pandemic,
when we happily didn't know of the looming and awful events to come,
when it seemed that time was in our hands, and on our side.

Now Brother Tic and Sister Toc won't let us forget
that we're moving forward, but not yet advancing.
We can't imagine an end to that measured ticking and tocking
Like Sysiphus, we are driven to repeat the act of listening
to this wordless song of quiet isolation.

~ Lois Angela Czyzewski

Life is Short; Life is Fragile
By Dave Polhamus

They met as a group. They met to talk about his life. They were not panning or bad-mouthing him, though some were ambivalent. They had just been to his funeral service and internment.

Several had worked with Keith for years. It was difficult to determine when co-workers had begun to notice him. When first hired, he had been in and out of the workplace for months at a time. Rumor was he was rehabbing at the local VA hospital. Back working steady, he kept mostly to himself, though, first thing every morning he'd make his way through the offices and work areas greeting co-workers. It was as if he wanted to ensure that there was a friendship, goodwill and rapport. He didn't spend a lot of time gabbing, just greeting.

"Good morning. Good to see you this morning."... "Good morning."

One person, then the next. "How are you, this morning?" ... "Good Morning."

Day-in and day-out, the process became predictable and eventually a nuisance for some. He was even mimicked and verbally abused. His daily greetings had caused some negative feelings, even now.

"G' morning, how are you?"

Today—a cool spring day, they had gathered at Metropolitan Coffee, a coffee klatch bar located in the basement of the building down the street. It had been overcast and breezy at the cemetery, and now in the confines of steaming coffee and hot chocolate it felt comfortable. There were more ladies than men, most wearing dark, conservative clothing—some in suits.

"Who all's going to be here?" Kay asked, at the door.

"I don't know, but it's good we could meet," Pete smiled. "What with no wake or anything, it's good we can talk. Uh, it's like needing to scratch an itch."

In the background, drinks were being created. The whirl of coffee beans in a grinder howled-out conversation. The espresso machine hissed a loud crescendo. Someone banging on a folded towel on a counter sounded like a muffled gavel bringing a meeting to order. Robust coffee brewing aroma sated the area.

Betty munched a chocolate-covered biscotti stick, brushing crumbs off her lap. Amy was settling into one end of a faux-leather couch. Jack wasn't saying much, yet. Mark initiated small talk.

"I have to admit, Keith's every morning greetings drove me crazy, but I'm sad he's gone. And his eulogy... that was different. Nobody does a eulogy anymore."

"Yeah, mostly now, it's the open-mike and 'What did he do that means something to me' stuff." Betty nodded. "The eulogy worked, though."

"I gotta' tell you, those dirge songs tore me up," Kay rolled her eyes. "So slow, so old, so traditional. Yeah, Keith drove me up the wall too."

"At least it wasn't the usual, Rock of Ages or Amazing Grace," Jack said. "You know, he wrote his own obit? That's what I heard."

"Yeah, and I bet he paid big bucks for that horse and buggy hearse team to carry him to the cemetery. What a kick," Scott said. "That was a nice touch, a novel idea. A horse and buggy. Dramatic. What a great way to go out!"

"Yeah, it was," someone agreed. "Certainly not the norm." They sipped caffeine and warmed up.

"I liked the Taps," Marsha said. "It's not every vet who gets Taps at his graveside. It looked to be a high school kid, who played. Yeah, Taps are good."

"I think you're right," Scott nodded.

They talked of the guy from Bayard, Iowa, who gave the sermon. The people from

Colorado who spoke—they must be cousins. Someone remarked that Keith was a private person, no wife, no girlfriend. Just a dog.

Amy talked of not knowing much about Keith. He worked alone in the shipping and receiving department at their company. Only time anybody saw him, he was delivering stuff to their work station. That, and his usual greetings. She wondered, aloud, if his daily greetings were his way of asking for a connection, or for belonging—maybe approval. He was always polite.

"Hey, anybody wanna refill?" Scott offered. "We've only just begun," he smiled, pulling up out of his overstuffed chair. Betty had another biscotti, this one tasting of licorice, or sweet anise. Pete asked for a Mexican mocha. He liked the hint of cinnamon and pepper, he said. Jack ordered a small mocha with a dollop of whipped cream—thank you.

They found seating, again. "The elephant in the room is called Viet Nam," Mark said abruptly."

"Uh, how so?" Betty said. "What happened?"

"You don't know?"

"Well, tell me."

"Keith wanted to serve his country," Amy said. "He enlisted, back in the mid-60s. He was loyal, patriotic."

"What was his M-O-S—his military occupation specialty?" Mark asked.

"Artillery, a forward observer," Jack said. "That's what he told me."

"So, what's a forward observer?"

"Well," Pete began slowly, "Judging from the title, I bet he had good eyesight. That, and maybe he had an aggressive, or forward personality. Maybe he was always looking ahead." He smiled demurely. "Or, just maybe, just maybe, he was a seer, a prophet, someone who could look into the future... you know, dispense omens."

The group groaned—some smiled. For Betty, it was an emotional release and she laughed unconditionally.

"I don't know if this is a good time for jokes," Scott remarked, lightly.

"A forward observer is with an artillery unit," said Jack. "He's out front near the action. At the proper time, he radios coordinates in, then calls an artillery barrage onto the enemy. He's got to be focused and pay attention to detail, or he'll eventually call it in on himself. Don't want that."

"Nope. So, he was good at that," Kay chimed. "What else?"

"Well, he was under an Agent Orange strike, once. You know, the stuff Dow Chemical used to make—denuded the jungle."

"So, you're saying that's what's responsible for his melanoma—the cancer?"... this from Pete.

"Yeah, that was nasty stuff," Jack said. "Back in the late '60s, the American public hated Dow Chemical, didn't they. I heard Dow went broke." There was some surface discussion of the hippie movement and protest demonstrations. One mentioned that Agent Orange was responsible for his cousin's being born with autism. He said that his uncle had served in Viet Nam and had been exposed. They agreed, they didn't like Dow Chemical.

"Keith was a POW," Mark said, abruptly. "About three years. Those little fellows in black pajamas had him; a six foot-square cell."
"Oh, my," Marsha whispered. "Oh no."

"Our human resources manager said that's why he came 'round to greet us every morning—the result of that experience. A psychologist might say... uh, that he wanted... friendship—acceptance, connection," Mark shrugged. "Maybe it was his way of saying it's a great day to be alive. Maybe he thought life is short, life is fragile... don't know. What do you people make of it?"

"Keith never seemed bitter, never complained of mistreatment," Amy said. "He never talked of the North Vietnamese in derogatory terms— you know—gooks, slopes, dinks. He resolved it, I guess."

"Oooh. I'm so sorry. I never would've known. I'm so-o-o sorry," Betty managed, shaking her head and tearing up. "I had no idea. I didn't know that was... that was his relationship, his bonding; his greeting us. I admit, I hassled him. I teased him. I was so blind. I'm so embarrassed." She leaned into her hands, now sobbing openly, loudly. Tears flowed. Someone handed her a handkerchief. Weeping—emoting, shaking her head. Ashamed?

"It's alright, it's alright," Pete assured her, standing and gently petting and patting her back. "We're all as guilty as anyone—others hassled him, too. None of us can cast the first stone."

Finishing their drinks, they trailed off. Some left together. Some alone.

Grateful

Looking backward – Looking forward
thumbing through our ups and downs.
I see sadness – I hear love,
the beauty and the beast are one.

Infectious enthusiasm clears a path,
for taking hold and hanging on.
Respect the tranquil, bring on the dance.
Move slowly, as we strategize our task.

Life's serious side can hinder our route.
Push away the frustrations, clear the doubt.
Come back to laughter, it cures the cause.
Rectify the compass, to life's circle and beyond.

With any conjoined journey,
the merry-go-round of life goes forward.
So – bring on goodness, bring on song,
bring on dancing and the journey – goes on.

Travel onward,
giving tenderness the lead,
with pulsating hearts,
our love story breaths.

~ Elizabeth Orton

Hubris

It feels wrong to say
I don't know
Or I'm in over my head

Who am I letting down?
Pioneer ancestors,
Can-do Americans

Who throw caution to the wind
Dodge bullets
And other impossibles

Like Icarus flying too close to the sun
We hope not to burn, not to fall
Not this time, not us

We wear scattered victories
Like badges, really only proving
We didn't die

Daredevils may break bones
Addicts recover
And broken hearts mend

Or not.
Moderns gasp at tales
Ending in shear failure

Maybe Icarus
Should stay home
Warming his hands by the fire.

But will he?

~ Rachel Rich

Haiku

Empty school buses
driving up and down the street
during quarantine

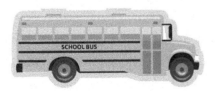

~ Kris Bluth

The One Armed Man from Pincher Creek

By Tony Hyde

(Pincher Creek, Alberta; June 1963)

I walked into the bar in Pincher Creek. It was about 5:00 p.m. and there weren't too many customers. Sitting over in the corner, I immediately recognized Clifford John Foster. He was known to everyone as C.J. He worked for Alberta Gas Trunk Lines, out of their Calgary office, the same as I did. We had only met in a work environment before and had never had much of an opportunity to talk socially.

C.J. was a tall, erect man in his early 60s. He was a sharp dresser, always wore a well-brushed cowboy hat with a large brim. His pencil thin moustache was trimmed and his string tie gave him an air of refinement in a world of rough cowboy-types. When he walked, he had sense of purpose about him. His cowboy boots always clip-clopped on the walkway with a steady rhythm. The craggy lines down C.J.'s face and the roughness of his hands told the real story of years working around the Canadian, Texas and Oklahoma oil fields. His refined manner belied the time spent in gin mills and whorehouses all over the Western States and Canada.

I sat down at C.J.'s table and ordered a beer. In true Albertan fashion, two beers appeared in front of me. The law makers, in their wisdom, had passed a law that prohibited the sale of beer in glasses any larger than 8 ounces. Bartenders quickly overcame this limitation by automatically serving up the two glasses with every order. The only persons affected by the law were the guys who had to wash up the dirty glasses.

Soon after my arrival, several other farm hands came into the bar. They were a noisy bunch. While they weren't totally belligerent, they certainly altered the previous tranquility of the place. A few words were exchanged with some of the other patrons. C.J. sensed things could get ugly in a hurry. This is why he always had a chair with its back to the wall, usually in a corner. If anyone came after him with a chair or a knife, he'd know about it and wouldn't be caught blind-sided. Things in the bar settled down without further incident.

C.J. related to me how he'd seen a similar incident in this very bar many years before. A guy by the name of Clem Thompson used to run this bar then, C.J. recalled. A man in the bar started pushing the other patrons around looking for a fight. Well, it didn't take Ole Clem long to size up that this guy had one too many drinks. The fella was about 6' 2" and more than 200 pounds. Now Clem was a good-sized man himself, but he only had one arm. Clem came around the bar, behind the trouble-maker, grabbed the crotch of his pants, hoisted him up onto his toes, put his shoulder into the middle of his back and ran him 30-feet or so out through the bat-wing doors into the street.

I sat, trying to visualize this scene with the one armed man tackling the bar bully. "How'd he lose his arm?" I asked in amazement.

"Two more beers over here," C.J. ordered in his characteristic raspy voice.

I could tell this was going to be a long evening and perhaps I shouldn't have asked about the arm.

"Me and Clem used to run booze across the Montana line in the late '20s," C.J. continued.

"We used to get $500 a run, which was a lot of money in them days. Well, word came down that a run was to take place this one night. It was my turn to make the run, but I had a bad feeling about things, so I called and said I couldn't make it. So Clem got called to come down to the warehouse to drive the Ford down to Shelby, Montana, from Lethbridge. They loaded them old cars with as much booze as they could possibly carry."

C.J. paused to sip his beer. His eyes were off in some far off place, dredging up old feelings and memories. He continued. "Clem gets across the border ok and he's heading south, when a car comes up from behind him, pulls out to pass him and then runs him off the road. The car remained upright, but Clem was shaken up some. He gets out of the car and before he can make sense out of the situation, one of the two men in the other car pulls a gun and shoots him twice, once in the left arm and the other in the upper body. Clem sank down on the ground and passed into unconsciousness. The two men quickly unloaded the Ford, transferring the booze into their car. They left Ole Clem there to die."

C.J. let the seriousness of Ole Clem's situation sink in before he continued.

"Clem comes around and finds himself in a pool of blood, his left arm is shattered. His first thought was to get his booze back. He did some crude bandaging to his wounds, jumped back into the Ford and headed south. He drove like a maniac, fighting back the pain. Twenty minutes later, up ahead on the dirt road, he saw the car his attackers had used to ambush him. The car had mechanical trouble and the two men were trying to get it running again. They waved him down as he approached them. They were unsuspecting of the identity of the driver, believing Clem to be dead in the ditch back by the border. Well, Clem's arm is a complete mess, he'd lost a lot of blood, and he knew these guys were armed and ready to use them."

I interrupted at this point and said, "Why in the hell would a person who's just got shot twice, is losing lots of blood, go back unarmed, against these guys? The booze wasn't his. So he's out the $500 bucks, but at least he was still alive and could make another run sometime later."

"Son," C.J. said, "you don't understand! If a man loses a shipment like that he don't get a second chance."

"Well, how did he survive this situation?" I inquired of C.J.

"The first man steps out onto the road waving his arms above his head to slow the oncoming car down. The second man takes up a position behind him, to the side. He's the one with the gun. They're about to ambush their second Ford in the space of a half hour.

Clem slows down, making look like he's a Good Samaritan and then guns it, running down the guy in the road. Without stopping, he heads directly for the man off to the side. The gunman realizes too late who the driver is. Clem ran him down in the shallow ditch. The first guy was dead and the second guy survived, but was in bad shape."

"Again, my mind ran through the situation Clem was in. Here he was in a foreign country; he'd just killed one person, had badly injured a second in the pursuit of the illegal activity of bootlegging booze across the border. He was badly injured, unable to transfer the booze back into his own car and make a timely escape with his shipment."

"OK, C.J., how did he escape the electric chair or the gas chamber?" I asked.

C.J. could only shake his head and say "You have to understand how it was in Montana in them days. The county police came and took Clem to the hospital where he had his arm amputated. At his trial in the county court in Montana, the lawyer representing Clem got up and said, "Your Honor, my client is a victim here. He was only defending himself and trying to protect his property." The judge deemed Clem innocent of violating any Montana law and allowed him to keep the shipment... well, most of it. The judge, the sheriff and the defense attorney each got two cases of the hootch."

I turned to C.J. after he had completed the story and said to him that, but for the grace of God, he would have been in Clem's place. C.J. replied that there was no way that such a thing would have ever happened to him. He tapped the left breast of his jacket as he spoke. I quickly leaned across the table and whispered "Jesus Christ, C.J. Are you packing a gun?"

Ignoring my question, C.J. pointed his forefinger at me with his thumb cocked and replied, "Those sons' of bitches would never have made that first transfer, if I'd been driving."

Early Life on Rue St. Christophe
By Demetri Liontos

Years ago, while attending English college classes, one of my professors assigned a book by Lawrence Durrell titled *Spirit of Place*. It was a collection of essays on the notion that the place where you live, where you choose to stay, shapes who you are. I've forgotten much of my unillustrious college life and what I had for lunch yesterday, but not those essays.

Durrell's ideas on *place* as an imprint on our life are indelibly engraved in my mind. East End Montreal in the aftermath of World War II was where I spent the first 13 years of my life, and I can still remember vividly the sights, smells and sounds of that unremarkable area, just blocks away from the city's glamorous downtown. My parents were Greek immigrants who had to scrape by to provide for my three siblings and me. My father, a proud, distinguished-looking man, once owned a small hotel, a restaurant and an apartment building at different times. But in the chaos from the war and the Depression before it, he had fallen on hard times.

After a series of low-income rentals in Montreal's French-speaking East End, my parents finally settled us in a third story cold-water flat on St. Christophe Street. The flat was reached by a double set of staircases, one outside going straight up from the street to a second floor landing and our front door. Another flight inside curved up to the entry way. (In retrospect, I never questioned how my father—overweight and out of shape—handled the demanding task of simply going to work and coming home. A child's curiosity goes in different directions, I think.)

The building itself contained five other residences, a six-plex with three units on either side. Inevitably, there was much going up and down the stairs, and as a result, we got to know our neighbors quite well. I remember them even today by name and appearance and, as was my nature, liked them all in varying degrees. Madame Mandeville on the second floor was always heavily made up with bright lipstick and coiffed hair, and you could smell her sweet perfume as she went off—sometimes just to the corner store for cigarettes. Carmen, her daughter, was a pretty teenager who emulated her mother with similar makeup and fancy clothes. Despite our age difference (I was only ten or so) I had a crush on her, something I didn't share with my siblings or anyone else. It was cool to have secrets, even then.

On the ground floor lived the Savard family, and Monsieur Savard was the person I liked least on our street. He drank a lot of Molson's beer, was always smoking a pipe and liked to play his fiddle on their porch. I didn't mind the music, but it was rumored that he sometimes beat Madame Savard, especially after a few too many Molsons. I didn't like that.

One summer, their son, Serge, returned from the war, tall and impressive in his pressed army uniform. I was full of questions for him: What was it like? Did you kill anyone? Did you get wounded? Where were you? But my queries would have to wait until he had settled in a bit.

On Saturdays I sometimes delivered groceries for Monsieur Lemaire at the corner store. Soon after Serge had arrived, old Monsieur Lemaire had a delivery for me to take to the Savards—bread, eggs, cheese, mustard and several bottles of Molsons. I loaded the box in my wagon excitedly, as now I could ask Serge my questions! When I arrived and rang the bell, the door soon opened—my jaw dropped and face reddened. There, filling the open doorway was my war hero, dripping water head to toe from his bath--and standing stark naked! I had never seen a naked adult before and my eyes were drawn like a magnet to his black curly manly area. I plopped the box of groceries on the porch, turned my wagon and sped off to my home one staircase over. My war questions would have to wait.

Later that summer I was sitting, reading a comic book on the outside stairs when a group of men arrived and went up to Mrs. Moshonas' place next door to ours. There were three of them and I hadn't seen them before, but they smiled at me from the opposite landing as they rang and rang her bell.

"She's not there," I said as I heard my mother call me for dinner. Later I learned to my horror that a tearful Mrs. Moshonas had come to see Mom to tell her she'd been robbed of all her jewelry and silverware. I stammered and stuttered and told my mother that I'd seen the men, but thought they were friends visiting Mrs. M. A stern lecture followed on how to tell friends from burglars and, in time, Mrs. Moshonas herself forgave me my childish innocence.

The spirit of this place was imprinting on me. It was a time of making memories, of playing and fighting with the "French kids," and holding onto unasked questions. It was a time too when I could have been a hero myself. If only I hadn't been so innocent.

In This Time

I want to wallow thirstily
in the golden cup
of the California poppy
the way the furry, black and yellow bumblebees
fill this smooth, shiny space;
collect pollen jewels on my body and
in baskets on my legs
from the richly burdened anthers;
absorb the warmth of this
   July morning
–not too cold, not too hot–
drinking its essence,
bathing in its light,
carrying hope onward
with my translucent wings.

~ *Susanne Twight-Alexander*

On Finishing My Fence

Do you want to see my fence
I built it over Christmas
It turned into quite a project
Come
Walk with me
I'll show you

I started it years ago
Never finished it
I guess I really don't like fences
But I have a pond in the yard
   and there are little ones nearby now
So that's what I did over Christmas
I finished it

Fences reflect what is wrong
   with us, I think
They warn, "Keep out!"
"Stay on your side."
"You're not welcome here."
They shout, "Me!"
They shriek, "Mine!"
They whisper, "I am afraid."

Rivers and mountains
   are natural fences
Canyons and oceans
   and blackberry patches work well
Nothing so stark as chain link
   or cedar slats
No need for razor wire
No locks
No "Posted" signs
   whatever "Posted" means

You say it looks great
Well thank you
I changed some things
Things I learned from last time
But still, there are flaws
No matter how hard I try
I know where they are
I can show you a few if you'd like
I am thinking of cutting off my ear

~ *Marv Himmel*

Girls Just Wanna have Fun
By Mary Daniels

The year is 1962. Imagine 12 British teenagers, heading off on an educational holiday to Italy chaperoned only by their aging geography master and his matronly wife. This childless and totally naive couple had no idea how challenged they would be keeping tabs on a co-ed group of 15-year-olds who were suddenly out of the clutches of their conservative and proper English parents. Wally Fergus had been a teacher at our school for the past 22 years and this was his first trip chaperoning a group to Europe. Wally only had one lung and suffered spells of labored breathing. He was overweight and not particularly quick on his feet, and we all wondered if he was really up to the task. His wife, Edna, older than Wally by at least a decade, was a frumpy, spindly, grey-haired matron with a prominent hairy mole on her chin. You couldn't look at her without your eyes wandering immediately to settle on it.

We traveled by air from London to Basel, Switzerland, then by train through the Alps to Milan, then by coach to the tiny resort town of Toscolano. No more than a fishing village just ten years before, the town council had sanctioned a small hotel to be built on the shores of Lake Garda, nestled in the shadows of the Dolomite Mountains in northern Italy. This would be our central location for the next ten days while we took side trips to Brescia, Venice and beyond.

The tiny chartered airplane, full of noisy youngsters heading to various parts of Europe, took to the air from London Heathrow airport. Grubby and rattling, it lurched onto the runway, roared up to speed and finally lifted off into the bright morning sky.

With ears popping, all of us over-excited, squealing and wild, we craned our necks to see out of the tiny windows as we soared higher and higher over the English Channel. None of us had slept a wink the night before and we could hardly contain our excitement. Imagine this group of high-spirited adolescents, on the loose in a foreign country for the first time. What could possibly go wrong?

Our landing in Switzerland was bumpy as our pilot navigated around turbulent cloud cover, and finally bounced onto the runway in Basel. With individual ID cards in hand, our group deplaned onto the tarmac and shuffled through the airport to a waiting train. We were told to sit in the central part of the long train and stay in a group.

The train pulled out and chugged through the most beautiful countryside I had ever seen. I had read books about the Swiss Alps, but nothing could have prepared me for these incredible snow-peaked mountains and lush green valleys with cows grazing in the sunlight. I was transfixed. We stopped at several train stations along the way and were even allowed to get off the train a couple of times to stretch our legs. Railway personnel maneuvered connecting carriages, shunting back and forth, until we'd be on our way again through more picture-perfect scenes of A-framed chalets and church steeples dotting the countryside. My friend Maureen (aka Mo) had noticed a dining car situated towards the back of the train, and she and I took off through the long corridor hoping to get a cold beverage or a cup of tea. We finally found the dining car after walking through a dozen or more carriages and Mo ordered our drinks using her best French language skills. I was impressed. We were just pulling our money out when the train suddenly lurched backwards as the more forward carriages were uncoupled from the dining car. Right away, I realized we were in trouble and we quickly tossed our money down, grabbed our drinks and spilled out onto the platform in a panic.

In unison we screamed "Wait. Wait. Stop!" We caught the eye of one of the train conductors who looked puzzled as we ran for our lives to catch up with the central carriages. We just made it in time to jump on before the porter closed the last door and the train pulled away. We made it, but our drinks didn't. They had been thrown aside as we scrambled to catch up with the train. My heart was pounding as we took our seats amongst our group who wondered what on earth we had been up to. One of the boys spoke up and with great authority told us that the back part of the train was going on to Munich, Germany, while our section was heading for Milan. The group cheered us on, laughing, saying "Close call." Catastrophe avoided.

The train passed by Lake Lucerne, then the glistening blue waters of Lake Como, as we wound our way through Switzerland into northern Italy. There, the scenery changed rapidly as we approached the big city, exposing dark, industrial buildings and massive concrete blocks of tenement flats right next to the railway lines. From Milan, our group boarded a coach that passed through increasingly pretty vistas, finally arriving in Toscolano as the sun set behind the towering mountains that bordered Lake Garda.

We were all pretty exhausted as we grabbed our luggage and made our way to our dormitory-style rooms in the hotel. Boys were on the ground floor; girls on the top floor, three flights up. Six of us, all good friends, flopped down on our twin beds, unpacked our suitcases and freshened up before going down for a light meal in the dining room. We immediately discovered the back stairs and took note of the fire escape ladder, just outside the third floor exit door that led to a back alley far below. Mo suggested we keep that little bit of information to ourselves, and we all knew exactly what she meant by that.

After dinner, we took the stairs again to our room and checked out the adjacent bathroom. It was huge and contained a full-sized bath tub, two shower stalls, a double sink, a toilet and an odd-looking additional fixture next to the toilet. It looked a lot like a toilet, but it had a tap at the top with a dial and a metal handle on the side. We looked at it quizzically, as Karen explained.

"It's a bidet, your idiots."

"A what?" we all chimed in.

A bi-DAY!" She huffed exasperated. "You wash your bum in it."

"You what?" we said in unison, starting to laugh.

"It's a European thing," Karen went on. "It's very common here, but they haven't caught on in England" We all burst out laughing, as we each took turns straddling the porcelain oddity.

"I can see why they haven't 'caught on' so to speak" scoffed Jenny, as she straightened up. "It's just weird and I think it would make an ideal ash tray. We can just flush the cigarette butts down and voila, evidence gone!"

We all liked that idea. And that's exactly what we used it for. Now, none of us were heavy smokers, being under-age, but we longed to get our hands on some Italian smokes and check them out just as soon as possible.

As we readied for bed that first night, we heard Mrs. Fergus tapping on our door. She'd come up to say good night and explain the rules.

"Curfew is at 11. Lights out at 11:30. That way you'll be fresh and rested for the next day's activities." With no elevator in the building, she was a bit out of breath having hoofed it up three floors to give us this news. She detailed our itinerary which included art museums, a monastery somewhere up in the hills, afternoons on the beach, several excursions around the lake and a very long day in Venice.

"I will be up here every night to make sure you are safe and secure at 11:30, so please be in your beds at that time. Anyone disobeying the rules will be immediately sent home." She underscored this with a stern look to each of us personally. "Understand?"

"Yes, Ma'am!" we chorused back to her. With a satisfied nod, she withdraw and clicked the door shut.

We waited in silence until we were sure she was gone, then we burst out laughing and took a bet as to who would be the first one to be threatened with an early departure.

We had eight days of holiday and sightseeing. We were ready.

Each day at the beach, we toasted our lily-white bodies in the scorching hot sun until we could stand it no longer then retreated to our hotel to nurse our sunburns. Trips out of town by coach were interesting and fun, educational even, as we toured ancient ruins and stopped here and there buying trinkets and souvenirs. Secret missions to obtain cigarettes were common and each night we'd be dutifully waiting under our covers for Mrs. Fergus's bed check at 11:30. But as soon as she was safely down the stairs, we'd spring out of bed, fully clothed, and hustle down the fire escape, spilling into the dark narrow streets looking for adventure.

Every night, local teens congregated around the fountain in the town square. The boys all had Vespa scooters and they'd speed around the tiny streets with girls on the back riding side-saddle, their skirts flying up, their hair blowing in the wind behind them. We got to know many of the local boys and Maureen, Jenny and I all paired off after the first few days and could be found making out in the dark alleys with these gorgeous male specimens. By 2 a.m., we'd sneak back up the fire escape, split one last cigarette, flush it down the bidet and fall into bed giggling, sharing our latest misadventures. And the next day we'd get up and do it all again.

Hands-down, my favorite part of our holiday was the day we spent in Venice. What a magnificent place. We rode in a launch on the Grand Canal and toured an amazing glass factory. The brightly painted bridges and quiet side canals were enchanting and the rows of bobbing gondolas were a huge draw. We were told before we arrived in the city that under no circumstances were we to accept a free ride on

a gondola. Apparently, the young gondoliers were notorious for offering rides to young female tourists, whose fate could be read about in the local police station. We fed the pigeons in St. Mark's Square and bought all manner of souvenirs for ourselves and our families. I purchased a set of hand-blown glass goblets for my mother and a heavy leather bag that I carried proudly for decades.

Yes, we were offered free rides by the gondoliers, but we declined. We never did get to experience that particular mode of transport, but that day in Venice was truly magical. I had a little Brownie camera and took some photo's but not nearly enough. All that remain in my hands after all these years are half a dozen black and white snapshots and a really nice photo of my "boyfriend" Justie, which he enclosed in a letter he sent after I returned to England. I have no idea what the letter said. It was all in Italian and I didn't dare show it to anyone for fear of shock and embarrassment.

When I think now of what could have happened to us; 6 teenage girls running around till the wee hours in a foreign country, I shudder. Somewhere there's a photo of me sneaking a drag off a cigarette behind a bench in St. Mark's square. That evidence of our misadventures disappeared after years in my possession, but my precious memories will live on forever.

This is an excerpt from my memoir, titled "Flying Through Time, with Occasional Crash Landings."

Just Desserts
By Margaret Sargent

"Darn. Just when I get a day off, you have to work," said Angela, registering her displeasure.

"It wasn't my idea," answered her husband.

"I know. Just disappointing."

"Why don't you call Elaine. She's always looking for something to do."

Angie reached for the phone on the kitchen counter, and as she touched it, it rang.

"Hello?"

"Hi, Angie. Got any plans?" It was Maddie, another friend. "It's a perfect day to sit in my backyard with cake and tea and smell the roses. Everything's blooming. It's gorgeous."

"Well, sure. I was about to call Elaine."

"Oh, good. There'll be three of us. I'll break out the good tea service."

Angie called Elaine who said she had an extra tray of hors d'oeuvres she could bring along.

"It's settled, then?" asked Charlie, as he kissed Angie goodbye. In a flash he was out the door, briefcase in hand. Soon after, Angie and Elaine were standing on Maddie's porch.

"This'll be relaxing."

"Yes, and good timing. I'm bushed. Ray had me running all over the place last week, fixing his mistakes."

Angie agreed. "We could both use a change of scenery, or even jobs."

The door opened and Maddie ushered them through the house and out onto the deck. She waved a hand as if she were a presenter, and a beautiful patio table came into view, laden with little cakes, cookies, sandwiches, and a big pitcher of Long Island Ice Tea. Delicate tea cups sat next to small plates, making three elegant place settings.

"Well, well. Have you hired a maid?"

"Heavens, no. I don't want anybody pawing around my property. Anyway, it's not hard to keep the house clean when it's just me."

"Just little ol' you?" asked Elaine, teasing.

Maddie winked. "There's a man here every once in a while, but he doesn't get to stay long enough to cause any trouble. No fuss, no muss." She winked again as she placed Elaine's tray next to the finger sandwiches. "I think we have enough food, but we can always order Chinese later."

Elaine and Angie scanned the deck and Maddie's backyard. The whole scene was a confection.

"Your tea is delightful, and your yard is amazing. Delicious rhododendrons, azaleas, primroses—luscious irises—how do you manage all this?"

"Except for cutting the grass and pulling weeds, the plants manage themselves. I do throw a little fertilizer at them, of course. I'm retired, remember, so I have plenty of time."

They sat down, and Maddie poured the alcoholic tea into their cups.

"Don't you miss being married? I mean, to Bob, the second one? He was a lot nicer than number one." Elaine didn't know much about Maddie's marital situations. Maddie's face clouded. "Nice—right up until he ran off with half my money." She tried not to scowl and made herself brighten as she refilled their cups.

"We probably shouldn't discuss husbands," said Angie, having known Maddie for twenty years and two spouses.

"I don't mind bringing Elaine up to date." Maddie adjusted her napkin on her knee and took a sip of tea.

"Howard was abusive. Said horrible things, the last being that he was going to leave me and marry his yoga instructor. His further sin, one of omission, was that he didn't mention his huge bonus and severance package. He took off with the instructor and all our money. Just left. No trail. It took seven years before I could have him declared dead and receive the insurance money.

"Then Bob. He found out I had more money than he first thought, and he threatened to divorce me and take half—half of this house—half of Howard's insurance money. I paid him off so he would take less, and he ran like a gold medalist. Just like Howard. In another year I can have him declared dead as well. So, I'm not ready for another husband, dear chicks."

"Goodness," said Elaine. "Maybe I'm better off single."

"Hear, hear," said the three women and clinked their cups together.

The afternoon sailed by with the sensation of traveling on a luxurious cruise ship. Scrumptious food, good conversation and laughter. No fuss, no muss, no hurry—until it was time to think of sailing home.

"I want a tour of the garden first," said Elaine.

"Would you take her around while I do a couple of things here?" Maddie asked Angie as she covered the leftovers.

Angie and Elaine were drawn to a sweet smell pulling them in the direction of lilacs. Next were the rhodies, illuminated by the sun beginning to sink toward the horizon. A pink and cream variety fascinated Elaine, and she looked under the bush for a tag that might tell the variety name. There was none, but there was a small name plate that said Maxwell.

"That was Maddie's dog. I remember she buried him here and planted the rhodie over him," said Angie, "and here's Taffy under this one. That was her cat."

They discovered two more pet names and both thought it sweet of Maddie to mark their graves. Then Elaine spotted another strawberry and cream rhodie and without thinking, crawled under to see if she could find the name tag. She came out with a frozen expression.

"What's the matter?"

"There's a name plate that says *Bob*."

Angie's face froze, too. Neither spoke, and Elaine looked under the last rhodie because she couldn't stop herself. She came out shaking.

"*Howard.*"

"It has to be a joke," said Angie.

"Yes, of course. They ran away."

The two women composed themselves and returned to the house, ready to make their goodbyes.

"What the heck happened to you?" asked Maddie, noticing dirt on Elaine's trousers.

"I slipped." Elaine hoped that sounded reasonable. Maddie didn't register any alarm except for Elaine's safety.

In the car on the way home both women kept their eyes straight ahead and neither of them spoke.

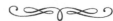

Aspyn the Tiger Moth
By Dennis Archambault

Once Upon a Time...

*W*here *does the time go?* Aspyn, the tiger moth, laments as it flutters above a bed of delectable flowers glistening with nectar.

A verdant carpet of natural splendor extends as far as can be seen and its beauty calms Aspyn. It watches as a light breeze kisses the petals of plants and grass into surging waves. Although it's a lovely view, Aspyn finds that it is tiring more each day from flying.

"I need to rest soon," it reflects. A nagging thought returns, "Am I nearing my time?"

Resting on a delicate fern that sweeps back and forth rhythmically, Aspyn takes a thoughtful breath. "When did it all begin?"

A lifetime of memories flood its thoughts, and with them, nagging questions that cannot be refused.

"Was I a good tiger moth? Did I betray myself or did I fully use and share the gifts bestowed me at birth, with no confessions that I'd get to them later, but didn't?"

A small whirlwind gamboling close to the forest's edge fetches the earliest memory with a jolt. A sudden nightmare returns of a deafening roar from a helicopter overhead blasting pesticide down over everything. Aspyn remembers itself as a fully-grown "woolly bear" caterpillar being blown off the juicy leaf delicacy and thrown far away from the other woolly bears. It slams into a curled leaf holding a large water droplet from the recent rain.

Spared direct drenching of the vicious poison, Aspyn watches as all the other woolly bears writhe in agony and convulse in final uncontrollable spasms, dying.

Aspyn's relief is premature as a deep, burning sensation grows. It realizes that some of the poison was ravenously eating at its skin. The rain droplet dilutes the noxious liquid as Aspyn swipes it from its skin... but,

too late. A veil of darkness intensifies. Strange images gather as Aspyn curled into a tight ball. A distant tunneled light growsintense. Through hooded eyes, Aspyn perceives a council of Ancient, translucent tiger moths descending and chanting as they envelop it. Their concerned faces are discernable through Aspyn's pallid eyes. Even so, with the poison leeching throughout its body, Aspyn's breathing slows and becomes erratic, sinking into numbness. The trees above Aspyn become delicate, edgy silhouettes that dissolve into the pastel blue wash of sky.

In an instant, Aspyn is above its body, watching its own still form. It is fascinated by the Ancient Ones placing their hands on its body and chanting a healing prayer. Aspyn studies the effect as its body grows more vital and straightening as their healing energy is absorbed. An Ancient One speaks to Aspyn telepathically, "You must return, your work is not complete."

Aspyn is repelled by the thought. "No! I'm tired of living in fear. Animals try to eat me and humans poison me. You know what I just went through! I'm a destructive pest and do nothing but destroy beautiful things... just ask them!"

The Ancient One smiles knowingly, "You are trapped in a story that others wrote. You cannot allow yourself to judge yourself by what people say. Stupidity and ignorance are always trumpeted. You must discover your own true essence, then you will find joy in your life and know of your own beauty. What you focus on is what you get. Always remember, inner peace comes when you face your fear." Smiling wryly the Ancient One added, "Besides, there is no choice here."

Aspyn is suddenly back in its body. Surprised at the feeling of its life renewed, Aspyn looks at the world around it, as if for the first time.

The beauty takes its breath. Dropping to the ground from the leaf, Aspyn moves through the tangle of high grass, dead branches and exposed tree roots. Nothing is too great that cannot be overcome. A giddy sense of vitality is seductive as Aspyn increases its stride.

Nighttime approaches and it is time to rest. Looking over a cliff's edge of shocking severity, Aspyn sees a small cabin far below. "Yes!" Aspyn smiles to itself. The way down is treacherous with loose rocks and dirt. Even Aspyn's numerous feet slip out from under it many times. By the time Aspyn reaches the bottom to the cabin, the last of daylight has faded.

Aspyn walks up to the cabin hesitantly. It has bad energy and a sense of foreboding, but the wisps of homey smoke from the chimney invite Aspyn to press on. Moving stealthily now, Aspyn peeks through a large crack in the wall. It sees forms dancing gaily, encouraging Aspyn to crawl through the opening to join them. Just as it is about to do this, a large cockroach scurries out of the same crack from inside. "Don't go in there," Cockroach warns.

Aspyn is taken aback. "Why?"

"Well... look at them," Cockroach snaps back. Aspyn peers at the faint figures. Diaphanous images of mice and birds twirl, and as they do, Aspyn sees that they have hollow backs. Cockroach says knowingly, "Yeah, no backs means that those are ghosts, and this is their feasting ceremony just before they go looking to take the living spirit out of whatever they find. And we're some of their favorites! We've got to get out of here before they quit dancing."

Aspyn and Cockroach rush to the darkest part of the garden, but close enough to see the cabin. Ghost figures sweep out from the chimney and fly off in different directions.

"That was close. Good thing I warned you," Cockroach says proudly, "and now you owe me." Aspyn splutters, "What do you mean?"

Puffing up and fluttering its wings in a display, Cockroach bragged, "I saved your life."

Aspyn is befuddled; this is all too weird, "You did, yes... and, by the way, when did you get wings?"

"All cockroaches have wings; we just move faster and are harder to catch on the ground... we're kinda clunky in flight." Cockroach looks around nervously, *Danger is about.*

They hurriedly search, away from the cabin, until they find a perfect place to rest for the night.

Dawn slides up over the horizon, awakening the two. Neither stirs. They look around cautiously. Cockroach says, "I don't move about much during the day."

Aspyn replies, "I do, now's the time when leaves open to their juiciest."

Cockroach stretches, becoming fully awake, "I'll leave you then... time for me to find a tasty garbage heap to burrow into."

Aspyn forces an appreciative smile, "Good luck with that."

Cockroach scurries away, calling over its shoulder, "Remember, you owe me."

Aspyn watches Cockroach dig into dank areas and move on if they're not suitable. Aspyn looks up at the canopy over it, being alert for birds and the occasional bat that has yet to find a suitable place to roost until nightfall.

After a trek up and over numerous plants, Aspyn comes upon a clearing. A garden spreads out before it. Salivating with excitement, a stunning geranium is closest. It is quite expansive at four feet tall and three feet wide with myriad, tender little leaves. Aspyn hurries up the stalk; it has been too long since he last ate.

Predators to caterpillars, two diminutive deer mice emerge below and chase each other, frolicking. Aspyn freezes in a clump of large leaves. The deer mice scurry away when a tabby cat takes an interest in their game.

Aspyn dares not move for hours. Stealthily, he leaves the garden as quickly as its feet can move without tripping over each other. Aspyn hurries to an old, gnarled oak tree with a large gash high in the trunk from where a big branch broke off in a storm. Aspyn climbs and impulsively enters the hole, but finds a hollow core and the reason the branch broke away from the majestic tree. The walls of the interior are still damp from the recent rain and it loses footing and falls into the deep crevice.

Aspyn lands heavily on a figure at prayer, causing quite a reaction. Showing no ill-intent, Aspyn holds up its hands to indicate no hostility, "Sorry."

Flipping back the hood of its robe, Praying Mantis rubs out the pain in one of its legs as it glares at Aspyn, "You could hurt somebody doing that!" But, Praying Mantis deliberately calms its anger by controlling its breath.

"The walls are wet," Aspyn apologizes. Nodding in agreement, Praying Mantis says, "Well… that's how I come to be here too."

They look up at the hole high above them. Each attempts to climb the walls, but they slip and this time Praying Mantis falls on Aspyn.

"Ooof," Aspyn exclaims.

"My bad," Praying Mantis replies, smiling.

"We're all even now," Aspyn submits.

"Not the right thinking, my little friend, there is no need to make even." Praying Mantis stands fully upright. The height difference is not that great except for the pointed hood now once again covering Praying Mantis' head.

Aspyn gives Praying Mantis a long look, "What's… that thing you wear?"

"It's the robe of a shaman magician," Praying Mantis replies.

"A what?" Aspyn asks.

"Shamans see into people, into their 'spirit body' and we find their true personalities and the issues that disturb their health, their joy of life, their energy field," Praying Mantis says candidly.

Aspyn snaps back, questioningly, "Oh yeah? Well then, what do you know about me?"

Praying Mantis studies Aspyn closely, so closely that Aspyn wants to crawl into a hole somewhere. Presently, Praying Mantis says quietly, "I know you have just been revived from death by heavenly spirits."

Aspyn's eyes open wide, as Praying Mantis continues, "and I see that you hold yourself in contempt… you don't love yourself, you think you don't have any value, that you don't have any gifts to share."

Aspyn's eyes tear, no one has ever before touched its heart so fully. "How do you know all this?" Aspyn whispers.

Praying Mantis smiles empathetically, "Shamans fill their senses with nature, every rustle of grass, every bird song, every whisp of a breeze. Each of these teaches us something. We believe what we see, not what others profess. We especially want to be aware of bad energy… that will save you."

Aspyn's mouth drops open, "I felt that when I got close to the cabin, but…"

"You went closer anyway?" Praying Mantis says frankly, "and that's your problem, you don't honor the deep knowing that you have. And if you continue to doubt your essence, deny your gifts, refuse your warnings… you will likely only end up as a meal, as you would have at the cabin."

Aspyn's head swims.

Praying Mantis offers, "You must learn the ways of nature if you are to fulfill your destiny."

Aspyn extends its palms upwards in a gesture for Praying Mantis to begin. Praying Mantis sits down and draws a circle around it as far as its index finger can reach, then it looks at Aspyn. "I don't have my shamanic drum so we must invite Woodpecker… it is much-favored by the divinities. Its pecking will be as a drum's heartbeat. You will journey on its sound, but first, we must find something here that we can use for our ritual."

Praying Mantis is satisfied as it picks up a leaf, "Now here's something that you know a lot about," as it hands it to Aspyn. "Hold it to your heart."

Aspyn does so.

Praying Mantis continues, "Now step into the circle." Woodpecker begins pecking on the tree trunk outside.

The moment Aspyn steps into the circle, Aspyn drops through space and wings through a magical world. Crystal dewdrops sparkle and wink, tall grasses smile, flowers bow in respect, ants wave from below, and crickets, standing in quartets, sing to Aspyn passing over them. The sky is alive with hundreds of frolicking tiger moths that fly in wondrous synchronicity. Aspyn watches them visiting every flower and becoming yellow with pollen and joins them. The flowers that Aspyn caress beam with dreamy, freshly pollinated grins. The sky is a profusion of colors that rainbows can only envy. Such joy, such freedom! Aspyn deliriously merges with the merriment of ecstatic abandonment. Woodpecker begins pecking a 'shamanic recall,' a beat that is faster and more erratic, that summons the spiritual traveler back from a journey.

Aspyn opens its eyes to see Praying Mantis smiling at it.

Praying Mantis offers, "You've been busy. Your energy body is luminous and quite attractive." Aspyn is giddy, "How long was I gone?" "A day, maybe a little longer," Praying Mantis replies. "Journeying time is not clock time. I was starting to wonder if you'd be back soon enough for us to leave, because I sense that moment is at hand."

Aspyn remains jubilant, "What I saw!"

Praying Mantis chuckles as it looks up at the gashed opening above them, "Nature is taking a hand and we must leave quickly."

The hollowed tree groans with an ominous cracking sound as thunder roils the sky outside and a violent wind torments the weary tree. They both hurry through the new oval-shaped, woodpecker hole to re-enter life outside as if for the first time. They breathe in the exhilarating scent of newly wet earth, again and again.

Inside, hollow sloshing sounds let them know their resting place is now full of water. The storm passes and nature settles back into its bustle of activity.

Praying Mantis turns to Aspyn, "How do you intend to use your life?"

Aspyn is startled—reflective—then hesitantly replies, "I saw a suspended cocoon nest that I made. Then... I was in it, swimming through a gooey, rich mixture of tissues, memory limbs and bodily fluids. And the jelly-stuff-like voice says that a more profound image of me... awaits me."

Aspyn is embarrassed at admitting something so strange and it avoids Praying Mantis' eyes.

"Wonderful work!" Praying Mantis exclaims, startling Aspyn, "and that allows me to go on with my life and leave you, my friend, with your *Becoming*. With no opportunity for Aspyn to say, "Thank you," Praying Mantis flies away.

Aspyn leaps from the tree trunk to enjoy its aerial journey vision, but it only plunges to the ground below in a cushioned bounce on matted grass. It finds a stately, tall plant whose broad leaves provide safety. Attaching a chord to the underside of a leaf, near the stalk, Aspyn follows a primordial urgency in spitting up a saliva-like mixture of hormones and mixing it with its own woolly bear hair. The encasement quickly forms one strand at a time, surrounding Aspyn into a protective shelter. Resting now from the rushed physical exertion, Aspyn's thoughts are as bewildering as those from its hallucinogenic trip from accidentally nibbling magic mushrooms. Aspyn struggles to make sense of its body assimilating a seething cauldron of molecules and membranes.

It abruptly finds himself outside its body again, but hovering close enough to see into its etheric body-cocoon and to perceive the life-legacy process evolving.

Aspyn watches Ancient Ones mingling in the swirling transmutation and harmonizing their vibrations to solidify the formless amalgam. Unassembled, in pieces, Aspyn's insides follow some invisible architectural plan with a heart forming here, lungs there, and wings expanding and evolving, all driven by a primordial destiny.

Days pass. Aspyn awakens to find itself back in its body and as though out of surgery. Aspyn is claustrophobic in its confining prison cocoon. The casing's protective rigidity resists change of any sort, but Aspyn pushes and stretches; its movements split the suffocating structure, and with a final effort, forces it wide open. Aspyn thrusts its body out of the empty casing and opens his wings for the first time.

It pumps internal fluids into the wing's veins, expanding them to be dried by the sun. They are a colorful tapestry of gossamer firmness. Perched on the lightly swaying cocoon shell, Aspyn flaps its wings for the first time and celebrates life with delicate fluttering. Freed from its woolly bear caterpillar life history and guided by a life energy that resonates throughout all of nature, Aspyn leaps into flight. The shamanic vision comes alive as Aspyn cavorts in ecstatic aerial inspiration. Swirling past one tree then another, hovering over one open flower and others, Aspyn is giddy.

Suddenly it senses danger and swiftly descends closer to the ground while scanning the sky above it. It sees a bat harassing something in the distance. Aspyn stares and sees its old companion, Cockroach, scurrying for its life. The bat is unrelenting. Aspyn remembers the Ancient Ones whispering about its new power and at once, Aspyn vibrates the tymbals on its abdomen. The bat becomes confused by the conflicting, pulsing vibration and flies away. Aspyn flutters over to Cockroach and alights next to it.

"Remember me?" Aspyn chuckles knowing it looks nothing like the woolly bear caterpillar that Cockroach knew. Befuddled, Cockroach shakes its head, 'No'.

"We were at the cabin together and you told me that 'I owed you.' Well, my friend, you've been repaid."

Cockroach is amazed, "You've changed!"

Aspyn smiles and laughs, "Good of you to notice." Then adds, "It's not wise to stay here. *Danger is about.*" Cockroach roars in laughter—those were its very words to Aspyn.

Together, they fly away into a sundrenched world of mystery, majesty and most of all, Joy!

Where is the Joy?

Washing the dishes, making the bed.
Doing my stretching and clearing my head.

Laundry and bills, visiting my dying mother,
Doctor's appointments and one thing after
    another.

Where is the joy? Is it in my dog's eyes when he
    looks at me lovingly?
Or the blue-sky day shining outside my window
    beautifully?

There is joy in my friendships which I cherish.
Joy in my serene, lovely home that I relish.

There is joy being with my husband when we
    dream and laugh.
The laughter so strong, I double in half.

There is joy holding my grandson, like no other
    joy.
He giggles and wiggles while he savors a new toy.
He reminds me of my son when he was that age.

Now that is pure joy! Some more of that please!

~ Nancy Moore

Finding Joy

The secret of long life is to live one day at a time
To make a memory while you are still in your prime

Think of your family when you are feeling very blue
Remember all those friends who have been so true

Be grateful for those years that are now in the past
Be thankful always for the blessings of love cast

Open your heart to children—all the girls and boys
Teach them to look to find in their life love and joys

~ Mildred "Millie" Thacker Graves

Ode to Trees
By Evelyn Searle Hess

During the heat dome, my husband David was working the Olympic Trials at Hayward Field in Eugene. As we currently have only one car, I transported him the approximately twenty miles to and from each day's competitions. On my way back to our home in the woods, a few miles north of Lorane, one hot day, I watched the reading on our car's outdoor thermometer dropping steadily as I drove south and west from Eugene. All that concrete in the city is a very effective heat sink, but replaced by green fields and trees, the air becomes friendlier. Cooler, moister air relaxed my neck muscles and invited good deep breaths.

One day, the Trials competition was suspended when the thermometer on the field reached 108F. David said that the track surface registered nearly 140 degrees Fahrenheit and athletes at the starting line burned their fingers in starting position. Studies have shown that unshaded asphalt can be as much as 36 degrees Fahrenheit above the temperature of nearby grass that is shaded from the sun by trees. Eugene's temperature that day peaked at a record 111F. The highest it got at home was 101, and under the trees, it was a full ten degrees cooler.

I was relieved to leave the city and more than grateful for our woods, but it was distressing to hear of the acute suffering—even deaths—of people without a way to escape the heat. Before we, as a society, wrestle with trying to find a source of energy and financing for a million air conditioning units, we might consider planting trees. Trees cool air by evaporating water through their leaves as well as shading the ground from the direct sun.

I've heard of people, understandably spooked by recent forest fires, having trees on their property cut down, thinking that to be a protection from wildfire. It might be surprising to learn that trees not only make the ground beneath and air surrounding them cooler, they also make the air *moister.* They can return up to 75% of their water to the air, the "tree sweat" making rain clouds that help water the forest and even travel on air currents to affect the weather farther away. Widespread clearcuts can make deserts. No trees, less rain... less rain, less water in rivers... less water for agriculture... less water for us to drink.

Most all of us know that trees and other green plants make the oxygen we breathe. Increasing numbers of us have learned that not only do all green plants help pull excess carbon dioxide from the atmosphere, photosynthesizing that carbon to make the sugars that feed them, but also that our Pacific Northwestern forests are one of the planet's best carbon sinks. Since 1980, forests have moderated climate change by absorbing about a quarter of the carbon emitted by human activities. That carbon is stored in the tree itself and, through the roots, it is also stored in the soil. At the same time that the forest is moderating the climate, it is providing homes for countless species—flying species, creeping, leaping and slithering ones, as well as those rooted in the ground. This is no small thing at a time when more than half a million species are threatened with extinction from insufficient habitat. And the roots of the trees, along with the roots of all the plants in the forest understory, help hold the soil in place. Bare soil flows downhill with the rains, eroding away precious topsoil that fills basements with mud in a downpour flood.

Beyond all those attributes that I can list dispassionately, I simply love our woods. Every time I come home I breathe a deep sigh and feel my chest swelling with joy as I enter our tree-lined driveway. Have you read the "Shinrin-Yoku" (translated as "forest bathing") studies? Time spent in the forest atmosphere has measurably positive effects in improving cardiovascular health, concentration, memory and energy, reducing stress and lifting depression. That's easy for me to believe. I experience it almost daily.

So if trees help our health as well as the lives of countless other species, and while they're doing that they clean the air as they absorb its pollutants through their leaf pores, provide more indispensible water, and moderate the climate, why wouldn't we want to spread the good? The famous biologist E. O. Wilson says we need to keep half the earth wild to preserve our planet's biodiversity. That's not hard on our lot, as more than half of it is woods, but how easy would it be in the city? Most moderate sized lots could probably dedicate at least a third of the property to green growing things, even if not technically "wild." Even your oats or prize petunias photosynthesize, and the apple tree casts welcome shade. Perhaps a third of the property could be under the shade of one or more spreading tree. A greater challenge comes with smaller lots and more developed places. But there can still be space for street trees, parking-strip gardens, roof gardens and balcony plants as well as designated pocket parks.

Communities in lower socioeconomic position often live where hot-weather temperatures are ten or more degrees higher than those in affluent tree-lined neighborhoods. Frequently polluting industries locate near these marginal communities and, without the benefit of filtering trees, residents breathe in the pollutants. As a rural resident, I wouldn't have an opportunity to vote for such city measures, but I hope there will be a concerted effort to get street trees and parks in areas of town now devoid of green space. I hate thinking of people breathing harmful air and I don't want to see another hot spell when whole communities are without the saving graces of trees.

Meanwhile, I'm so very grateful for ours. Their seasonal changes are my calendar. Their resins in the summer and leaf decay in the fall keep my olfactory senses delighted. The finches exploding from and swooping to their branches enthrall me. Near their roots I find orchids in the spring and from their branches I hear warblers sing. I mulch my garden with their duff and warm my house with downed trees and their cast parts.

The trees protect us from the wind like a sheltering parent and provide a cool respite from a too-active sun. They give us oxygen and clean air to breathe and their roots hold on to the soil on the hill above our house. Each day I thank them for being there and give a silent prayer for their continued health. As they help moderate the climate I only hope that we humans will put brakes on the spiraling climate chaos before it's beyond the trees' ability to effect.

one little victory

if my wish could be blown
... on candles
it's surely been blown
for years

through all of the struggle
all of the dreams
all of the pain
and the tears

to have that little bit
... of success
that I have something
to say

after all these years
... of trying
that something has gone
my way

just one little victory
is all I need
one little victory
for me

I've held on for so long
I've tried to remain strong
just one little victory
for me

in times of utter despair
I've still risen to the task
to try and
be strong

just trying to hold on
wondering
is it too much
to ask
optimism

has always been part of me
a smile
always on my face

through heartache and stress
and yes, even death
I've tried to just stay
in my place

just one little victory
is all I need
one little victory
for me

I've held on for so long
I've tried to be strong
just one little victory
for me

~ C. Steven Blue

Coming Home

She hears the whistle call her in
Like the harmonious sound of coming home
I hear the pounding steps get louder
as her hooves press harder into the ground

The smell of dirt and dust tickles my nose
a surrounding I know well
just rotten boards and baling twine
holding this life together

Her blaze is shining in the sun
My face lights up as it touches hers
The halter barely fits her now
But we are ready to fly once again

~ Linsey Kau (Haxby)
Groundwaters Vol 5 Iss 4 (2009)

Backyard Melodies

Within the darkness of the pond-slowed stream,
which glides behind our somewhat urban home,
the sound of chorus frogs arrives each spring,
and I'm relieved that they have, once more,
come.

As tadpoles do they practice with a hum?
Yo Yo Ma can pull a river's limpid flow
of music, always, with his artful bow,
that reassures, and calms, and tells me this.
In our chaotic year, from frog or cello,
the notes of pond or strings bring welcome
bliss.

~ Susanne Twight-Alexander

Paydirt
By Vicki Sourdry

The music of Tosca flowed through the hallways of the *Golden Pelican.* Maria smiled. That meant Chester had found something. He always played Puccini when he was happy. She preferred music a few hundred years more modern, but to this mining ship, Puccini was good. It meant credits in their account.

"What did we find?" she asked as she entered the small Control Room. They had been hovering over this new asteroid for a month, and with the radar had only found small amounts of metal, until now.

He was smiling. "Water. We found water."

Maria smiled. Water meant oxygen and hydrogen for fuel to sell to ships that docked here on their way somewhere else. It meant shielding from solar radiation. It meant water for their solar arrays. It meant water for living and growing. These asteroids were rare.

"How much?"

"Hard to tell. That's your job." His smile was infectious.

Maria sat down at her science station and began the tedious job of analyzing the find... quality, quantity, purity. Finally, hours later, it all looked good. She gave a report to Chester, and then said, "Looks like a good payday, finally."

He informed the crew of the find, and ordered Jasmine to land. Maria stretched to get the kinks out of her back from hunching over the computer for so long. "Ready for a break? I'm hungry."

"Sure." He called Fiona to come up and run the Control Room while they were gone.

They didn't have a set work schedule. They worked until they were hungry, then they ate. Then they worked until they were tired, and they slept. There was no night and day on the ship. They were attaching to an asteroid out in The Belt, beyond the orbit of Mars. It tumbled lazily in its long circuit around the sun. They were too far from the sun to have it dictate their cycles, but it did fill their huge solar arrays, in abundance. From the batteries, power flowed through the ship and its attendant cables and mining equipment. The more they worked, the more credits they made, and the sooner they could sell the operation and the ship, and go back to Mars to live comfortably for the rest of their lives. Asteroid mining was a sometimes dangerous and always lonely existence. Besides their shipmates, the only time they saw other people was when a ship docked to sell them supplies, when one came to buy fuel, or when a freighter came to buy their metals.

Dinner was pasta with re-hydrated cheese and something Chester called "mystery protein." A supply ship was scheduled to dock in a few days. Until then, they ate whatever was left in the larder. The cook doubled as an 'outside worker,' making space walks when repairs or maintenance was necessary. The ship was middle-aged, so he was outside more frequently these days.

Several days later, Chester checked the calibrations in the high-temp electrolysis converter. It was slow going, but oxygen and hydrogen were flowing into the separate tanks.

"I love the credits and benefits from water, but nickel is so much more valuable than the other metals." Marie said, keeping her eyes on the gauges.

Chester smiled, "Agreed, but it's also so much rarer. I've studied so many of these rocks with the radar, and they nearly all come back carbon. Useful, but we can't retire on it." She nodded.

There were ten people on the *Golden Pelican.* Chester and Maria owned the operation, and the rest were trusted, long-time employees. They had all been together for 20 years and sixteen asteroids. They all shared the profits.

Maria left the Control Room to run an errand in Life Support.

"Maria?"

"Yes Yuri? Great job on the probe placement yesterday, by the way."

The burly red-head blushed. "Thanks. I wanted to ask you if we could get something from the supply ship next time."

"Of course. Just put it on the list. You know that."

"Well, it's going to be a surprise, so I don't want her to know." Yuri and Jasmine had been together for more than 18 years. He had even made her a ring from one of their gold strikes... a totally devoted couple. Maria couldn't imagine Yuri being able to keep a secret from her.

"I understand," she responded with a smile. "What would you like to get?"

"Seeds. She wants to grow tomatoes." He said it almost apologetically.

"Oh my, Yuri, that would be wonderful! Fresh tomatoes would be such a treat." They had a hydroponic garden in the solarium, but it mostly grew leafy vegetables like lettuce and greens.

Yuri smiled broadly.

Maria laughed. "I'll contact the next supply ship and see what they have."

"Thanks, Maria!" Yuri walked with a spring in his step as he headed down the hallway.

Jasmine was their pilot/navigator/course corrector... a 'jane of all trades.' It was her responsibility to move them from one asteroid to the next when it was time, to make sure the ship was always space-worthy, to slow the orbit of the asteroid if it was too erratic, and basically make sure the ship was healthy and safe.

"Chester!" Jasmine's voice broke the silence in the Control Room a few days later.

"Yes?"

"We have a problem. There was a collision of two asteroids about 10 minutes ago. Now one of them is on a collision course with us. It'll sideswipe us. We have about an hour."

"Thanks. Mark it in the file. I'll get back to you shortly."

He called it up on his screen. Jasmine had highlighted the problem already. Maria came and stood over Chester's shoulder.

"Wow."

Chester took a couple breaths. "Shut down the converter. Get everyone inside. Red alert for collision."

Chester called Jasmine back. He saw the red light already flashing on the wall.

"Can we move far enough to miss?"

"I don't think so. But I've already started."

"If we move at top speed, where will it hit us?"

"I've calculated it will hit on the other side or the bottom, but I can't be certain."

"Do what you can. Let me know." He closed the connection.

In 20 years, they had never had a collision. Not even a near miss. "Damn," he said under his breath.

He looked at Maria. "Have Bobbie get the escape pod ready. We'll have to launch well before the collision to get free, and that might not even work. If it shatters the asteroid, who knows where the pieces will go."

"I'll contact all ships in the area to warn them, and have them pick us up if the *Pelican* is totaled."

"Yes." Chester was silent for a few seconds, then he switched on the intercom to the whole ship.

"Bad news folks. Asteroid fragment from a collision is heading for us. We're trying to move out of the way, but probably won't have enough time. We have," he looked at his watch, "about 50 minutes. Close down your stations. Get your survival gear and get to the escape pod. This is not a drill folks, this is real. If we have to launch, we need to do so in 30 minutes. That is all."

"Go get our stuff," Chester said to Maria. "Then go to the escape pod. Organize the others. They're good, but they'll be scared."

She nodded, finishing the "Mayday" call to any ships in the area, and warning them of the first collision, and maybe the soon-to-happen second collision.

"Love you," she said as she left the Control Room.

"Love you too."

"Where's Jasmine?" Yuri asked desperately.

"Trying to get us out of the way," Maria answered. "She'll be here. We aren't going without her."

"But we have to launch soon."

"I know. Chester isn't here either. Get everyone else settled in and make sure all gear is safely stowed so we're ready to go when they get here."

"Yes, ma'am."

Maria was worried about Jasmine and Chester too.

She finally keyed the communicator to the Control Room.

"Chester?"

"Yes?"

"We're ready to launch."

There was a pause.

"Good. Stand by."

"Are you and Jasmine coming?" She tried to keep the fear out of her voice.

"Yes. Just trying to get out of the way. We'll be there."

"OK."

When she looked into Yuri's eyes, she saw the same fear she was feeling. She smiled and gave a thumbs up. He smiled, but it didn't reach to his eyes.

Five minutes later, Chester and Jasmine came running down the hall and entered the escape pod. He sealed the door, and she immediately released the pod from the ship. She piloted it away, at a sharp upward angle from the asteroid. Speed increased quickly, and all the passengers were pushed deep into their seats. All eyes were on one of the screens in front of Jasmine. It showed the asteroid with the *Golden Pelican* attached. It was the first time in 20 years any of them had seen it from a distance. Maria laughed nervously. The others looked at her.

"It looks more like a butterfly than a pelican," she explained. And it did. The huge triangular solar array wings dwarfed the long 'body' of the ship, and the 'legs' stretched out to attach to the asteroid with cables and probes, and, eventually, with mining equipment to withdraw the metals or water found in the interior of the rock. It really was beautiful in its own way.

After about 10 minutes, they could all see a movement beyond and below the asteroid— the fragment from the earlier collision. The hurtling rock was spinning at a great rate, and hit the bottom of their asteroid, churning and shattering about a third of it into a million pieces, which spread out through space. The fragment had then unceremoniously stabbed itself into what was left of their asteroid.

The small crew in the escape pod breathed again. The debris from the collision mostly went 'down,' while they were 'up.' Best of all, the *Golden Pelican* was still attached. The spin of the asteroid was significantly slower than it had been, barely turning at all now.

"Well done, Jasmine!" Maria said with a huge sigh of relief. Applause erupted in the small escape pod.

Chester got everyone's attention. "We are still in jeopardy, people. We need to get back to the *Pelican* and see what happened." Everyone knew it was true, and no one knew if the ship would still be livable, or functioning, when they got back. But for now, they had survived.

The next two hours took them back to the *Golden Pelican*. During that time, three ships had responded to their Mayday signal and contacted them, offering help. Chester told them the situation, and put them on 'stand by' to help if the ship was unrecoverable.

As the pod finally nosed into its berth, the crew began to unharness and grab gear. They all had oxygen masks on and tanks hanging from their belts in case the ship had been breached.

Chester evacuated the air from the lifeboat into its holding chamber and pressed the pad to open the door to the ship. Air flowed in. That meant there was no breach, and the recyclers were still working—at least in this section of the ship. A good sign.

Over the next twelve hours, everyone had a job to do—check their areas of expertise and repair if necessary, report any failures to Maria in the Control Room, and see if they all still had a home to live in and a job to do.

All in all, they were very lucky. Life support and navigation were undamaged. The solar arrays needed some repair, but amazingly, most still worked. Repair parts could be purchased, transported and installed; and Gerald, their cook/maintenance expert, was hopeful. He checked everything, inside and out, and patched some damaged areas.

Industrial connection to the asteroid was an issue. Most of the cables and tubes had been blown out. Yuri worked tirelessly to repair and reconnect them.

The hydrogen and oxygen tanks had breached, so their "payday" had evaporated, literally, into space. It had left the *Golden Pelican* without anything to sell to passing ships. They would be living on the credits in their account until they could get new tanks. That account was the retirement for the entire crew.

Chester and Maria thanked the ships standing by to help and released them from their "Mayday Obligation." Over time, life returned to normal, but without income from the asteroid. It had little to offer the miners now.

The supply ships came and filled their larders, and replacement parts were either purchased or ordered. Freighters skipped them.

Days later, Chester suggested that they check out the fragment that had caused their emergency in the first place. They couldn't see it, but knew that it was a huge piece of rock, embedded into 'their' softer asteroid. They would have to move the ship to the fragment. Two of the crew suggested that they cash in what they had and return to Mars. With the collision, it would be less than they hoped and expected. But they were ready to retire, even if it meant they would have to work once they got to Mars. They had all been thoroughly scared. Chester and Maria thought seriously about it.

"What do you really want to do?" Maria asked. "Deep in your heart."

Chester looked at her, and inward to himself. "One last try. It almost killed us, but I want to see what it has for us."

Maria hesitated, and smiled. "I do too. Then we're done." Chester nodded.

They called a crew meeting. Maria spoke.

"Any of you who want to go, are certainly free to do so. The *Argus* supply ship is coming in five days, and they will take you to Mars if you wish. We will have your portion of the ship account transferred to whatever account you wish. However, if you wish to remain, you will have your account increased by whatever we find on the fragment. This will be our last asteroid. Chester and I are retiring after this. I hope you stay with us. We have been a team for a long time,"

The vote was unanimous. One last expedition.

Everyone shut down their stations and stowed their equipment. Yuri unattached and stowed all the cables and probes. The solar panels were folded and stowed. Jasmine planned the move carefully. It all took six days.

"Prepare for disengagement." Jasmine's calm voice rang through the ship. "Three minutes." Chester got eight affirmative responses. Everyone was harnessed and ready.

There was a slight jerk when the last of the anchors was released and the maneuvering thrusters kicked on. The *Golden Pelican* moved slowly around the asteroid. Jasmine piloted it down around the bottom to a position above the new rock. Chester used the radar to determine its composition. After about 10 minutes, he smiled.

"Puccini?" Maria asked.

"Puccini. It's nickel/iron. We hit paydirt."

"No, paydirt hit us," Maria said with a relieved smile. The music of Madame Butterfly flowed through the ship.

Social Distancing of the Stars

I can relate now to the silence
Of the social distancing
Of the stars

Like when I used to meditate
... Deeply
Or when I would climb up waterfalls

Listen to the mountain spring
How softly it speaks
To your inner ear

In the densely populated
Memories
Of Mother Earth

Wisdom sings
Listen closely

So you will never forget
Bathe in the refreshing
Water of Life
And come clean

~ C. Steven Blue

My Secret Garden

My secret garden is a green sanctuary;
when I visit there, it restores my soul.
The wind in the trees witnesses the solitude.
I go there in the cool of the day.

The birds are chirping their own songs of praise.
My green sanctuary has no stained-glass
    windows.
The tall trees are like a cathedral reaching to the
    sky;
and when the wildflowers are in bloom,
there are Trilliums in every corner of my room,
nodding their pure white heads and bright green
    leaves.

They are a reminder of another Trinity.
The fresh air flowing through the fern whispers
    its own story.
I am so blessed by natures witness.
It brings me peace and that is eternal.
I cannot stay in my green sanctuary.
I must share it with the world.
It is always open to everyone.

~ Rosanna Martin

Elder

Teach me, dear stone, of my soul.
Tell me of light and dark and light...
and water.
Tell me of tides, and thunder,
the swift footstep of creatures,
the love in my heart.
Teach me of the deep, deep earth. And air.
And surrender.
of movement and stillness.
of origin and journey,
of form, and texture and color...
of sparks.
I take you with me in blood and memory,
in hand in pocket
pressing and turning
until within becomes completely without.
Teach me, dear stone, of my soul.

~ Judy Hays-Eberts

Komila Chandra
By David Erickson

The Bean Counter's atmosphere is bright without glare and just crowded enough at any time to suggest the site's quiet popularity. Komila is seated, as is her custom most days, alone at a small high-top near a street-side window, cup in one hand, foldie in the other, scanning headlines without much interest.

Not for the first time, she marvels at the coffee's convincing aroma, its heat in her nostrils, and the visceral certainty of each luxurious sip. She sets the cup aside, her fingertips grazing its surface as she releases the handle. Its ceramic context is undeniable. That such nuanced sensations as these can be conveyed within a construct never ceases to intrigue her. The craftsmanship of the experience here is among the best anywhere, and she looked around deliberately before choosing this one.

Likewise, the continuity of the scene proceeding streetside, beyond her window seat, is an anomaly of sorts in virtua. Unlike most fee-comp nodes, as The Bean Counter has ever been, the exterior activity and architecture is immaculate and convincing. She's watched carefully over the course of many subjective hours here at her favored table by the window—always hers, no matter the time of day nor the volume of clientele, worth the extra simoleons. The virtual tableau through her window view proceeds without apparent loop or even a subtle reordering of recognizable components.

It has become her preferred entry portal, a casual, unpretentious ambiance from which she can decompress after work, review and select from a menu of experiences, meet with friends, play, relax, commune. The value of such experience is proven to be therapeutic.

She swipes across the foldie, shifting all the content into a corner, scrolls through a short list of personal messages without reply, and schedules a day trip with her friend, Yunie, to visit a mountaintop monastery in Nepal this weekend. A breathtaking teaser assured her the monks themselves have developed a masterful virtual reflection of the vertigo-inducing site.

No one seems to pay any attention to Eric as he makes his way between knots of patrons engaged in animated exchanges and others, like Komila, in quiet pursuit of personal interests. He stops at a polite distance from her table and graces her with an open smile.

Komila's avatar is of the current trend for many older citizens of the virtual milieu, an unpretentious representation of the corporeal without excessive post-corrections. She appears a slightly plump, fortyish woman with pleasant, dark-complected, East Indian features. She wears an ornamental bindi with a small peridot on her forehead. She doesn't stand, but stares at him over her cup with a narrowed brow.

"Whoever you are, everyone knows that face. You should go away."

"You are correct, Mrs. Chandra," he says. "That is why no one else would try to wear it here but me. You are also correct to be skeptical. Here is my validation."

A Character wouldn't know her name outside of a scenario and this isn't one. Komila has an unclocked moment. The documentation is authentic; unless the concrete foundations of AsReal have broken down, there is no question. It really is him.

"You're really him," she says and wishes she could have those words back. She places her cup in front of her. "Why are you here at my table, sir?"

"I apologize for the interruption in your experience, Mrs. Chandra," he says. "I have a matter of personal importance to discuss with you."

He has a likeable, boyish face and all the lines in it turn upward, as if they've done it often. A good-looking man, as famous for his asocial behavior as for his numerous accomplishments and, if one can believe, accounts, questionable, possibly terrifying motives.

There are so many things she thought she might say to this person, should the implausible opportunity ever arise. Flustered, she settles for, "Go ahead."

"This venue is far more open than I prefer. More so than is prudent for such a conversation. Will you spare a few minutes of your time to accompany me so we may speak privately?"

Komila searches the nearby tables in the window's reflection to see if heads have turned toward her noteworthy new acquaintance. None conspicuously so, it would appear.

"What about, Mr. Gerzier?" She pronounces his name with the proper French-Canadian enunciation, rather than the American bastardization so typical among those who do not like him, and there are so many. "I am, as you may imagine, confounded as to why you would need to speak with me at all."

"Your son, Rahm, Mrs. Chandra."

Her peridot tips into the furrow between her eyebrows and she allows herself to give the surroundings' reflection a more critical review. She considers a number of responses as she does so, some of them civil. She isn't concerned for her safety; wherever he might take her to 'speak privately' must exist, if that's the right word, within AsReal. As bizarre as this moment has become, she reminds herself, she is in no real danger from this man. Or anything, really. Her Autonomy and Exit rights guarantee it. Aside from any of that, what does the notorious Eric Gerzier have to do with her child?

"May I ask where we are going?"

"My home. And I apologize in advance for the abrupt transition."

"What?"

The coffee shop motif dissolves and Komila is weightless a heartbeat before the site's physics capture and settle her into an overstuffed chair.

"Oh!" she pipes and cannot get that back either.

Eric's chair faces hers at a discrete distance.

"Again, Mrs. Chandra, I apologize," he says, "but this was the first opportunity I've had to reach out to you. Are you all right?"

She's had rougher transitions. They say the more coherent the communication between AIs on either end of a transfer becomes, smoother, less visceral responses will become commonplace rather than exceptional. Sometimes it seems like two pilots trying to land the same aircraft, each only able to control the opposite side of the plane. A soft landing like this is a memorable one. Her personals have followed her as well, as they should, cup steaming on a side table, clutch and foldie next to it.

"I'm fine, thank you."

Her first assessment of the interface is a quick one. Impressive presentation, stunning aesthetics. Her natural curiosity would draw her straight in, but she knows enough not to be spellbound by a site's glamour until it's time to do so. The nature of this particular interaction precludes it anyway.

"I'm not sure whether to be flattered or afraid that you even know who I am, Mr. Gerzier. What is your interest in my son?"

"Rahm has made direct application to my Promethean Project School. It is unusual, given his age... twelve next week, is that correct?"

"No."

"He's not?"

"I mean no, I will not co-sign his application. I will not allow him to join your cult army. He is a boy. He does not understand what he is doing and you..." Komila is surprised that she is able to keep her voice level, "You cannot have him."

Eric's expression does not alter, except maybe around the eyes, as if perhaps she'd stung him with that 'cult army' jab. She expected him to look angry or something, but he doesn't. She's waiting for his rebuttal. It doesn't come. He just sits there and twinkles at her. She notices herself noticing that this irritates her quite a bit and knows that's not a good place for her words to come from, but here they come anyway.

"I have heard things about your students and your school," she says. "Even if they're not true, the accusations disturb me deeply. It is common knowledge, I'm told, those enrolled in your school lose their American citizenship and that alone is reason enough to decline your offer." She watches for him to react, a hint of a smirk or scowl, a hasty denial, something to confirm her words. If anything, he looks solemn.

"I have asked to speak with you like this because it is the School's responsibility to notify you of your son's application within a very specific and prohibitive timeframe. Any number of my associates could deliver this information to you in a formal setting, but this is personal to me. It is precisely young people like Rahm for whom the School was designed. I consider it a courtesy to bring you into the moment personally and as directly as possible. This I have done. In similar fashion, I have made it possible for you to bring your husband, Madhu, into this moment as well, if you wish it."

Oh no, she thinks.

"No," she says.

Dammit, she thinks. Madhu will be all for it.

"Very well," Eric says. "A moment ago, you mentioned declining my offer. I have made no offer. Rahm has made application, quite on his own initiative, and I am following protocol.

"He is a gifted young man. That much is obvious. He has a window of opportunity to understand and develop those gifts. The fact that he understands this and has taken responsible action, at an age when an overwhelming number of his peers are adrift, is significant. The Promethean Project School was created to nurture talented young people like Rahm, help

them focus their abilities toward overcoming the challenging aftermath of the so-called End Times. You have, no doubt, seen some of the work that's being done around the globe by my 'cult army.'"

"I know you're trying to change the world by bullying governments into doing things your way because you think no one can stop you."

"That is an unproductive exaggeration. We are striving to help heal the damage we have done to the planet and we are not alone, but we have taken bold steps others cannot. We are not trying to change the world, Mrs. Chandra. We are changing how we live with it, if we can.

Komila knows it will be unproductive to say, "You sound just like Madhu," but there it is anyway, right out there, word for word. Her peaking frustration, both at her own impetuous speech and at this shadow celebrity's obvious ploy—attempting to weave Rahm's uncharacteristic and troubling recent behavior into what she knows to be twisted facts about his own lofty actions and motives—have given her medications in Real a test. She can feel her anxiety spiking. "What I mean is, I see no reason to continue this conversation. Rahm is not of age to make this choice for himself and I will not change my mind."

She stands, and Eric with her. "Will you have your agent return me now, or must I exit here?"

"Your previous frame will be restored, of course, Mrs. Chandra. Before you go, I will ask you to share this with your husband."

Eric extends an open hand with something in it she's heard about. She doesn't reach for it.

"What's in it?"

"It is the complete four-dee record of Rahm's application exam submission to the School. I am still following protocol, Mrs. Chandra. As a minor, Rahm understands he is not legally entitled to Privacy and, by his submission, has allowed this record to be made. It is your parental right to have it." He holds the thing between them in the steepled fingers of one hand.

"Is this the original and only iteration?"

"The original, yes. The School will retain a copy for its records, of course."

It is the size of a robin's egg, but angular, and its surface seems to be indistinct, shifting in conflicting Escher-esque motion. It is unpleasant to look at.

"Of course," she says and plucks it from his fingertips. It squirms in her palm. She snatches her clutch from the side table and releases the weird thing into it, snapping it closed even as her cup bounces and coffee splatters the carpet.

"Oh!" Hand over her mouth, furious at her gracelessness and the mess it's caused, she reminds herself this is virtua. There is no mess, no good reason to feel foolish. She looks at her cup on its side, the dark blot contrasting with the carpet pattern, splattered drops on Eric's shoes.

She expects to see on his face the look her father would show her whenever she spoke or acted without thinking. He showed it to her often. Instead, Eric's eyes are kind. She can't remember ever seeing a validated four-dee of him without an expression of good-natured patience. Her favorite channeler often likens it to the vacant look of a lobotomy patient. Ha ha. Komila isn't seeing that today, up close and personal. Yes, this is vee, but she reminds herself, this is a Person, not a Character. His manner seems effortlessly genial and respectful. Even here, he maintains a polite distance and demeanor, not quite the arrogant, polarizing figure as he's been depicted. She has a brief glimpse of how her information stream has narrowed, and her views with it. She wonders what's become of her old skepticism and inquisitiveness. And she is curious.

Behind the man, the entire long wall from floor to ceiling is cabinetry crafted from some rich vermillion wood. An eclectic assortment of mementos and artifacts, some of them recognizable, and objects of either artistic or inexplicable purpose dominate open shelving. Books stack, stand, or slump between them all. Nearby, a wide stair curves upward to a mezzanine and what appears a spacious, softly illuminated common area beyond. At the far end of the study, a single painting commands the wall, an energetic abstract backlit to allow translucent elements to stand out in colorful relief. Turning to see what's been at her back the whole time, she barely realizes her tari has begun walking toward it, a single, monolithic transparency spanning the entire length of the room. A few steps carry her to what seems a precipitous edge. Beyond is an undulating sea under a crystalline half-moon. Dark, roiling surf scours the lagoon below.

Komila realizes she's allowed herself to be drawn in against her best intentions and drags her attention from the view, back to the contradiction of the man.

"I understand your reticence," he says, "and I don't presume to know the precise narratives that dominate your perception of my work. I trust you haven't predicated all your hopes and prayers upon their guidance alone. More immediately, however, I trust you and Madhu will choose to understand why Rahm has made this decision. I believe he wants that understanding from you more than anything today."

She wants to ask why he thumbs his nose at laws and governments where he has no right to involve himself at all. They say his workers are given implants and become robotic. And does he really grow inhuman creatures in tanks as laborers and soldiers? And why, maybe the most telling question of all, does he care what one disturbed little boy does or doesn't do? Her opportunity to probe the celebrated recluse will never be any better than this and Komila is disoriented once more to find herself in the Bean Counter, seated alone at her high-top by the window.

There is a small node the size of a pea behind her right ear—not really; it's a AsReal thing—but she presses it just so and the gesture initiates the exit protocol. She is in a

cubicle, a soft-cornered booth as immaculate as it is austere. A luxurious reclining couch covered in a tough synthetic hide is central and a low, integrated shelf runs the length of one long wall for personal belongings. These, a charging stack on the shelf, and a double hook at the door to hang her coat and hat, represent the only differences between a virtuary and a closet.

She reaches for her tiny handbag and her foldie within. The back of her hand brushes the vorp. It is still obnoxious. She opens the foldie to its margins and a three-dee three-sixty of Eric Gerzier's study displays on the seamless matte surface. A linking icon accompanies the image with a personal note from the celebrated recluse in a casual, cursive script. It seems merely a polite close with no answers to the questions she was not even allowed time to ask. She folds the sheet into neat quarters and slips it into her clutch. Well, maybe she will ask them.

She cups her mask to her face and it seals below her eyes and under her chin. A breath in and out to test it, she steps into the hallway toward the exit with a purpose. There will be no more socializing in virtua for Komila today. No time for further diversions of any kind. Nor will there be, as much as she is committed to maintaining her rigid fitness regimen, time for an energetic workout. She's got something in her clutch that will make Madhu just absolutely shit himself.

Fifty Butt

The other day,
My neighbor's precocious peach-fuzzed son
Tailed me up the stairs.
At the top he said, "You have a fifty butt."

"Fifty butt? Really?
So, what's a fifty butt?"

He went on,
"A fifty butt happens to lots of guys your age.
There's nothing there.

Your Levi's back pockets just hang.
There's nothing on the other side of 'em,
Nothing there—
Just the shape of your wallet."

Well, okay. Fifty butt?
If I have a fifty butt
And there's nothing there,
I also want to know

Do I have a fifty belly?

~ Dave Polhamus

Black & White and 1965

Back when
the girls
couldn't stop
screaming at the

handsomest
cameraman
ever to film–
Paul McCartney

~ Kris Bluth

Living Away from Home
By Ruth Kanagy

When I was fourteen, I left home for the first time to go to boarding school. After almost eight years of Japanese education, my parents thought I should solidify my English knowledge. I did not resist leaving home, since other missionary kids were doing the same thing.

So in the fall of 1966, I packed my suitcase and took the train three hours west to Sapporo, the capital of Hokkaido. Huge department stores clustered around the train station; cars, buses and taxis filled the wide boulevards—a contrast to the rural town surrounded by rice paddies and volcanoes where my parents lived.

I moved in with the Blossers, missionary colleagues of my parents, who had turned their home into a hostel so missionary kids from outside Sapporo could attend Hokkaido International School. "Uncle Gene" and "Aunt Louella" took care of seven kids besides their own three. There were eight girls and two boys aged five to fourteen. My best friend, Gloria, whom I'd known since age four, and I shared a bedroom upstairs in the roomy house. We stuck together like peanut butter and honey.

Every morning I climbed down from the top bunk and stumbled toward the window. The sun glinted through the lace curtain, spotlighting specks of dust in the air. Gloria crawled out of her bottom bunk and joined me, rubbing her eyes and shaking loose her wavy brown hair. Looking out the window we sang, *Oh what a beautiful morning, oh what a beautiful day...* Our sleepy voices croaked like toads. This was our morning routine, rain or shine... just because it was weird.

After breakfast ten of us kids grabbed book bags and lunches and walked past single-family houses and empty lots to our school in the suburbs of Sapporo. The two-story concrete building held classrooms for fifty students in grades one to nine—Americans and a few Canadians, mostly children of missionaries.

Our ninth-grade English teacher was Mrs. Merz, who had gray permed hair and oval glasses. She came from the American military base in Chitose, an hour away. She stood upright and appeared ill at ease facing us.

"Class, for your next homework I want you to write a composition based on personification," she said.

A boy raised his hand. "What does personification mean?"

"It means to take an inanimate object and write a story from the point of view of that object," said Mrs. Merz.

That evening I wrote in my notebook about a day in the life of my book bag as it got jostled around on a crowded city bus. The next morning I tore out the sheets and turned them in.

When Mrs. Merz handed back our compositions she paused next to my chair and looked at me intently. I was surprised to see 'A+' on my paper.

"Ruth, you write very well. You should consider becoming a writer," she said.

I glanced up, startled. Instead of saying "Thank you," like a normal American, I started laughing. I tried to calm myself and rearrange my face into a serious expression, but the giggles kept shooting up from my diaphragm. I couldn't stop. Mrs. Merz arched her eyebrows and pressed her lips together. I looked down at my desk and wished I could disappear.

Several days later I found out that she told the principal that she never wanted to teach missionary kids again because we were so rude! That was the first demerit against my character—"demerit" was an unfamiliar word. Looking back, I think my laughter was a Japanese response of embarrassment. To be polite in Japan requires negating any compliments.

At the hostel, "Aunt Louella" talked fast and moved fast and ran an efficient household. She had a no-nonsense silver streak in her dark hair that swooped back into a bun. She hung a chore chart on the wall with our jobs for each day: setting the table, clearing the table, washing dishes, cleaning the living room, and making school lunches for ten. If we did a good job, we got a purple orchid sticker by our name on the chart; if we didn't, we got an onion.

"Ruth and Gloria, it's your turn to make lunches for tomorrow," Louella said.

"OK," Gloria said. She turned to me. "Let's make peanut butter and jelly sandwiches."

"That should be simple enough," I said. We opened two loaves of white bread and set them on the kitchen counter.

I slapped peanut butter on a slice and set it face up on a chopping board. Gloria slathered grape jelly on her slice and put it face down on mine. One, two, three, four sandwiches... the stack grew. Soon we had a giant tower of bread oozing brown and purple goop.

Grabbing a table knife, I started sawing through the precarious pile. The knife shifted to one side as I cut through the slices. The tower collapsed and pieces of bread flopped all over the kitchen floor like a game of fifty-two pickup.

"Oh no." Gloria said.

"Don't tell anyone. They'll never know."

We got down on the floor and started picking up the gooey bread. We slapped the pieces back together, wrapped them in waxed paper and put them on the counter for the morning rush to school. I hoped no one would find out, but the next day there was an onion sticker on our chore chart.

Several days later Gloria and I decided to bake peanut butter cookies.

"Let's make a double batch," I said. Following the recipe in the *Mennonite Community Cookbook*, Gloria and I measured flour, shortening, eggs, baking powder, sugar and dollops of peanut butter. We mixed it together in a big bowl with a wooden spoon. We scraped the edges of the bowl and patted it into a ball. I lifted the huge ball of cookie dough and set it on the kitchen counter.

"Hey, this looks like a bowling ball," I said. "I'll roll it to you."

I launched the sticky ball toward Gloria. The ball of cookie dough wobbled on the counter, knocked over the salt and pepper shakers, and leapt onto the floor.

"Whoops."

We wiped the debris off the dough and rolled it out and shaped it into cookies... baking it at 350 degrees kills any dust balls and cat hair, right?

Gloria and I also developed a secret signal to communicate with each other in stealth. When we saw someone saying or doing something we considered silly we tapped an index finger on the wall, keeping a straight face and stealing glances at each other so no one would notice.

One afternoon when I came home from school I found a white envelope on my desk. It was addressed "To Ruth." I opened the envelope and unfolded the hand-written letter.

Dear Ruth,

We are happy to have you join the hostel this year. You add a spark of energy and life to our 'family.' I am concerned about several things. I often hear noise from your room after 9:00 p.m. lights out. It disturbs the quiet when everyone is trying to sleep. I also notice that you and Gloria sometimes whisper and act silly at meals and during devotions. I know that you are new this year, while the other children have been living with us for three or more years and are used to the daily routine. Gloria was so well-behaved before you came. I'm afraid you're leading her astray with your behavior. I hope that you will change your ways and cooperate. I am praying for you, Ruth.

Aunt Louella

The words seared onto my heart like a branding iron. My face grew hot. I wasn't sure what, but it seemed there was something wrong with me. An adult had judged that I was defective. Gloria was the good one. I was not.

Was acting silly to release tension so wrong? I never spoke of the letter to Louella, Gloria or to my parents, but kept it hidden deep inside.

From that time on I pretended I was normal, but felt like an imposter. The imposter syndrome would follow me for years.

Meditation at Brice Creek

Across the footbridge rapids undulate
and slide down over granite ledges
into deep green pools.

A bird chirps an afternoon melody
and the shade cools me
under a canopy of old Doug fir.

The light breeze blows,
and a raven squawks.

Big black fly buzzes
and a butterfly hovers.

Farther up the trail
water ripples and
   gurgles
in the shallow
   streambed.

A bend in the creek sings a lullaby
and old wounds open and close
like shafts of light in the ancient forest.

On a flat boulder is a good spot to
lie back and dream and then take a dip
in the cold clear water.

The sun sinks lower
as it moves farther westward.

Tall shadows follow me
on the trail among the silent groves.

Sunlight fades into dusk
as the moon's gravity pulls
the currents

and white water swirls
in the eddies.

~ Thomas Avery

Wet Diamonds

Rained this morning,
came down hard.
From gray-black clouds
with droplets large.

Upon conclusion, of this good dousing,
the clouds began to pull apart.
The gentle movement of fluffy clouds,
brought a soft light blue, into view.

My neighbor's stocky, leafless tree,
gathered oodles of wet diamonds for all to see.
Hanging from barren branches,
waiting their turn to moisten Mother Earth.

Birds gather on the leafless tree,
with their magical melody of song.
Also, chattering as they do
then fly away to something new.

A marvelous view, my window gives.
Perhaps the birds can see me too.
Moments in nature, are most often free.
Free as a bird, one might say.

Wet diamonds continue,
to drop from the tree,
as the sky begins to darken anew,
taking away, all soft blue.

Mother Nature leans in and works hard,
giving the earth both bounty and charm.
Another shower, now on its way,
where birds and wet diamonds will soon play.

~ Elizabeth Orton

Sometimes Hope Bubbles

Sometimes hope bubbles,
Small, carbonated droplets,
Sitting in the glass.

~ Kathryn Fisher

Christopher: Fire and Rescue
By Melinda Bender

"**D**addy, read to me! Read to me about rescues and Christopher, Daddy!"

She tugged on my sleeve as I was tucking her in. Looking into her freckled face framed with curly red hair, I couldn't say no.

"Ok, let's read!" And I opened the book and began reading *Christopher, Fire and Rescue...*

* * *

Christopher loved shiny red engines, fire engines.

"Hey, Christopher, what do you want to be when you grow up?" His dad had asked when Christopher was small.

"A firefighter, Daddy!"

Christopher's dad was a firefighter as were his grandfather and his great grandfather. His grandmother had even been in charge of making her famous biscuits on special firefighting occasions.

Christopher was destined to be a firefighter. However, at an early age, the townspeople knew how directionally-challenged Christopher was when finding locations. One day while coming home from school, which was around the bend from his home, daffodils caught his attention. Christopher wandered over to another street to smell the lemony scent and became lost.

A neighbor helped him home and, crying, Christopher stammered, "Mommy, Mommy, I couldn't find my way home!"

"Oh, honey, you will learn," his mother whispered.

Another time, he ventured up the hill in search of robins; again, he was lost, and a volunteer firefighter found him. Their town was small, and the townspeople looked after Christopher, guiding him home. Most hoped Christopher would learn directions as he grew older.

"We can't destroy his dreams!" the mayor exclaimed.

As Christopher grew older, his family and the townspeople doubted he would ever be a firefighter. He would never make it to a fire! But they did not have the heart to tell him.

When Christopher graduated from high school, he promptly reported to the fire station and began the training courses. The town of 700 people was small enough to have one full-time firefighter, a fire chief and a few volunteer firefighters.

"Son, we really only need one firefighter in our town. Until I retire, maybe you can work with Hank at the hardware store and volunteer with me at the station in the afternoons."

Christopher hung his head of curly red hair and said, "Ok, Dad."

"Son, as you know, most of our calls are saving kittens in trees and finding lost children."

Christopher volunteered with his dad and learned how to become a firefighter. He was skilled. However, his dad and the townspeople continued to worry about Christopher's sense of direction.

After a few months, Hank, the hardware store owner, realized how sad Christopher was becoming. Hank's hobby was drawing.

"Hey Christopher, would you like to see one of my drawings and help me out with some of the locations?"

"Sure, Hank!"

Hank showed Christopher a beautifully hand-drawn map of the city with names and pictures of people's houses and pictures of landmarks. Betsy's Pie Place had a delicious picture of berry pie. For the next few weeks, they worked on adding newcomers and new businesses to the map. As Christopher helped Hank, he grew to know the town's street names and locations.

One day while Christopher was helping his father at the station, his dad twisted his ankle while polishing the engine. A frantic call came into the station.

"This is Betsy, and my kitten is up in a tree. Help! The birds are upset because their nest is near, and they are diving at her. Please, help my kitten!"

Christopher's dad's ankle was swelling more and turning blue, so Christopher yelled, "I got this, Dad!"

The engine screamed out of the fire station, and Hank's map was on the passenger seat. When Betsy's kitten was safe, Betsy hugged Christopher and said, "You are wonderful, Christopher! You are ready to be a firefighter!"

And Christopher's freckled face was all smiles.

The next week, while Christopher's dad was healing, another call came into the station.

This time the call was from the high school. Christopher knew the location, but his map helped him get there more quickly, and people lined the streets giving him encouragement.

Hank continued to draw more maps for Christopher. The townspeople reported new people moving so that Hank could add them to his map.

When Christopher's dad retired, Christopher became the fire chief. To this day, Hank's maps are always with Christopher, and the townspeople line the streets to help direct Christopher to the needed locations.

* * *

As I closed the book and kissed my daughter's cheek she said, "Christopher is you, Daddy!"

"Yes, Christy, good night."

"Read it again, Daddy! I want to be a firefighter too!"

Perception

His lingering gaze sees not
the feet slippered for comfort
that once dazzled in dancing shoes,
the sagging breasts
once jutted proud,
the grayed thinning hair
once tossed bright in moon beams,
nor the furrowed brow
hard won with pain.

But he sees her eyes
once seductive
behind shuttering eyelashes,
now serene in the calm of wisdom.
Her morning smile that awakens
to the promise of a day to ponder
ideas and thoughts and wonder.

He feels the hand grasping firm;
It once rested feather light on his arm,
Feels the communion of shared knowing
in a glance unseen by others.
A brushing hand once electric in touch
now a gentle reminder of their oneness.

There is the catch of breath
in his tightened throat,
only distant memories of
the hurried passions of youth,
the hours rushed past
now grown into quiet depth.

A precious Gift of time and thought
yielding her maturity.

~ Gus Daum
Groundwaters Vol 5 Iss 3 (2009)

Hiking

We passed on the trail–
pulling up masks, eyes smiling.
"The new greeting," he said.

~ Susanne Twight-Alexander

Looking at Myself, Looking for Myself
By Alexandra Mason

For the past month or so, I've been sorting through decades of snapshots and organizing them into albums. This is not a task I've jumped into with joy. The piles are amassed on the Civil War trunk we use as a coffee table, and there they stay, unbothered for days at a stretch. Four album books are finished and full, waiting to be packed neatly away. Empty albums sit waiting to be broached. Frankly, the task has unsettled my mind and muddied my emotions.

I've made my way through black and white Kodaks from the 1950s, where I am a hopeful curly-headed little blonde girl, mostly looking happy and comfortable with the world—but there is the promise of angst just around my eyes.

I like this little girl. She looks away from the camera with a clear sense of being-in-the-moment and expectancy. For her, things seem to be as they should. I've also gotten through smaller piles of fuzzy and formal photos of her ancestors, serious-looking folks in formal attire. These are mostly family portraits or wedding shots, but a few of them capture my forbears seemingly in a moment of daily life. They are clad in work-dresses and coveralls, standing against unpainted farm houses with broad prairies and endless horizons opening up behind them. In these shots they are hardly ever smiling.

Some of these relatives I recognize by sight, mostly my grandparents. In their faces I see familiar features, patterns of my own cheeks or chin. My imagination bogs me down, as I try to animate these stills with a sense of their world at that moment, a young Grandma Olson on her wedding day, for instance, or a youthful but matronly Grandma Klein surrounded by four sons and a handsome husband by her side. What were their thoughts about the future? How did they envision their prospects? I believe their expectations were far different from mine. 'Happiness' was a less-expected or more amorphous ideal, and simply 'getting on' occupied most of their time.

Maybe I underestimate them. Perhaps they harbored romantic and idealistic dreams. I seem to be turning into Grandma Klein in my general looks, although she was far more proper and well-behaved than I am. In one photo where she is about my present age, in her seventh decade, standing next to Grandpa in front of a red Mercury, I see the play of a piquant humor around her mouth. I am enormously glad that they both look happy. Other ancestors I recognize only as they have been introduced to me in pictures and through oral lore, the family mythology. The photos, the stories, and my own memories all become mingled, and I'm no longer sure what I truly recall.

Only a couple of photos exist from my teenage years. I was the third child, and with cameras using film, people took fewer photos than they do today, as developing was expensive. There is one photo of me in a lovely aqua-colored prom dress, long and straight taffeta with an empire-waisted velvet bodice of a slightly darker shade. I have tortoise-shell glasses and am sporting some sort of hairpiece plunked down on top of my blonde flip—at fourteen, I look nerdy and on the verge of womanhood. The boy, my date, is not to be seen. I cannot recall who he was, even though dates with particular people seemed so important at the time. What remains in memory, rather than an entire evening like this 'Snowflake Ball' I was about to attend, are isolated moments, metaphorical snapshots themselves, impressions of people that seemingly captured their essence. There I am nineteen and getting married—a whole photo book, again black and white to keep costs down.

I see myself during the seventies, a married woman, slim and quite blonde, hiking and visiting the L.A. sights—Disneyland, Universal Studios, La Brea Tar Pits, the UCLA Sculpture Garden, the L.A. Art Museum—and in some shots including our cars, the 1970 two-tone Ford Maverick and the 1970 yellow VW bug. There I am in cap and gown, my mother with me, she looking younger than I am now. Ah, she would have been only 50. Her face was still unwrinkled, forty-four years later at her death. There I am five years later in front of husband Paul's and my first house, in the snow, in Albany, New York. And there are shots from the New York City years. I seem to be growing rounder through these pictures, noticeably more so after the divorce. Here are pictures of my fortieth birthday party. There are several gatherings at that Albany house with people I hardly recognize now or do not recall—I think they were students, perhaps. I must have experimented with my hair, naturally an ash-blonde. In some of these shots I have auburn hair; in some, more of a straight-on reddish shade. Unless my hair is cropped quite short, it is wild, fuzzy.

As these photos progress through the years and become closer in time to now, I actually feel more distanced from them. I see that I was busy and active. I see lots of travel shots, both in the U.S. and abroad. I see images of myself smiling, and I know that person for a long time was surviving as if under water—not that she would have wanted to continue that first marriage, when Paul stopped having the energy or desire for daily contact. The symbol of New York City replaced me in his priorities—I recall it was present as a siren song of possibility even when we first met, a magical mantra for him. But I can see that she is unmoored, floating. I see people, good people, hugging her. Bless them. She needed nurturing. She was lost from her path.

I do not want those middle years back, yet I no longer feel that I am the one who lived them. I don't recognize this woman as myself. Going through all these archives is painful business. I'm relieved when I reach the Carl years with my second husband, and I see how much fun he had through his last decade and a half on earth, with me. There he is, a large man, sitting on a child-size low bench a foot off the ground waiting for the Pendleton Underground Tour, or pretending to kiss the statue of a saloon girl in Wall Drug in South Dakota. He loved the silly and the absurd. The picture I most shudder to look at is myself as one of the attendees at Carl's funeral. I look weary, terribly bloated, almost deformed from myself. Now, eighty pounds lighter, I find it hard to see the me in that poor woman. Her self-image and how she looked are worlds apart.

Throughout all these later photos I feel an unsettling sense of duality. I recall several of the events in which I am pictured, and I know that person as myself, yet these images lack that full presence I sense in looking at myself as a child. I wonder if parts of my potential as a woman have been stripped away by my thirties and forties and fifties, parts of me torn off in a child I gave to other parents, in another child fallen of its own accord into the toilet after three months of germination, in scads of potential egg-children ripped out with my ovaries in a standard hysterectomy, parts of me torn off by being a westerner in the east and later, by the battering of a pervasive workplace discrimination that culminated when I took an administrative position in a rural Oregon community. The woman in these later photos seems under siege, that angst near her eyes now fully present. She needs somehow to reclaim herself, despite what a former woman student just wrote to her: "You were a guidepost to me of what a woman can be."

~~~

At age fifty, after a solitary walk on Seaside beach, I returned to our rental house and wrote my first poem. It's not very good, but it sets the cycle in motion. That entire year of sabbatical, the poems kept pouring out, on nearly a daily basis after a beach walk. After Carl died, some eight years later, poet Ruth Harrison found me in a grief group, invited me to her writing circle, and somehow I began to rebuild myself through weekly poems in order to manifest my years of literary training in a complete, unified identity. Writing has begun to re-establish all the connections between body, mind, knowledge, emotion, past, hope and the continuity of lives. Like Roxane Gay, "I buried the girl I had been because she ran into all kinds of trouble. I tried to erase every memory of her, but she is still there, somewhere. She is still small and scared... and perhaps I am writing my way back to her, trying to tell her everything she needs to hear." I am writing to save that little girl in all her expectancy and potential. And now, in photos from the past couple of years, I see her peering out at me again, the hope once more in her genuine smile. I think she's running on the right track now.

The Switch

At some point
when the store of enthusiasm runs low
when life becomes repetitive
even dreary and sometimes empty
comes a transformation from
growing and becoming
into knowing and dying
and that long slow slope into the infinite

The headwinds of youth
become the tailwinds of aging
time picks up speed
bravado and wisdom
pass each other like
strangers on a crowded street

And sometimes
just for the hell of it now
you feel comfortable
picking out mismatched socks
and leaving your fly half-zipped
or driving too slowly
knowing it pisses people off
and they can do nothing about it

~ Marv Himmel

The Waves, They Crash

The waves, they crash
Building speed as they hit the shore

The views from the rooftop
Blue skies, sunshine & clouds
Swirling sea air

On a hot summer day
A peaceful, easy feeling abides
Along with the tan

This is what serenity feels like

~ Oswald Perez

My Life—1941 to 1949—The War Years

By Reida Kimmel

I was born nine months before Pearl Harbor. My mother had been told that she could not have any more children. She was, after all, almost 40 and had three teenaged daughters away at school. Like those of most women of her class eighty years ago, her days were filled with club activities, volunteer work and managing a large household. One afternoon, while knitting at the Red Cross headquarters, crafting heavy sweaters and caps for the British seamen who were already fighting the War, she suffered a familiar thumping lurch in her belly. That was me! She fainted. I was born on time—my time—at a small hospital down the street from our house. Embarrassingly, I arrived before the doctor.

Our home at 210 Gardiner Avenue, New London, Connecticut, where I spent my first eight years, was huge, gray, old, but not ancient, situated on a double lot. Its soil furnished vegetables for two families—ours and the Cannistrarro's. I remember walking the rows with Daddy, eating peas and raspberries. Surely, there must have been other good things in the garden, but I do not remember them. Instead I remember the rich scent of moonflowers on vines climbing beside the big porch and the vanilla perfume of the avenue of heliotropes. They are from the magic past. Neither plant has ever consented to grow in my garden here in Fox Hollow.

Somewhere outside the house there was a door to the basement covering the chute into the coal room. A truck came at intervals, backed up to a basement door and slid a load of coal down into the coal room. From there it would be shoveled—by whom, I never knew—into the furnace to heat hot water. Water heated rooms as it flowed through the radiators and provided all the water for our family of seven. The coal room must have been well-sealed because the rest of the basement was the laundry room. In the days before dryers, clothes dried on lines in the basement all winter. In summer we had lines outside. Rugs that hung outside in the kitchen yard suffered beatings with special sturdy, woven rackets. For other cleaning jobs, brooms, mops and the 'carpet sweeper' sufficed. Doing laundry was no casual task. Sometimes Razzy, aka Mrs. Rasmussen, the lighthouse keeper's wife, came to help. We had a wringer washer which filled and agitated and emptied without human labor, but then the clothes had to be fed through the terrifying wringer, several times, I remember. "It could break all your fingers little Miss."

Dried clothes and linens were ironed down in the basement. Everything—even entire sheets—had to be ironed. Luckily, the basement was a pleasant place. I never helped. I sat reading books like *Legends and Tales from Italy* about good little girls who grew up to be saints. I still have the book. It has not helped me much. Neither my deportment nor my ironing skills have improved over the years.

Houses can offer shelter and comfort, but even an innocently bright and spacious home can hold fearful surprises. I learned, very young, to be wary. The house had three stories besides the basement. The top floor had two rooms—one with twin beds. The other must have been my sisters' play room. Capacious closets housed toys of no interest, erector sets and chemistry kits. There were no dolls, no teddies. There was, however, a large and beautifully furnished doll house. It had been my mother's. I loved it. The book cases, shelves stuffed with dull books for dull children, held a few truly wonderful books: *The Red Fairy Book, The Lilac Fairy Book,* and *Mother West Wind Stories.* Early in my reading career, I read the story of Blue Beard, and convinced myself that he and his beheaded wives resided in the cabinets with the erector sets, I stopped playing in the attic unless I had company.

The next floor down had all our bedrooms. Daddy and Mother had rooms separated by a bathroom. I shared with my father for four years until my sister Chi married and I inherited her room, where a terrifying, big tree filled with evil spirits groaned and twisted in the wind outside. I slept in an antique crib from which it was challenging, but possible to escape. Sometimes I was allowed to sit in bed with Mother, who had her breakfast of white toast and black coffee brought to her every morning. She would read to me from Dickens' *Child's History of England.* I loved all the ancient characters—the Venerable Bede, Lady Godiva and King Alfred, who burned the oat cakes. Jack Frost painted the upstairs windows with lovely ice patterns all winter long. You could not see the ice until morning, because every evening we covered all the windows with heavy dark curtains—blackout curtains. Even more than the rationing, they were the sign that indeed there was a war going on, and it was right at our doorstep.

You see, we lived two blocks from the Thames River, just downstream from an important submarine base and the U.S. Coast Guard Academy. Across the river was a factory that built submarines.

My sisters, Chi and Anne, were often away at school and college, working or married. The youngest, Diney, had a little room and a bath she shared with Dell, who was, along with my father, the most important person in my life. Hard working, tough and competent, Dell was our cook, housekeeper, and child minder—everything. As a child in Ireland, she had carried messages about troop movements from farm to farm—dangerous business for a little girl—but she was very proud of her contributions towards Irish independence. Later she immigrated to the United States, training, and then working, as a cook at a lavish estate on Long Island. The Depression years saw her in Connecticut in my parents' employ. My sisters had been raised by full-time child care persons, who departed to serve as WACS and WAVES, which I am sure was a lot less harrowing than working for my mother. Dell took over my care. If my parents were otherwise employed, she took me to Mass and then to visit her friends on her Sunday afternoons off. Her 'gentleman friend,' Willie Sullivan, was a plumber and, as such, had extra gasoline rations. But mostly we took the bus, and then walked about the two downtown streets to shop, or sometimes, to see a movie. Dell never punished me, but she taught strict moral lessons. Never steal. Never lie. Never cheat. Once I stole some metal pieces from the trash bin at the 5 & 10 Cent Store. I was discovered, and the next trip downtown saw me returning the trash and apologizing to the store manager. A shaming like that is a lesson learned forever.

The kitchen was our kingdom. Remembering the gas cook stove, I think of the sumptuous meals Dell prepared on that beast. It was set on curved and footed legs, like a Chippendale table. A pilot light ignited with a match 'turned on' the stove. There were four burners and a single, but large, oven. Daily, with this cumbersome tool, Dell brought forth meat dishes and several cooked vegetables for lunch and dinner, as well as desserts, obligatory in the old days when no one was fat. For Thanksgiving, there were two pies—pumpkin and apple. For Christmas, we had mince pie as well, and steamed pudding, dark with molasses and rich with slivered almonds, Gravy, hard sauce, sauces for the vegetables were all produced on four little burners, and in the oven, a roast, stuffed turkey with brown crispy skin, or roast beef or roast lamb... Well wait a moment! Those red meat roasts had to wait until after 1945 and the end of rationing. Instead, Dell contrived casseroles and elaborate little French dishes, meat pies and fish. One summer Daddy and John Cannistraro bought 100... or was it 300?... chicks to raise in the garage to supply food for the families. The garage flooded, and most of the chicks died. I played, inappropriately with others, but why wouldn't a chicken appreciate the swing I made for him? More died. None laid eggs because, surprise! they were all males. Then my sisters refused to eat the chickens, claiming, falsely, that they all had names and were too sweet to kill. So we were back to chowder and baked beans.

I sat on the edge of the sink and helped to churn butter from the cream that Diney had fetched on her bicycle from Dimmock's Dairy in nearby Waterford. I squeezed orange food coloring from capsules and stirred it into lard-white margarine in order to transform it to a palatable yellow color. Everyone hated margarine. At least we could have butter and cream sometimes. We were a lucky family, with fruits and vegetables stored away and pantry shelves filled with jams and jellies, pickled peaches, spiced pears—all wonderful treats in the larder for the long winter. We were lucky, too, in having a real refrigerator. Many families had ice boxes in which a huge block of ice was stored to keep the food on the shelves above cold enough. Ice could be delivered every week or it could be purchased at the Ice House uptown. Daddy sometimes got ice there for parties.

The rest of downstairs was taken up by the dining room, the 'little living room' where Daddy kept his *Organic Gardening and Farming* magazines, and where he read aloud to me articles about dinosaurs and Neanderthals. How we wished that the Neanderthals were human, and now we know they were! The 'big living room' had the piano and the fireplace. It was the Christmas tree room, where Santa visited and ate the cookies and milk I left for him. But downstairs came with real terrors. Beside the front door was the coat closet. Admittedly, it had a small window, and a dim light, but it was the dark awful place where I was put when I had been 'Bad,' to stay and wait until punishment was meted out. The room smelled of shoes. I still hate the smell.

I do not keep shoes in my closet. I have no memories of what I did when I was 'Bad,' but I truly do remember the cold fear of awaiting punishment. I doubt that my delicate mother ever hit me, the imprisonment was punishment enough, as we both knew.

The big warm house enveloped us, hiding our family's sickness and anger. What did my sisters know? Why did they wait so long to talk to me? Diney, gifted musician with a head full of fantasies, was shipped off to Charleston to live with Granny and go to secretarial school, because she had become engaged "inappropriately." When Diney returned, she married the boy next door, who really was unsuitable.

Chi married as a teenager, quitting college to wed her handsome pen pal, a naval lieutenant. A very talented poet, she has written the stories of her own and our family's heartbreak and tragedies. She knew or intuited much of what was wrong with our family, but not until her own marriage was troubled for the same reason.

Anne, placid beauty, artist, writer, teacher and loving mother never spoke of the unhappiness until she and I were old.

And Dell could never tell. When Dell was home, we listened to the radio—Beulah, Amos and Andy, and all the soap operas. Saturday nights I lounged in her room next to the big brown Motorola, listening to the Hoagie Carmichael Show. But if Dell was out, I was alone with my parents. Daddy was away a lot during the week. He managed a mill that made sleeping bags for the military—Alaskan issue. This war essential job kept him—a captain in the National Guard—from serving in the war. He also owned a print and dye works in Massachusetts, and he had an office and shared apartment in New York, because business took him to the Garment District regularly. When he was home, he gardened, puttered in his shop and was involved in church and the beach club business. On weekends there were always parties—endless cocktail parties—dinners out and dancing—lots of drinking. That is what you did in a Navy town. Daddy drank a lot, smoked a lot, probably died of it, but I never saw it take him down.

My mother, a tiny woman, who descended from generations of 'teatotalers' was a different story. She was filled with anger at his 'adventures' in New York. After three whiskeys, she turned nasty. I, a child shrinking in the pantry, did not know what was the matter. I thought her anger would soon extend to me, swallow me up, smash and claw me. And I could not escape. I could hide in the pantry, go to bed and cover my head, but somehow, I'd be caught... I was sure. I never really knew that all the anger was not about me. The flying plates were not aimed at me. And no one told me what was the matter. I was a teenager before my sister, Chi, talked with me about alcoholism, how it can poison the lives of even the most talented, productive people. She knows the tragedy of seeing it destroy her husband, and later, two of her three children. Mother may have craved love, but she pushed people away, saying terrible things, destroying her victims' self-esteem, poisoning love. My miseries seem so trivial compared to Chi's. My fate, so happy, compared to poor Diney's, who with a kind and simple heart, took care of Mother's every need and demand, only to be rewarded with complaints and insults. I was angry—for myself, for my sisters. I still am, but at least, I'm also understanding and pitying. It has been a long road, but I am no longer afraid; my house is an open house with no hideous secrets, no lies, no need to hide.

That's a lot to say in today's scary world.

Late Night

The late night hours comfort me
As I walk outside.
The quiet of the houses relieves me
Of the weight of Covid pressing on my shoulders
And my mind.
There is no one walking at this hour,
There are no hellos, avoidances, nor masks.

The moon, nearly full, is stunning in the silence.
I can stop, look up, breathe deeply without the
    normal watchfulness
Pressing on me.
I like that.
It feels restorative tonight.

I miss my freedom,
To walk, to talk, to touch a shoulder or a hand.
It feels so long ago.
Am I forever changed, or temporarily altered?
I don't yet know.

The coolness of night
Clears my head for a time.
Looking at the dark houses
I wonder who lives inside, what stories they hold.

Changing towns just before the pandemic
Has robbed me of deeper friendships... for now
    at least.
I don't know them.
They don't know me.

And so I walk.
Wondering.
Reflecting.
Grateful for the night, the coolness, the silence,
    the moon.
Grateful to leave my house for a time.

My heart is both nourished by family here,
Yet, hungry for more.
The night reminds me of this.
More what? I don't know... just more.

~ Kathryn Fisher

The Shadow Warriors
By Jerry Brule

My back was already so scarred that the whippings no longer caused me incredible pain. An Ashanti Prince couldn't scream. That had enraged Jeb, the overseer, even more, and he redoubled his efforts to break me... to submit.

My crime today was helping Mary pull her ten-foot-long cotton sack. Mary was pretty and I loved her. That was probably why Jeb had raped her and told me never to talk to her. Now she was heavy with his child. My helping challenged his authority and reminded him of his shame.

They tied me up, as usual, spread-eagled between two posts. Again, Jeb had the other slaves gather around to watch. But this time, he hesitated. Jeb felt the heavy scars on my back. Then he stood in front of me and studied the pattern of the tribal scarification on my cheeks and chest. "Ah bet you're proud of these scars, ain't 'cha?" he said. "Ahm gonna add a bit to 'em today."

Jeb was proud of his skill with his bullwhip, with the metal studs on the ends. He slashed me like a panther and then the pain rolled over me. I tried going inside my mind, but was brought back to the horrible reality with each bite. I plotted my revenge and planned where to run. The Earl of Dunmore, the British governor of Virginia, had promised slaves their freedom if they fought against the rebels. I had no love for this foreign country, and the British couldn't be much worse. Their troops were close now, and the slave chasers would probably figure I went that way.

The Cherokee Nation was attacking settlers entering their territory Westward. They had allied with the British in the revolutionary war. I thought Cherokee tribes would be closer to my own African tribe. Jeb went away and I hoped the torture was over. I had slumped down, allowing my bonds to support me, but then he came back with a box of rock salt. Grinning he ground the crystals into my wounds. I passed out from the pain.

It was night when I awoke. Mary had washed the salt out of my wounds. She was crying, and she kept saying, over and over, "I'm sorry," as she sewed up the deepest cuts where the flesh hung down.

"Ain't nothin' you did," I said. "It's all on Jeb."

She slathered on an herbal salve that felt better and said, "The salt hurts a lot, but it might keep the wounds from going bad," as she bandaged me.

"Thanks," I said. "I'll be back for you." She smiled and slipped away.

I longed for sleep, but I couldn't. Jeb wouldn't expect me to show up for work tomorrow, so I had to go now. I sprinkled ground pepper in my tracks for dogs as I slowly hobbled through the fields to the river. I had noticed a log that had run aground the other day. By rocking it, I worked it into the current, then clambered on top and passed out.

When I came to, the moon was still shining. When I saw a rock outcrop, I struck out for it, so I wouldn't leave tracks. I stumbled West for three days, and then Cherokee scouts found me. I was close to death already, and they were curious who could have done this to me and took me to their camp. The women were impressed with the suffering I had endured and nursed me back to health. I helped with 'women's work' whenever I could, but they laughed at my helplessness, so I spent much of my time with the children. They would teach me words and their culture, and I would teach them English and about the American and African cultures.

When I felt better, I borrowed a bow and went into the woods to hunt. I am good at this, and I usually returned with a deer or sometimes a pig. This made me feel useful and gained the tribe's respect.

Two or three of the braves could speak English. One young teenager named Sequoyah was especially curious. I told him that the British had promised slaves freedom if we fought for them. I longed to raid the plantation to free the slaves, to save Mary. "If the slaves and the Indians could join up with the British, they could drive the bad white men out of the area," I said.

"Are there any good white men?" The brave asked.

"The plantation owners and the rich are bad," I said. "But a lot of the poor whites are just trying to survive."

"They steal our land and kill our people," he said. They have no respect for the earth or the animals. They have no honor or harmony."

"Yes, most of them are bad, but I have met a few good ones," We had some white preachers and teachers come through that tried to help us slaves. I think education makes the difference."

"What do these people try to teach you?" Sequoyah asked. "Our elders teach us our culture and traditions."

"They were trying to teach us to read. The preacher wanted us to read the Bible, and the teacher wanted us to read other books, but learning to read and write also allows us to write to people in faraway places."

"What is in these books?" Sequoyah asked.

"The Bible teaches us right from wrong, but that and other books also teach us the wisdom of our ancestors.

Sequoyah talked to his father, who spoke to Dragging Canoe, the Cherokee war chief. He hated the settlers that kept moving onto their land and didn't think much of me either. Dragging Canoe had already worked with the British to attack settlers, but wanted to learn more about the possibility of slaves rebelling against their masters. "What happens if slaves run away?" he asked.

"They have a police force that the slaveholders pay to recover runaways," I said. "But they are all joined by local militia groups, and they bring dogs to track us."

"And what happens if the police force does not come back?" he asked.

"Then they send in the army."

They helped fifty slaves slip away, and I shot Jeb dead when he discovered us. Thirty police and militia came after us. The Indians ambushed them, took their horses, clothing, and weapons. They scarred the cheeks of the survivors and warned them that they would be killed if they ever chased slaves again. Plantation owners sent out 300 troopers.

The troops were harassed by invisible braves picking off the officers. Once the Indians allowed themselves to be seen, and a patrol of soldiers chased them. They were ambushed, and none returned.

For two nights, we kept them awake, shooting into the tents, especially of the officers. We were nearly invisible at night, and patrols sent out with torches to find us, were killed, one by one.

Exhausted after another sleepless night, they stumbled on—for a while. The British army were waiting for them at the top of a rise with 400 men and canon .The Indians and former slaves flanked them from the cover of the woods. Dragging Canoe thought the British were dumb to just stand up without cover and take turns firing, but the British thought that was civilized warfare. Two hundred of the rebels were wounded. Half would die, and a hundred surrendered. Only twenty British and two Indians were killed.

General Curtis wanted to just shoot the wounded prisoners. He couldn't care for them, and didn't even have the food or the personnel to guard the rest. Lieutenant Brown pointed out that the Continental Army treated their prisoners well and could have prisoner swaps to get British soldiers back. Dragging Canoe said that they often used prisoners as slaves.

I was shocked when I heard that. I thought we Negroes could live in peace with the Indians. I didn't know that they advocated slavery.

"Is this Cherokee justice?" I asked Dragging Canoe. "Are we to become your slaves now?"

"If you adopt our customs and work hard, you can be adopted into the tribe," he said.

Turning to General Curtis I said, "I thought you promised slaves their freedom if they fought for you,"

"That's true," the General said. "If you prove your worth, we will grant you freedom when we are finished fighting."

They left the wounded to fend for themselves. About a third of the able-bodied troopers decided to fight for the British. A third became slaves of the Cherokee, and the rest were marched to the coast and kept on prison ships.

Among us slaves, I joined Mary and most of the women and children with the Cherokee, and most men stayed to fight for the British. I later learned that the tribes had a long history of enslaving their enemies. They also looked down on black people as inferior.

It was a new culture and more work, but much better than the plantation. I have come to believe that there is no real sanctuary.

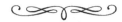

My Left-Handedness

10% of humans are equipped with this blessing or
    curse
We are unique
And artistic
A study says we may even have better verbal
    skills

My friends…

So keep an eye out for our group
We will be the ones
In this right-handed world
Who will not easily be able to:

- Use scissors
- Sign our name at a checkout counter
- Use a laptop
- Remember numbers
- Knit
- Or use a spiral-bound notebook

~ Lona Feldman

Sailing

I sent a ship a sailing
a sailing toward the sea
And oh it was a lovely ship
a lovely ship to me

It sailed toward the sunset
the sunset golden and low
It took off in the current
the current made it go

I watched it with a purpose
a purpose of sweet release
A part of me was moving on
Moving on past all reach

When the toy became so small
so small as it sailed away
At last I turned my eyes from there
from there and then that day

I paused a time to wonder
to wonder what next to do
I saw an eagle's wings outspread
outspread against the blue

I knew then what I'd forgot
what I'd forgot was yet true
I had wings of my own to stretch
to stretch, and off I flew…

~ Judy Hays-Eberts
Groundwaters Vol 7 Iss 3 (2011)

yellow quilt

I sit in the wicker chair
on the veranda.
the yellow quilt
made from your old clothes gathered
all last year
covers me like the promise of summer.
leftover popcorn is scattered
for the birds that will come
believing I am asleep
as I wait for warmth
and your return.

~ Emily Hart
Groundwaters Vol 8 Iss 3 (2012)

The Heartbreak Kid
By C. Steven Blue

An excerpt from my forthcoming memoir, *Heartbreak Kid: on the Streets of Hollywood in the 1960s*, written completely during the pandemic of 2020.

1960:

My whole family loved music, and from an early age I loved all the arts—music, painting, drawing, writing and, of course, dancing. As far back as I can remember, I always had big dreams. Teachers used to catch me staring out the window, daydreaming. Yes, I was a dreamer with a vivid imagination that encouraged my desires.

In reflection, 4th grade really seems to have been a milestone in my early creative development. I had gone to Longfellow Elementary School, named after the poet, Henry Wadsworth Longfellow. My 4th grade teacher was Mrs. Kime. One day she read an epic poem to us, written by our school's namesake, titled, "The Song of Hiawatha." I loved the poem so much that I read it over and over. I wrote my first poems in her class when I was 9-10 years old.

Mrs. Kime really encouraged reading and writing, and she convinced me to join the book club at the library across the street from school, which also had a poetry club. My favorite book was *King Arthur and the Knights of the Round Table*. At home I would build forts out of cardboard and pretend I was Sir Galahad. I created a little handmade book of poems in her class and drew a picture of Sir Galahad on the cover. Because of her encouragement, I won my first poetry award at age 12.

1965:

I had just graduated from junior high and would be starting high school in the fall. Little did I know it would be the last innocent summer of my life.

In the very first week of summer vacation, Mom let me take a backpack and sleeping bag and hitchhike to the beach for almost a month with my friend, Gary, from school. I didn't know it then, but Mom was already gearing up for the breakup coming in our family, and that's why she let me go, even though I was only 15.

Many families of the richer kids from school had summer rental homes on the beaches of Southern California: Laguna, Balboa and Newport. Our plan was to hitchhike down there and party with our friends up and down the coast all summer.

First we hitched down to Laguna Beach, where the family of my friend Liz had a vacation home. We stayed there for a few nights. Liz and I hung on the beach all day and on the second day, I fell asleep on the beach and got a severe sunburn on the back of my legs, right where the knees bend. I ended up with large sun blisters on both legs. That night, Liz's mom gave her some cocoa butter, which she rubbed on my legs. When they finally healed, the skin on my legs pealed like crazy!

After leaving there, Gary and I worked our way north, staying with other friends and their families. Sometimes we'd even sleep on the beach in our sleeping bags, which you could do in those days.

Our friends' families would sometimes feed us lunch and dinner and sometimes, to get some breakfast, we'd wash dishes in a local restaurant at the beach or on Coast Highway.

During that summer, one song echoed along all the beaches—"Like A Rolling Stone," by Bob Dylan. It was his first electric rock-n-roll song and the biggest hit of 1965! It became an anthem of our generation and some say it is the greatest rock-n-roll song of all time. What a glorious summer it was!

In the previous month, right before summer break, and just before I graduated from junior high (9th grade), I had been given a fantastic opportunity because of my dancing. At our school's Friday night Canteen Dance, there was an announcement that our school would have an opportunity to be represented as part of a forthcoming live TV concert event, to be held in Hollywood in July, a month after school let out for summer. I was one of the best dancers at school, so I was invited to apply to be in the dance contest at "The First Annual 'POP' TV Music and Dance Festival." I was accepted and my friend, Beverly, who was in my class and also one of the best dancers at our school, got accepted to be my partner. We were both very excited. The first, second and third place winners of the dance contest would get to appear on live TV, as part of the show. We couldn't wait for summer!

Right after Gary and I returned from our month long hitchhiking excursion on the beaches of Southern California, it was time for the TV show. I was excited beyond any expectations I ever had for dancing. The concert event was to be broadcast live on TV in July, and it was held at the Hollywood Palladium. Besides the dance contest, there was a "Battle of the Bands." The winners of both would appear on TV along with famous Rock-n-Roll and POP performers such as Donovan, Sonny and Cher, Bobby Vee and The Dixie Cups. The star of the show was Chuck Berry.

Bev and I came in third place in the dance contest. We, along with the first and second place winners, got to be on the stage dancing on live TV as Chuck Berry played to the gathered crowd. It was the most bitchin' thing that had ever happened to me. I was dancing on the stage, twirling my partner, while Chuck Berry was doing the "Duck Walk" just a couple of feet away!

In September, I started high school at a brand new school, Blair High. I took a drafting class and it became a new obsession for me. It was just like art, but more technical. I really got into it, and I could see myself in the future as possibly being an architect.

I made new friends at school. One of them, Paul, was a regular dancer on *American Bandstand* and we were the two most popular boy dancers at school. He asked if I'd like to go on the show and I said, "YEAH, for sure!" He took me with him to one of the tapings and I got to dance on the show.

High school was shaping up to be a lot of fun, but just as it started, Mom kicked Dad out of the house. She had had enough of his abuse. This is what she had known about when she let me hitchhike to the beach.

Dad got his own place in the south of town and I'd have to go over there to see him. He was teaching me how to drive his car so I could get my driver's license as soon as I turned 16. When I went over to his house for a driving lesson, I saw that he already had a new girlfriend. I didn't even want to know about it! I ignored her as much as I could. Dad had given me our old '54 Ford coupe which wasn't running. I had plans to fix it up and it would be my first car. That was never to be...

1966:

Through the end of 1965, I had gone to school with all the same kids from kindergarten through junior high, hanging out with all the same friends from my earliest years until my middle teens—playing, dancing, surfing, then beginning high school. It would never be the same again!

In January, right after I turned 16, Mom told me we were moving to Hollywood—just the two of us. My sister was already pregnant by her boyfriend, so she was getting married and moving in with him. Mom and Dad agreed that I would go with Mom, and my brother, Bob, would go with Dad. Our family was totally disintegrating.

I had only just started high school, but now I had to leave everything and everyone I knew and start over in a new, unfamiliar city. I didn't have my driver's license yet, and the Ford was still not fixed. Mom said I had to get rid of it, as there was no way to take it with us and no parking at the new apartment building where we would be living. I felt anger building inside of me. I was discouraged more than I could express, so I didn't—I stuffed it, instead. To make it even worse, Mom told me she had a new boyfriend, and he would be living with us. My heart sank!

When you are young, time moves slow. A year can seem like an eternity, but right then, the world around me was changing too fast, and it caught me up like a whirlwind. Suddenly, my family was gone, as were my friends I grew up with. I moved with Mom to Hollywood and began the second half of my sophomore year at Hollywood High School.

Hollywood was where *American Bandstand* was taped and Paul got me on the show again. Because I lived so close, I became one of the regular dancers on the show. Soon after, I became a regular on *Shebang* and several other TV dance shows that were popular then.

1967:

That summer Mom sent me to Arizona to spend a couple of weeks with her mom, Nini, who had moved from Phoenix to Seligman, Arizona, in the middle of nowhere on Route 66. Nini had moved because she got married again. Her new husband, Guy, owned the Standard gas station there. I took with me my portable record player and as many of my 45s as I could get inside it, as well as some LPs in my suitcase.

Being a city boy, I had never been to a small town like Seligman before. It had a railroad station, post office, market, one gas station—my step-grandpa's—one school—kindergarten through 12th grade—a barbershop, and a highway hamburger stand with a jukebox. That was about it. You could almost hold your breath while driving through it.

Whether you stood in front or behind grandma's house, you could see the horizon in every direction. I had only experienced this vastness once when we traveled from California to visit her in Phoenix when I was younger. But standing there in the middle of the world, *Wow!* It was breathtaking! To the west, you could see some mountains, but they were so far away it was almost just a crooked horizon line. Then, in every other direction, it was just flat, as far as you could see!

Behind Nini's house were the railroad tracks. If you lay down and put an ear to them, you could hear a train coming before you could ever see it on the horizon. Then, when it finally got nearby, the sound was so enormous that it baffled the mind. The silence of a vast desert, then—*Bam!* It was fantabulous!

That year, the graduating class from Seligman High was the biggest ever in the school's history—seven!

I learned there were some local teenagers around my age, because they hung out at the hamburger stand, listening to rock-n-roll on the jukebox. I would go there most afternoons or evenings after dinner to hang out and listen to music. Believe it or not, several of the teens recognized me from *American Bandstand* and *Shebang*, so I became a local celebrity that summer. They invited me to go with them out into the desert at night to their favorite spot, where they would build a fire and just hang out together as teenagers. I brought my records and portable player, and we all danced in the desert sand.

If you wanted to go and see a movie, you had to drive to the next town, Ash Fork, which was 30 miles away. Nini let me use her car and go one time while I was there, and I took a couple of the local kids along. It was really exciting driving fast through the desert, down the straight, flat line of Route 66. I don't remember what movie we saw, but we had a bitchen time, and they showed me around Ash Fork while we were there.

There was a clock radio in the room where I slept. Lying in bed at night, I'd try to find some rock-n-roll music on it. I could never find any FM stations but, surprisingly, I was able to get Wolfman Jack on AM. He was legendary and seemed to be able to broadcast to anywhere from some giant broadcasting tower nobody could ever find. I could always pick up his station in L.A., but to hear him out in the middle of the desert in Arizona just blew my mind!

It rained some that summer, and the rain was warm, like shower water. You could see lightning strike all the way to the ground, far away, way out in the desert.

Mom had let me take the train to Nini's. It was quite an adventure to begin my summer vacation, as I'd never been on a train before. I wish I could have taken the train home too, but at the end of my vacation, my sister and her husband showed up to visit. They told me Mom had sent them to take me home.

On the way home, heading west on Route 66, I made my sister stop on the side of the highway, and I got a Route 66 sign off a pole out in the middle of nowhere! I couldn't have done that if I'd taken the train. Oh... I still have the sign today!

"Peace Between Us - Toucan" created by C. Steven Blue in 1968.

self portrait

gazing at the crystal mirror
what do I see
memories and longing in my eyes

all my life...
reflecting back at me
is there to realize

what is true
what I've been through
it's all there to see

but you cannot touch a reflection
like you can't hold the wind
that blows through the tree

all I can do
is to look and see
the things that shine back at me

like the memories of feeling free
of walks by the sea
of you and me

leaning on the sky
gazing in the mirror
seeing you there
seeing me here

leaning on the sky
gazing in the mirror
now the things I see
are crystal clear

~ C. Steven Blue, 1978

"Perch in the Corner" artwork created by C. Steven Blue as a youth in the 1960s.

Storytellers
By John Henry
"I Feel Like I'm Fixing to Die Rag" - Country Joe McDonald

I was sitting in one of the back seats at the wake of Tilly, my mother-in-law. Story followed story, mostly coming from one of her six children. Most of the stories were short vignettes with a funny or sad ending. Her six children loved her and had seventy-odd years to pick and choose from her exploits. I'd already heard a number of these tales of their blessed Mom several times and all the weeping and comforting going on interrupted the disjointed anecdotes. Each of the children shared the spotlight, taking turns regaling the grieving audience, affirming Tilly's goodness, kindness and saintly love.

I kept losing the thread of the story-line after the first half-hour. My mind was glazing over; the buzz of the wake reminiscences were about sweet Mother, all goodness-gracious, not rough and tumble Tilly Babcock.

Some stories you hear are port-holes into life-affirming, death-defying and times in between. There are storytellers who can implant their story so it leaves something indelible. I can testify that this has happened to me a few times... not recently, however. I've settled down—a two-beer-Johnny, setting my cruise control at five miles per hour over the limit, money in the bank, college fund for the kids. I'd lost access to the germane storytellers and even the knack of listening for soul food.

My mind was cruising great stories in my life. Some had knocked my socks off at the hearing and lost their import, others still give me a grin or a shudder. My mind left Tilly's storytime. I recalled some adventures when I was a young renegade exploring life. Back then, I was ever open to the stories of reality.

One summer I rode the range with the Bar Q outfit in Eastern Oregon. I sat by the campfire at night where gristled cowpokes prodded the embers on chilly high desert nights and yarned cattle drives gone by. I was a greenhorn and discovered only later that tales that the old wranglers told about wolves, stampedes and rustlers were spun high, wide and handsome. I was new to the trail and their doom and gloom made me shiver and shake, but served their purpose of keeping me vigilant and wary, making me a better fledgling cowboy.

Dennis, the itinerant Colorado barnstorming preacher, had the gift. Some said his stories fed their soul with manna. He got a tent full of people drinking in words of salvation, guaranteed for eternity by stories of a two-centuries-old Jewish carpenter. He was darn good at making all the listeners jump on board the flight to heaven. I met him in a bar, gambling and carousing the night before the tent revival. I can't say Dennis' stories lost any of their power because of his human weaknesses.

I've been to Alaska fishing for King Salmon, been to prison for hitching a ride in Georgia, done combat duty in Afghanistan for months on end, wielded a chainsaw in the Canadian tall timbers, and sat at the feet of an Indian guru in Poona. I mention all this itinerant wandering because, as a younger man, I was in places where I heard some mind-altering stories of human wisdom and folly. I've found it's more likely to happen when you're doing stretches of time where you can listen fully to the whole story without your mind yammering a to-do list. Of course, it's crucial that the stories are so alive inside the teller that they spill forth and cover you outside-in, too.

The preacher from Tilly's church finally arrived to say a few words at her wake. Most of those gathered bowed their heads for his invocation while a few of us hightailed it out the side door. The preacher was known as long-winded, meandering and consumed with pomposity. I'd slept through a few of his sermons already and joined the escapees.

My wife's Uncle Hiram, her Daddy's younger brother and the black sheep of the family, was sitting on the tailgate of his Dodge truck drinking moonshine out of a jug. I hadn't seen him inside the funeral home, so I assumed he was paying his regards to two-fisted, foul-mouthed Tilly from the parking lot. Hiram has star-quality, magnetism that gathers a crowd. The shine helped attract a few of us, too.

Hiram took a swig and passed the jug. I choked and exhaled some flame from the white lightning with a few harsh coughs. He laughed with the other escapees and proclaimed, "Guess I made a good batch of corn liquor. Gets right to work on your innards and cleans your pipes."

The weather was quickly gaining an attitude adjustment—the wind was whipping the tree branches, some lightning was streaking the deepening purple sky, and big drops splattered the escapees, who scurried back into the funeral parlor. I passed the jug to Hiram and was about to follow the crowd. He gripped my wrist and mumbled "Climb in mi casa, amigo. What's your hurry? You can weather the storm with me."

Inside the truck, we were sitting back, leaning against the canopy sides listening to the rain drum on the roof. Hiram put a cork in the moonshine. He began humming Country Joe's 'I Feel Like I'm Fixing to Die Rag'. He looked up and mumbled, "That song spoke sense to me in the Nam war. Reverend Martin Luther King and Mr. Bobby Kennedy spoke sense too, but I had a hormone surge when I got drafted and laughed at them. I knew better than the truth-sayers. While I was living the invaders' nightmare, these two gents preaching peace were both assassinated. I was off playing war games in Uncle Sam's sham." He sighed and continued, " Life's all so darn black and white. You get your little self born out of the black and after a short white spell, it all goes black again." He smiled and got back to humming the rag.

We were back sipping shine, watching the streaking lightning show. I asked, "Hiram, you been around the world a couple of times. Now, you're old as dirt, even older than dead Tilly. You ready to enter the black tunnel at the end of your time. Ever get any clue what's on the other side?"

He responded, "We just BS'ing over this jug? You passing time til the rain stops and go back inside and pretend to be sad? Or you want to know for real if there's something I might of figured out?"

I surprised myself and answered, "Cork the jug, Hiram. Tell me what you got in the vault. It don't bother me if it ain't the way I sway, or the way I'd like it. I might not have a use for it; but give me the scoop before me or you are on the dark side and I miss the chance."

"So nephew-in-law, what you got in your kit bag that I might use? You got a story to share?" We laughed and he guessed right, "Too busy working and being Dad and husband? You missed the danger signs of becoming your own prison." He twisted his mustache and frowned. He pulled on his long white beard and looked deep into me until he decided which story was circling for a crash or a landing.

"OK. I'll tell something from my tour in Nam back in '69. Use what you can of it. I extended my year duty in the war so I'd get an early out from the army. I hated being under the gun, but I hated spit and polish worse. Day follows day if you're lucky, and I was finally done with all the following order crap except for the paperwork. I got orders to leave my combat unit, get up to Saigon, and get on an air-conditioned jet for the homeland of good and plenty. Soon after I arrived in California, the army and I would hurriedly say good riddance and both be better off.

"I rode a deuce and a half truck with five other nervous grunts sixty kilometers down Highway One to Saigon, the capital of South Vietnam. A short ways inside Saigon, there was a wreck, or the VC had staged an ambush, or some other obstruction up ahead to my return journey to life, liberty and the pursuit of happiness. We were stuck in a traffic jam which was a sniper bullet or a grenade waiting to happen. I panicked, jumped down from the truck and ran for cover. I looked back and the truck I'd been on was driven up on the sidewalk and in jerks and crunches continued on its way.

"I walked on the stinking, crowded Saigon streets in the sweltering afternoon. I found an outdoor oasis selling beer on ice. I sat in the shade on a low stool drinking a few cold ones, my first in months. A young soldier eased out of the shadows behind me. He stammered he was running from death. He'd been in Nam for two months and was scared stupid. I asked him how he thought he could get out of Nam and be safe again. He cried in the beer I bought him and answered, 'I can't go back, can't go out every day waiting for my buddies or me to get whacked. I can't take it anymore. Going AWOL is my only out. They won't take me back alive.'

"I looked at the pathetic deserter, a young kid scared crazy. An hour or so later, I couldn't listen to his whining and fear any more. He kept begging me to help him. He told me he was screaming in his sleep when he could sleep. He was wetting himself. He couldn't stop crying sometimes. He broke down all hysterical and threw himself at my feet, clutching my legs, begging me for his life. I finally had it and threw him a bone, 'Kid, shut up. You got no place to run, no place to hide. But... but, I've a ticket home in my pocket. You decide. I've done my time and earned a ride out of here. You want me to stay in Nam in your place? I been here for over fourteen months in a combat unit and am as crazy as the Mad Hatter. You want out so bad you'll take my ticket back to the real world and leave me in your place?'

"He looked at me like he'd gotten everything he ever wanted from Santa Claus and here it was March in the Nam war. He exclaimed, 'Thank you, thank you. I might feel bad later; but you know how to stay alive. You'll be OK. Please, I need to get out of here or I'm dead. Let me go home in your place.' He looked at me with soft wet puppy eyes.

"I was numb, in shock. I gave him my orders to the airport and then home, exchanged my dog tags for his, proof that he was me and I was him. I swapped my boony hat for his helmet and rifle. I gave him some money so he could get a taxi to the embarkation point. I wrote down important personal data: my birth of date, etc. He shook my hand, and said, 'You are a saint to do this. I'll never forget you. I swear I'll lead a good life and do good things. You've saved my life. I'm so grateful. I can never thank you enough.'

"I wished him luck and told him that I'd find the MPs in a week, if they didn't catch me first, and go home. I'd say I'd been hit on the head and robbed. I advised him to use the free pass wisely. Stay cool. He was about my size and coloring. This might work getting him out of Nam. I felt weird; I didn't give him a free pass because I was sympathetic or liked him all that much. I felt no loving kindness, no compassion. He didn't ask for my home address and I didn't ask his. I bought a few beers and was going to get a hotel room to sequester in. I planned to sit in that room ordering out for food and beer for a week. I was a war criminal with a loaded weapon again. Why did I not want to return home and my real life? Why did I give my orders stateside to a suicidal, AWOL, chicken-shit, wet-nosed kid? Had I finally done something good in Nam? All these thoughts zipped through my brain in a flash.

"A loud blast put me back into the real deal time and place: March, 1969, raging war, Saigon, Republic of South Vietnam. I dropped the beer bottles and ran toward the explosion and billowing black smoke. A mangled taxi, twisted and on fire lay in the middle of the road. A charred corpse lay nearby the metal wreckage. I was the first gun on the scene and the civilian Vietnamese wisely withdrew. I bent down and the corpse had some singed GI boots and shredded remnants of a jungle uniform on him. I saw charred dog tags on the road. They were still hot; they were mine. The dead kid I'd given my return ticket to the free world was KIA."

My wife was standing at the tailgate with her anger shining bright as the lightning. She snarled, "Uncle Hiram and you getting drunk out of a jug of moonshine while we're praying for Momma's soul. You stop acting like spoiled teenagers and come in right now and show some respect for the departed."

Hiram answered her, "Darling, we're on our way. Ain't nothing between us and Tilly but a short span of light. Like Country Joe, the prophet of the 60s, said, 'Well there ain't no time to wonder why—Whoopie! We're all gonna die'. I'll meet you young folks on the other side."

I followed my angry wife toward the funeral parlor as I heard Hiram start up his truck and drive away. I thought that I was on my own deciding if Hiram's gripping story was a useful portal or a cul-de-sac.

When Things Go Right

I write
Happy thoughts
Leave the sighing behind
Smile and joke
Much kinder
With more patience
Relax and look forward
When Things Go Right

When Things Go Wrong

I fuss
And boy do I sigh
Agitation
No creativity
Or desire to be alive
Or live to be 100
What it is
Is what it is
Can't appreciate
Or take care
Or keep organized
When Things Go Wrong

~ Lona Feldman

I Come From

I come from
the end of a short
gravel road
fifteen miles from
the nearest grocery store

Dad planted six fruit
trees when he bought the property
he told me five of them
were mine

today, a fifth-wheel sits where
my dream bedroom
was
I can still picture
the window of an
imaginary loft bedroom I sketched
in my notebook pad using no. 2 pencils
Dad sharpened with a pocket knife

when we go to see him,
we camp down the road, by the river
I play with my toddler in the sand
the same sand where I used to bury treasure
with the neighborhood boy, Johnny
right upstream from where I got sucked down
into an unforgiving whirlpool... twice

I build fire
carry water
by the river

I come from
a place
not a town
more like a speck
of water
on the map
than a dot

~ Terah Van Dusen

This is a National Poetry Month poem I wrote, inspired by Kirsten Fountain's poem/concept, "I Come From."

The Chief Advises
by Dorothy Brown Soper

Welcome to the Akan world! This story is an excerpt from my middle grade novel, We Are Akan, Our People and Our Kingdom in the Rainforest, Ghana, 1807. *The setting is the council room of a chief's home after a day of hard work by many to prepare for an important festival that will take place the following day.*

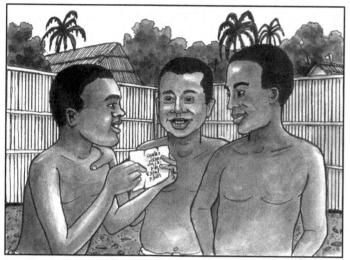

Kwami, Kwaku and Baako.
Illustration by James Cloutier

Three boys, ages 11-13, are resting in the chief's courtyard after a meal. Kwame, the chief's son, Kwaku, the son of the chief's elder sister and likely heir to the chieftaincy, and Baako, a slave who belongs to the chief, are good friends who work together daily.

A few Akan references are included in the text. Chiefs are often addressed as 'Nana.' Each chief has a spokesman whose title is 'Okyeame.' Words from Twi, the Akan language, are included and translated when used.

Seeing the Okyeame approach, the boys stood up immediately and greeted him respectfully, their heads slightly bowed, "*Maaha* – Good afternoon, Okyeame."

The Okyeame returned their greeting and said in a soft voice, "Come with me. Nana wants to talk to you." The boys stiffened, not knowing why the chief was calling them.

"Did we do something wrong?" Kwame asked.

"Is Nana angry because we looked at the black stools?" Kwaku wanted to know.

"Does Nana know that I climbed trees carrying a machete?" Baako was worried.

"Come with me," the Okyeame repeated softly.

They found Nana in the council room, sitting in his royal chair with Elder Kofi standing at his side. The chief smiled as the boys entered and greeted him. He returned their greeting and spoke in a quiet voice. "You worked well today to repair the roof of the stool house and drive the ants away. The elders and I are pleased."

The Okyeame and Elder Kofi clapped their hands saying, "*Yoo* – agreed."

"*Meda ase* – thank you," the boys replied.

"You will soon be young men," Nana continued. "You are healthy. You work hard. You are learning the ways of the forest, how to farm, and how to hunt. The elders and I want you to be leaders of our people. Let us help you. Hear what I say.

"Learn your history at the *Adae* ceremony tomorrow. Listen to the blessings and the stories. Follow the Sankofa bird that walks forward while looking backward. You see one at the top of the Okyeame's staff. Sankofa birds let the past guide their future.

"Elders say that if a grasshopper's eyes extend beyond its eyebrows, it becomes ugly. When a grasshopper opens its eyes wide, it is looking down on people. This is a warning. Never look down on people. Respect your ancestors, your elders and your friends. If

Sankofa bird

you do, they will respect you and help you.

"Learn to think carefully and speak well so you may convince others of your ideas.

"Elders say that one head does not hold consultations. Make important decisions only after talking to others.

"In your friends we see your character. Your actions and theirs will show us if you can be leaders. I hope that you three will remain friends and strengthen each other.

"Kwame," Nana continued, "you are my son and you belong to your mother's clan. Honor her when you decide your future. Work hard to learn the skills that you'll need. Always consult with your Uncle Kwasi.

"Kwaku, you are the son of my senior sister. You belong to my clan and you are the eldest son who might become the next chief. The Queen Mother selects the chief and asks the elders to approve. Show them that you are worthy. In the *Adae* ceremony tomorrow listen to the reasons that we honor our grandfather chiefs. Learn what a chief must do.

"Baako, you are the son of *nnonko* – slaves. You have shown strength and skill in your work. You see your father's diplomacy as my foreman. Study him well. You are earning your freedom."

The boys remained quiet, struggling to understand the advice and why Nana was giving it to them at this time.

"I invite the three of you to join my delegation to Kumasi for the *Odwira* festival," Nana explained. "The walk is long, but you're strong enough and you can help carry supplies. Leaders must make this trip. In Kumasi, you will see people from all parts of our kingdom. You'll see foreigners from outside of our kingdom. You will witness the chiefs pledging loyalty to the *Asantehene*—the king—and learn why our kingdom is powerful."

The boys looked at each other and showed their pleasure with smiles, slight jumps, and small hand claps. There was no need to talk. They all wanted to go to Kumasi. "*Meda ase, meda ase*," they repeated.

Nana continued. "After a few more *Odwira* ceremonies, you will be young men. Kwame and Kwaku, you each owe allegiance to your mother's clan. As young men, you will move to the home of your mother's senior brother.

"Kwame, you will move to the your Uncle Kwasi's home. Kwaku, you will move to my home. Baako, if I adopt you, you will owe allegiance to my clan and move with Kwaku to my home. In your new home you will help build a new sleeping hut. You will stay there until you marry and move to your own home. In this way we keep our families strong."

The chief folded his hands in silence and the Okyeame spoke to the boys, "Nana talked to you directly and that is a compliment. You may go now." The boys returned to the courtyard where they hugged each other and patted each others' backs.

"We're almost young men!" Kwaku cheered.

"We'll always be friends!" Kwame shouted.

"It's my dream! I want Nana to adopt me! I want to be free! I want to be Akan, but I'll never forget my mama and papa," Baako said with both happiness and apprehension.

Nana, the chief, on the right, steps out of the council room with his spokesman, the Okyeame
Illustrated by James Cloutier

Skin of our Teeth
By Lee Boutell

In December 1973, Betsy and I planned a holiday trip to visit families, driving my VW camper van to Kansas City, then flying to Virginia. Betsy reserved flights. My friend Denis would drive the van back to Eugene from KC.

Like me, Denis loved the orange and white van. He helped drive. We stopped in Boulder, Colorado, to visit my buddy Frank who offered us a place to stay. We ate at a restaurant near campus and had some laughs. I asked why the place seemed so empty and Frank said students were leaving for the holidays. Betsy and I crashed in his spare bedroom and Denis took the couch.

In the morning, Frank knocked and woke us up, "Coffee's on! It's snowing, so you might wanna get going before it gets bad."

I looked out the window to see everything covered in several inches of snow. It was coming down hard.

"Wake up, Bets. We gotta get going!"

We grabbed a quick bite and Frank showed us the map to I-70. He said because of the oil shortage, the roads didn't get plowed right away. They plowed only in extreme blizzard conditions, but apparently not this time.

After the Arab oil embargo shook the country in October, fueling up became much more difficult and expensive. Lines of cars waited hours for a tank of gas and stations continuously ran dry.

Fuel prices doubled or tripled, and the era of cheap gas was gone forever.

After our goodbyes, we hit the road with Denis driving. Roads, trees, mountains—everything—lay covered with six inches of snow as huge flakes fell, limiting visibility. With three people breathing and fogging up the windshield, I continuously wiped it down. I'd grown up in Kansas blizzard country, but it'd been a long time since I'd seen conditions this treacherous.

We pulled onto the interstate and the outside road noise sounded eerily muffled, in strange contrast to the loudness you'd expect from a highway. We could only hear the pulsing chatter of tire chains going the other way. We sat nervously, almost afraid to speak as Denis piloted Jason through the blizzard, up and down hills of compacted snow, in a half-speed procession of morning traffic to Denver.

As we rolled around a curve and down a long hill, through the foggy windshield we suddenly saw brake lights ahead with vehicles skidding, veering left and right. Traffic had come to a complete stop a couple hundred yards ahead. As we watched vehicles start plowing into each other, Denis hit the brakes, our tires locked and we skid down the hill as if in slow motion. We felt helpless, watching the brake lights of a big white van growing larger and larger until, BAMMM!—impact at 20 mph.

I quickly turned to look behind and saw a big sedan in a slide heading our way. "Hold on! We're getting hit!" I yelled. WHAMMMMMMM!—impact at 20 mph. I heard a few more crashes. Our engine had stopped and it became eerily quiet in the falling snow.

"Everyone okay?" I asked quietly. We were all fine, just shaken up.

I looked at Denis. He seemed stunned, immobilized. "Nothin' I could do," he mumbled, staring straight ahead.

"I know," I said. Maybe I should have driven. Denis grew up in California and didn't know snow. But it might have happened to me too.

The van's nose was punched in. His gently rounded front got flattened after smashing the big van. Our gas, clutch and brake pedals got pushed in and up, close to our knees. The slanted steering column now stood completely vertical. At least the windshield survived.

I managed to force open my jammed door to check damage to the rear. As big flakes fell, I gingerly traversed compacted snow to find our bumper and engine door got crunched in. The bumper hung precariously on one bent-up bracket and the engine door hung by one hinge. The van wouldn't be going anywhere, but it could have been much worse.

I went to talk with the driver of the sedan behind us. A middle-aged man with glasses rolled down his window, shaking his head.

"Are you okay?" I asked.

"We're fine, how about you?" he asked.

"We're okay. Guess I need your driver's license and phone number," I said.

He handed me his license and insurance card, saying, "Don't worry. We've got no-fault!" I liked the sound of that. No-fault insurance was a recent innovation that prevented lawsuits and delays after an accident, simplifying the settlement process.

I took down his info and went to the driver of the van we hit, a 30-something working man with dark hair. He stepped out and said he was all right. We looked at the back of his big Ford van and it didn't look damaged, just a barely dented bumper and a slight orange paint smudge on the back door.

"Don't worry about it. It'll be fine!" he said. Apparently the Ford was built far sturdier than the VW.

Having no insurance, I felt relieved. I brushed off my head and shoulders and slipped back into the van, slamming the door until it latched. I gave the damage assessment and said we got lucky with no liability for hitting the guy in front and the guy in back would cover damage to us.

As the snow fell, we sat and waited. It would take hours before help arrived. At least 40 or 50 vehicles sat on the freeway in disarray like a disorganized, jumbled parking lot. Vehicles with heavier damage would need to be towed away; certainly the van would. It could be a long time sitting in the cold.

With no engine and no heat, snow covered the van in a deep layer of white. None of us had worn adequate clothing and it grew colder. Betsy said, "We should try to get to the airport." I agreed. At that point flying would be our best bet to get to KC. We certainly wouldn't be driving.

On the shoulder of the left lane, a few vehicles behind us, sat a big bus, undamaged. The driver had wisely used the concrete barrier to stop the slide by rubbing its big tires against the barrier. The illuminated sign atop the bus read "Denver."

I walked to the bus through deepening snow to see if the driver would let us warm up inside. Maybe we could catch a ride once traffic resumed. He opened the door and I climbed in with my cheeks glowing red, shaking off snow. "Could we maybe catch a ride to town? We don't have heat and we're freezing. My van got crunched pretty bad. You going to Denver?"

"Yeah, we can take you downtown."

"Great! Is that anywhere near the airport?"

"After downtown we're headed to the airport."

"No kidding? That's where we're going."

"No problem," the driver said with a smile.

"I'll get my friends!" Betsy, Denis and I grabbed our bags and left the poor snow-covered orange van on the interstate, crunched between a big Ford van and a heavy sedan.

Boarding the bus, I asked the driver, "What's the fare from here?"

"No charge."

"Thank you!" we said and found some open seats. We warmed up to the reassuring purr of a running engine. How lucky that we'd found a ride to the airport sitting just behind us. I hoped Betsy and I could get tickets to Kansas City soon, before flights got canceled because of the blizzard.

Denis said, "Don't worry about the van. I'll take care of it." I gave him my parent's phone number and the guy's insurance information and told him to let me know how it goes. Denis would be spending some time in Colorado.

"Think we'll get tickets? The airport is probably jammed with students leaving town," I said. "It'll be hard to get a flight."

Betsy said, "I don't know, but we might already have reservations."

"Whaddaya mean?" I asked incredulously.

"I made reservations from Denver to Kansas City, just in case. I think it's for today."

"That would be amazing!" We sat in silence, wondering if we could be so lucky. After an hour we saw traffic start moving along the left shoulder. Half the crashed vehicles sat quietly covered in snow in the traffic lanes, but the left shoulder opened up and cars started pulling into a slowly moving line forming in front of us. Good news!

The driver put the bus into gear and slowly pulled forward through the snow. Good thing it had chains. As we passed my van, Denis and I looked back sadly, saying goodbye. Our driver slowly negotiated through scattered vehicles, weaving through a passageway of damaged cars. Once we got over the hill, traffic opened up, the bus gained speed and we were on our way to Denver.

We made it to town safely and, after a brief layover, we rode on to Stapleton International Airport. We thanked our driver friend and got off with our bags. He wished us luck.

Betsy knew the airport and guided us toward the ticket window. To say it was crowded would be an understatement. Hallways, corridors and waiting areas were packed full of people and not an empty seat could be found. Students lay on sleeping bags and sat on backpacks scattered on floors throughout the terminal. The over-crowded scene had the feel of an urban refugee camp. People looked frustrated, angry or bored.

At airline ticket counters the display boards indicated that flight after flight had been canceled. "This doesn't look good," I bemoaned.

We found the United ticket window and stood in a long line of students and vacationers. Finally making it to the counter the attendant asked, "What's the name and to what city?"

Betsy gave our information and the attendant checked the flight roster. After a minute she said, "Here you are. Your flight departs in 40 minutes if it doesn't get canceled. You checking bags?"

I couldn't believe our luck. Weeks ago Betsy had reserved tickets for this day just in case, and we showed up in time.

We checked our bags and said goodbye to Denis. He said, "I'll get the insurance settlement and fix the van. See you back in Eugene in a few weeks." I hoped so.

Walking to the gate, we saw nearly all flights had been canceled. Dazed people walked around in confusion, some swearing out loud. Long lines waited at every pay phone to call loved ones about changed plans. We overheard people expressing frustration being stuck with nowhere to go, no relief in sight, and just before Christmas.

"I sure hope our plane makes it out of here." I lamented.

We boarded and took our seats. From my window, I watched a crew working in the falling snow, de-icing the wings. Passengers sat nervously with baited breath, praying the plane would depart. Finally we heard the captain announce that we'd been cleared for take off. Passengers erupted in applause and shouts of joy. I looked at Betsy and she grinned. I gave her a kiss.

Sometime after take-off, the captain announced that we'd been the last plane out of Denver. All further flights coming or going had been canceled. I shook my head in disbelief. Such luck!

As we circled the darkened skies before landing in Kansas City, the captain announced that the same storm had arrived there, bringing freezing rain. Local conditions had become extremely hazardous, even worse than Denver. He said we'd been cleared to land, but we'd made it just in time. He said no more planes were taking off from Kansas City and only a couple more would be landing. I gave thanks once again.

I didn't like the sound of local conditions. Freezing rain is more dangerous than compacted snow, much like a skating rink everywhere, making even walking hazardous. I called home and Dad answered. I told him Betsy and I made it to town and we needed a ride home.

He told me he'd been watching the weather report and couldn't risk driving all the way to the airport and back in rush hour traffic. The normal 45 minute drive could take hours. His Toronado had studded snow tires but even so, a long drive through the Kansas City hills was too dangerous. He said to catch the shuttle bus that would drop us off a few miles from home, then to call.

"Okay Dad. Talk to you then."

The bus to Overland Park had chains, which felt reassuring. After a short wait, we rode through the freezing rain in a slow-moving procession leaving Kansas City toward the suburbs of Johnson County. We saw abandoned vehicles that had skidded into ditches and one wrecked on a tree. After an hour and a half, we finally pulled into Overland Park. The freezing rain continued as we carried our bags across the ice. I worried we could slip and fall.

I called Dad and he said he'd be there as soon as he could, saying, "Good thing the Toronado has front wheel drive, otherwise I wouldn't even try driving tonight." Betsy and I watched the sleet fall. Cars, buildings, trees all looked like giant popsicles.

When Dad pulled up, we carefully made our way to the Toronado. He popped open the trunk and I threw in our bags. As we hopped in, I introduced Betsy.

"So glad to see you, Dad. We had a rough day getting here. We wrecked my van this morning and had to leave it on the interstate. We got in a huge chain reaction accident."

On our drive home we saw only a couple other cars on the road. It was just too dangerous to drive unless you had to. I filled Dad in on our narrow escape from Colorado, about leaving Denis with the van, catching a bus to the airport, amazingly getting tickets to KC on the last plane out, and landing in KC just before they closed the airport. "We're really lucky we made it," I said.

"You're also lucky you got to Overland Park when you did. A half hour more of this and I wouldn't be out here, even with studded snow tires."

When we slowly pulled into the driveway, I got a warm feeling all over when I saw Mom smiling and waving at the front door. We'd finally made it home, a few days before Christmas.

Though we had to abandon the van on a snowy highway, Denis would deal with it (and he did). I had my sweet girlfriend at my side and we could finally unwind and enjoy the holidays with our families.

Betsy and I were unbelievably lucky getting to Kansas City on that day. We made it by the skin of our teeth.

Dream or Nightmare: A Dichotomy of Sort

By gael Doyle-Oroyan

I woke up wondering if that experience deserved consideration as a dream or a nightmare. I sat up, ran fingers through my thinning gray hair and headed for the shower.

With hot water streaming down my body, it all came back. I relived the experience as I walked through the pearly gates, met by a serene, mystical park-like setting... blue sky, beautiful large trees casting shadows across the green lawn extending as far as the eye could see.

I moved forward, full of hope, wondering if I might find them... my daughter, my parents, and my daughter-in-law's mother and her parents... all such very special people and all gone for more than a decade. They had all died and I missed them so.

Surely, I could find them here in heaven. I'd reconnect, hold them in my arms, expressing my love, sharing that I considered them my angels now who looked over me. I'd see them in the clouds occasionally when I walked. I always smiled then and thanked them for communicating with me.

Raised in a Catholic family, I believed in God and the church principles until the time I sought help from a priest to hopefully stop a divorce from the father of my children. The priest took me in his arms and tried to kiss me. I pulled away as hard as I could and ran out of the rectory and away from the Catholic Church for a long time.

Now, I moved forward and noticed a large crowd of people sprawled on the lawn. Some sat on benches obviously engaged in animated conversations. Others sat quietly dozing, reading, writing. I moved closer, but did not recognize even one person. Looking around, I saw more people, the largest collection of men, women and children I'd ever seen gathered anywhere in my entire life.

Emotions whirled within. *Am I really here in heaven? Where are my relatives? How do I find them?*

I approached three women sitting on a bench, dressed casually in pale colors, talking in a relaxed manner. I asked them, "Do you know Colleen, my daughter; or Ed, my dad or maybe Marion, my mother? How 'bout, Gloria, mother of my daughter-in-law or Nonnie and Papa, Gloria's parents?" I provided all their last names too.

The women shook their heads, looked at me as if I might be a bit off my rocker. "No," they chorused. "We don't." I thanked them and walked on, asking over a hundred people within the next few hours. Nobody knew anyone I asked about.

I finished scrubbing my body, turned off the shower, stepped out, took my towel, proceeding to dry, dress, and comb my hair. In my mind, I continued through this heavenly place looking for those dear to me. There are too many people... totally unbelievable. And, if this is truly heaven, how is it that people don't know each other? I've always believed that a true and incredible magic exists in heaven.

Big cities are located throughout the world. Perhaps I should have been prepared for the biggest city ever. Interestingly, I saw no high-rises, traffic, crime, hate; just millions of people in simple attire and lots of room... so much open land for them.

Frustration and concern versus a feeling of peace and joy argued inside me. I so wanted to find and see those who'd meant so much to me on earth—my daughter who died of diabetes complications before her 31st birthday—such a sweetheart; my father and mother who raised me and taught me so much; Gloria, my daughter-in-law's mother… I wanted to share with her the fun, silliness, craziness and struggles that my son and her daughter were experiencing now that they'd grown up enough to realize they were meant to be together. We needed to laugh once again at learning when we were neighbors and the kids were young teens; they had practiced kissing with one another and my son had learned how to unhook a female's bra with her daughter's consent. These two had now been married over a decade after reconnecting. This followed each divorcing a "wrong first spouse."

Gloria died before these grown up, well-educated kids married on a beautiful beach in Hawaii. She would have been so delighted.

And, then, Nonnie and Papa were such wonderful grandparents. They served as role models for the kind of grandparent I hoped to be. They loved their grandchildren so dearly. The children also loved them.

It was so sad that I found none of them. It made me mad. What is this "heaven" place really all about? Where are all my loved ones?

Maybe, with all respect to heaven, I like it here on earth and want to stay where I am—at least for now—with other special people in my life who are alive and that I love. I need more time to enjoy my wonderful husband, my son and his wife, and my daughter and her husband, their children—my grandkids and great-grands.

My brain suddenly takes a different turn. I need more time to think about all of this. I really don't think all those missing loved ones are in that other place down below.

Although, I recall someone once saying, "I'll be going to hell instead of heaven because all my friends will be there." Maybe there is some truth to that after all.

Oh well, "there is always room for at least two truths." I guess what I experienced could be considered part-dream, part nightmare—a dichotomy of sort. Amen!

A Gift to Self

In comfort I sit with propped up feet and a cup of
   hot tea by my side.
A small candle greets me with flickering flame,
bringing a touch of light to a darkened room.

I relax in the stillness.
Giving permission,
to wandering thought.

Memories flicker,
like the flame on the candle,
creating muffled laughter and moistened eyes.

A whiffle of scented warmth,
relaxes and dismisses my memory voyage,
as I sip and swallow my perfectly brewed tea.

The brightness of day has wrapped itself,
in the dark-black blanket of night.
Providing celebrity stars their moment of timeless
   dazzle.

Feelings of ease – warmth – cozy, position
   themselves,
as I lay hold to the twinkle-twinkle of night.
Relishing each minute, while sipping my perfectly
   brewed tea.

~ Elizabeth Orton

Pandemic Pearls
(aka Pen"damn"ic Pearls)

- Don't drink coffee in a recliner.
- Don't expect anything, especially a thanks or a reward.
- Always have something pleasing to look at.
- Clean a little every day.
- Try not to retaliate, it never works.
- Follow the Doctor's orders to the letter.
- Keep coffee and milk on hand for a latte.
- Enjoy the rain, Oregon has lots of it.
- Accept what you see in the mirror, that is you.
- Water your flowers and deadhead them.

~ Lona Feldman

The Papaya: Recalling a Favorite Fruit
By Tom Oroyan

In April 2021, our good friend, Madge Walls, from Medford, stopped in Eugene to visit and stay overnight on her way to see family in Wilsonville. Gael and Madge are longtime friends and we've visited once or twice each year before the COVID pandemic. In fact, as a former student of gael's writing class in Hawaii some 50 years ago, and now a published novelist, Madge has shared her experiences with gael's memoir writing classes at Eugene Senior Center on several occasions.

We hadn't seen Madge for over two years—not since her move from Wilsonville to Medford. She now lives at Rogue Valley Manor, a nifty senior resort-like center that has all amenities one can ask for. We did hear from her, though, when she asked gael to edit her latest book that is about to be published. She was on her way to meet with her daughter-in-law, a graphic designer, for the cover design of her new book.

Christmas card designed by Tom Oroyan of the Hawaiian-version of the "12 Days of Christmas" song

Madge's short visit was a memorable one. We went to an evening dinner and an evening show at the Shedd Institute of Performing Arts. We enjoyed our visit—as they say in Hawaii, where I grew up, we engaged in 'talk story,' meaning we were able to catch up on news and gossip at the dinner table.

I was still sleeping when gael said goodbye to Madge early the next morning after breakfast. Madge, who also grew up up in Hawaii and attended Punahou, has never been short on Hawaiian manners. She not only insisted on paying for the drinks at dinner the night before, she also left us a few *Mahalo* (thank you) gifts, including a couple of 'cozie bowls'—bowl-shaped pot holders used to remove hot bowls of food from the microwave and, to top it all, she gifted us a fresh, plump papaya… to me, the equivalent of Hawaiian soul food.

It was a whole, firm and roundish fruit, 6" to 8" in length, fully ripe, mostly golden yellow in color and it sent my saliva reeling. I haven't had papaya for what seemed like ages. Both gael and I enjoyed the fruit that morning. I wolfed down a slice of papaya and asked gael to be sure to save a slice for the next morning's breakfast. In Hawaii, papaya is not eaten just for breakfast; like mangoes, they are eaten anytime, day or night. In Hawaii, it is considered an 'ono' or 'onolicious' fruit anytime.

Since gael and I grew up in the islands, the papaya has always been a common food item. While living in Hawaii, we didn't have a papaya tree at our house, but relatives, neighbors and friends would share the fruit from their garden or yard with us.

I can vividly recall a nostalgic scene while staying one weekend with my sister Vicky and her family in Manoa, a hilly district with a vista of the city at the outskirts of Honolulu. While sitting at the kitchen table, enjoying the view and eating brunch, Sis asked me, "*Eh Brah*, you want some papaya?"

I said *Fo Shua!*—local lingo meaning "For sure; go for it!"

With similar enthusiasm, she stepped out onto the kitchen porch, reached over the railing and plucked a papaya fruit from the tree. "*Wah *lah!*" she said as she cut it open, cleaned out the tons of black seeds and laid half the delicious fruit in front of me. Part of the unforgettable magical scene was that the twenty-foot-tall tree she got the fruit from grew adjacent to the house, within easy reach from the second floor porch of the family home. Her in-laws lived on the ground floor.

It's funny how we take things for granted, that though we grew up with the fruit that has become part of our life-style, things come and go with time and place. I had almost forgotten about how much we depended on the papaya in our daily lives. Madge's gift brought back sweet memories...

I can recall some special dinner dishes in which Mom used green or half-ripe papayas in her stew recipes with pork or chicken. Onolicious! Today, on the Mainland, one can find similar cuisine or dishes using papaya in local Asian restaurants. We recently ate at a local Thai restaurant which featured a dish of shredded papaya salad with chicken. It was delicious, but so spicy hot!

During our cruises in the past years, gael and I spoiled ourselves at breakfast; papayas automatically became part of our order. It went great with my regular order of lox or smoked salmon, hot steamed rice and scrambled eggs.

I found, however, that not everyone likes papayas as we do. Jim Fall, a staff architect who worked at the same firm where I worked part-time while attending University of Oregon in the mid-'60s was an exception. During a work break one day, we had talked about the Oregon fruits—apples, strawberries and boysenberries—we liked. I mentioned the fruits of Hawaii and found most were familiar to him. Jim said he had tasted pineapple and mangoes, but he had not eaten or tasted papaya. As a treat, I brought some papaya to work, cut in cubes with a tooth pick in each, to share. The half dozen staff I shared them with liked the papaya, but when I went over to Jim's cubicle and offered him seconds, he said, "No thanks!"

Then I asked, "How'd ya like it?"

Jim quickly replied, "No offense, but I nearly gagged! It's too sweet and perfumey; I just couldn't eat it!" Well I guess you can't please everyone's tastebuds.

Basic research shows papayas also have medicinal benefits. They have high levels of antioxidants, vitamin A, vitamin C and vitamin E. Not only the fruit, but the whole papaya tree, have been found to benefit good health. The leaves and bark are used medicinally, as well.

My brief research of this fantastic fruit provided some interesting history that I did not know about until now. Papaya is not indigenous to Hawaii. Papaya may have been introduced to the Hawaiian Islands between 1800 and 1823 by the Spanish who settled in Hawaii. Others believe that it came to the islands via Asia and the South Sea islands before the Europeans appeared here.

The name 'papaya' comes from the Taíno word *papáia* that was changed in Spanish to papaya, the spelling most used worldwide. The Taíno were an indigenous people of the Caribbean. European sources in the late fifteenth century, found that the Taíno were the principal inhabitants of islands spanning an area from Cuba, to Jamaica to Puerto Rico and the Bahamas. The Taíno were believed to be the first New World peoples encountered by Christopher Columbus in 1492.

I also ran across another fun bit of more recent papaya historical trivia. The fruit may have inspired a 1940s popular song titled "Princess Pupule Has Plenty Papaya." The song was written at a party in Haleiwa, Oahu, Hawaii, by Doug Renolds and Don McDiarmid and was published by Harry Owens in 1940, as one those humorous wartime songs written about a crazy well-endowed princess sharing her abundance. Depending on the mindset, some may find it naughty.

Also interesting is that the papaya once played a role in the Hawaiian version of the "12 Days of Christmas" song. Instead of lyrics of the traditional song's first line that goes, *On the first day of Christmas my true love gave to me, a partridge in a pear tree...*" the Hawaiian pidgin version goes, *Numbah one day of Christmas my Tutu gave to me... One mynah bird in one papaya tree...* ('Tutu' means 'grandmother' in Hawaiian.)

So, with this festive ending of my memoir, I have asked my dear wife gael to include papayas on her next grocery list!

Mona Lake Channel in Autumn

Along the rock-strewn moat
Where sun shafts turn citrine waters platinum,
Squirrels send an alarm to other denizens
Of the maples and oaks with their insolent chatter.
"We are not alone," they cry.

Amid the deer trails of sand,
Breezes stir the skeletal tree canopy,
Choreograph the magenta and gold leaves
Death dance spiral to the branches' repetitive beat.
The end is near, shivers the air.

Swallowed in watery ripples
Then lifted on a frothy wave,
Forest's summer clothing drifts down the lake,
To pile as worn discards along the shore.
A promise of renewal or of the grave?

Across the sentinel canal
Battened down summer cottages squat,
Their vacant windows stare as if accusing us
Of abandonment.
Summer will come again, whispers hope.

As autumn's wind perfumes the air
With the winey scent of overripe blackberries,
It is time to draw the curtain
On pleasure and begin the harvest.
And the gleanings will sustain life for another season.

~ Jeanette-Marie Mirich

Lost Coast

We had stopped for dinner on the drive south,
so hoist our packs in the dark
and stumble along the beach for half a mile or so.
Ground cloth spread,
sleeping bags unrolled, we shelter behind a log,
lulled to sleep by the muffled cadence
of waves against the shore.

Breakfast is cooked as sunlight breaks over the
    treetops.
We continue our northward journey.
No rush.
Two more nights ahead, on this 25-mile route.
Going north is supposed to be more difficult
because of prevailing winds
but we are basically wind-free.

I've never before backpacked on a beach--
patches of fog burning off,
a baby seal left waiting while its mother forages
    at sea,
gulls calling and drifting
    overhead,
taste and smell of salt,
constant sound of the
    surf,
sunrises, sunsets.
One afternoon we strip to
soak in a sandy tide pool.

Car keys are exchanged somewhere around the
    midpoint.
After a brief synopsis of adventures, and taking
    photos,
they continue hiking south and we to the north.
They'd been frighteningly caught in a little cove
by an incoming tide,
drenched by ocean spray.
We waited that one out in the shade of shrubs
along one of the small streams plunging
from the steep hills of the King Range.

Forty plus years have passed.
I am grateful for the memories.

~ Susanne Twight-Alexander

In Search of Serenity

His Levis low on his hips,
a stogie he holds in his lips.
His smoke relit, he falters a bit
then sneaks from his can a few sips.

There's none can fail to see
on the surface he seems to be
unsteady afoot as slowly he puts
more ground 'twixt him and me.

His bike he walks beside
unfit for him to ride.
He's doubtless a loner. Perhaps a stoner?
He has a secret to hide?

His countenance stern and sad,
he looks as if he had
a sleepless night—a beggar's plight –
alone on a concrete pad.

He looks like a man of the street
slow-weathered by summertime heat,
oft battered by rain and weary of pain
from walking on shoeless feet.

I must get his attention fast
before my chance has passed.
It's not too late. Can't hesitate.
"Hold on," I cry at last.

"Just where will you be found
when you reach where you are bound?"
He hears my voice, he makes his choice
and slowly turns around.

He rearranges his cap.
I slowly close the gap.
Then what I see unsettles me–
those words upon the flap.

He has a friend somewhere
and may be tramping there?
The words I see could be the key
to the pain he seems to bear.

'Be Brave, My Buccaneer'
I read as I draw near.
Is he on track, and coming back
to someone he holds dear?

"A minute to talk?" say I.
"I guess," his blunt reply.
Before we talk, in silence we walk
till one should break the tie.

"This may sound rash," I say,
"but, looks to me today
a lot of stuff that makes life tough
was somehow sent your way.

"When first you came to view
I mulled a question or two.
And now we've met I hope you'll let
me ask a chosen few."

Responding to what I said
his reply is a nod of the head.
He's tired of walking, so for our talking
we need to sit instead.

We park on a bench nearby
and sit there eye to eye.
"You seem to be a dichotomy,"
I offer by and by.

"Yet, please don't be offended.
I harmlessly intended
to ask if it's true that deep in you
both grief and love are blended.

"Although you seem to be
alone in this galaxy,
on the cap you wear, the words declare
something else to me.

"So now that we have sat
and settled on this chat
please share with me here privately
the myst'ry of your hat."

Unsure just how to start
he gestures, hands apart.
"You think I'm a book wherein you look
and think you'll find a heart?

"No, not any more, my friend.
I'm not a love/grief blend!
I loved in the past both deep and vast
until the very end,

"but since I lost my wife
a shamble is my life.
My love now dead, I know instead
eternal pain and strife.

"My world's a horrible mess
an' the doin's my own, I guess.
Wherever I travel my plans unravel,
an' I hate it I must confess.

"On my bike, as you can see
I tote along with me
the stuff I possess, no more no less
in search of Serenity."

He cleared his throat, then spat.
"Oh yes, the hat... the hat.
It reminds me of her, an' my senses blur
whenever I think of that.

"We had a house on a hill,
myself, two kids an' Jill.
A storybook life, a man an' his wife
with dreams to yet fulfill.

"One day our boy was grown
an' took off on his own.
He grabbed his bags, put on his tags
an' left us home alone.

"While he was over there
we had a daily prayer:
'Please guard his soul an' keep him whole
throughout this whole affair!'

"But God just turned his head.
Had other plans instead.
I couldn't at first accept the worst,
that he was really dead.

"My wife more troubled than I
imagined the truth a lie.
Her thinkin' was skewed, her world unglued,
her endless cry was, 'Why?'

"Convinced he'd not be back
we worked to get on track,
but it was tough to sort his stuff
'cause mem'ries that hurt we unpacked.

"We emptied his bag on the floor
an' began our troubling chore.
It's funny the things a soldier brings
to ease the horrors of war.

"We found his teddy bear,
a book he carried there,
his high school ring, some trinket thing,
an' the hat you see me wear.

"The hat was a gift from his sister.
That night he hugged an' kissed her
an' tears in his eyes said his good-byes
an' joked he already missed her.

"But... back to the hat on the floor.
Her words I couldn't ignore:
'We really can't share it, so you must wear it
since he is here no more.

"'Goodbye, my buccaneer.
I'll miss you forever, my dear.
My soldier's gone and to carry on
I may not be able, I fear.'

"I didn't know if she meant
on leavin' this earth she was bent.
Then, bein' distraught perhaps she thought
she'd find him wherever he went.

"The truth is this my friend:
Disturbed to the very end,
my precious wife soon took her life
just as she did intend.

"So miserable was she
her grief transferred to me,
then with her gone I traveled on
by numbin' reality.

"Most nights at the Lucky Star
I carried my drinkin' too far.
I gambled away my weekly pay,
yes, even my house and car.

"In awhile I was deep in debt,
an' my future course was set.
Bankrupt and friendless, I sleep with the homeless
beset each day with regret.

"We once were a family of four,
but we're nothin' any more.
The two are gone, an' two move on
all casualties of war.

"I hear she's out of jail.
Guess someone posted bail.
But where she'll go I wouldn't know.
I hope I can pick up her trail."

A smile appears on his lips.
He takes a couple sips.
"If only she had a responsible dad
we'd rescue each other," he quips.

"So where do you think she'd be?"
I asked eventually.
"Well, long story short, she's not the sort
to be found so easily.

"The day her mom passed away
her spark began to decay.
Though never a quitter, soon it hit 'er:
Someone has got to pay!

"Her spirit never the same,
more angry she became.
After one episode she took to the road
an' laid on me the blame.

"I said my love is dead.
Truth is, you were misled.
I love my girl, my precious pearl.
Forget whatever I said.

"I'm hopin' to restore
the bond we had before.
So, done with talkin' I gotta get walkin'
an' back to my search as I swore.

"In partin', I say to you
my vow to her holds true:
I'll end my quest when I hold to my chest
my daughter, Serenity Sue!"

~ Wayne Westfall

Pennies from Heaven
By Kelli Graves Krueger

As I was walking into work one morning recently, I spotted a penny on the road. I quickly picked it up, put it in my back pocket and continued to my work area. Later on I decided to look at that penny to see what year it was. It was dated 2011—the year I turned 50. On my birthday that year, we had a family get-together at the cabin and the following day we headed to Loveland, Colorado to visit some relatives.

Finding pennies has become a new hobby for me. It all started when my Dad, Selwyn Graves, passed away on September 2, 2016. On the day of his funeral, I found a penny for the first time that I can remember. I'm not sure now what year that penny was, but it held meaning for me. After that, I began finding pennies in odd, random places.

At work one day, I happened to get a Diet Pepsi out of the pop machine. I put in two $1 bills for the $1.25 pop, and when the change dropped into the change slot, there were three quarters and a penny.

Curious about finding more pennies after going so many years without picking one up off the ground, I decided to "Google" it and see if there could be some meaning to my new hobby. I discovered that people actually do find pennies in random places that they claim are from loved ones who have passed on.

Now, whenever I find a penny, I pick it up and say, "Hi Dad!" Then I look at the year. The date usually has some significance for me if I think hard about it. Hardly a day goes by that I don't think about Dad and I like to believe that he is sending me his love.

I know my mom, Millie Graves, and sister, Vicki Doughty, have found pennies in random places over the years since Dad passed, too. I have a jar that I keep mine in now. It has "Pennies from Heaven" painted on it. My daughter, Amanda Krueger, found it for me online. I haven't counted how many pennies I have in that jar yet; maybe someday I will.

I think my family sometimes thinks I'm a bit crazy because I get so excited whenever I find a penny. My hairdresser calls me the "Penny Lady" every time I go to see her. Up until now, I have told only a select few about this secret of mine. Now, I've shared it with many.

Montana Keystone Cop
By Rene Tihista

My hometown of Nashua, Montana, reached its apogee of population and prosperity in 1950, when the census revealed that 943 people resided there. Nashua's municipal government consisted of a town council and a sheriff. The sheriff's duties included handling the town's water and sewage system and whatever other civic responsibilities besides law enforcement a town so small, required.

Our sheriff in 1950, Walt Whitmeyer, was a dour middle-aged man who wore a grey Stetson fedora and spoke with a slow deep-voiced nasal drawl. My brother Jerry, then a teenager, did a dead- on impersonation of Walt that amazed everyone. As with most small towns, everyone knew each other, yet Walt carried on an open affair with Greta Buchler, the baker's wife. Both were married and the subject of gossip, yet for some reason Walt's wife aroused more sympathy, at least from my mother, than Greta's husband did. I never understood why. For the most part, Walt was respected except for Jerry and his buddies, who sometimes spied on the couple rendezvousing in Walt's Ford while hiding behind the stockyards.

Walt left Nashua rather abruptly around 1951. I'm not sure why, but I believe he had a stroke (Greta Buchler could raise a man's blood pressure). The town was without a sheriff for a while until Clayton Vreland was hired. I guess the town council was desperate because Vreland turned out to be the sorriest excuse for a sheriff that could possibly be imagined. Keystone Cops were FBI compared to Vreland.

Clayton was a skinny guy of medium height, maybe forty or so. Our new sheriff also had a serious drinking problem. In fact, one night in the Nashua Bar, Clayton was tossing down shots with beer chasers so enthusiastically that the bartender, Pete Z., made him hand over his pistol and handcuffs before he got too drunk. Clayton didn't have much sense when sober, but drunk, he lost whatever minimal prudence he possessed and once picked a fight with a big farmer named Vick Weinmaster, a nearly fatal misstep.

Picking himself up off the floor after Big Vic quickly planted him there, a bloody and enraged Clayton ordered Pete Z. to give him back his gun. Wisely, Pete refused because he accurately guessed that the potted sheriff intended to exact revenge on big Vick with lead. The whole episode finally ended with some of the bar patrons taking Vreland home to his nearly-widowed wife and family. He retrieved his pistol and handcuffs from the saloon the next day when he was sober.

Probably the most farcical example of Vreland's Keystone Cop ineptitude happened during a ferocious mid-winter Eastern Montana blizzard. Two desperados, apparently without much more sense than Clayton, robbed a bank in Glasgow, the county seat, fourteen miles west of Nashua. In pursuit, County sheriff's deputies phoned Clayton and requested he apprehend the robbers when they passed through Nashua on Highway Two. The bandits' car slid off the road in the howling blizzard just before reaching White's store and Texaco station, not far from our place on the outskirts of town. Clayton temporarily apprehended the shivering bank robbers at gunpoint when they staggered through the blowing snow into White's store where our crafty sheriff was waiting.

While holding the desperados, Clayton imprudently laid his pistol down on the counter to rub some circulation into his cold hands. One of the robbers promptly picked up the gun and pointed it at Vreland. The tables were turned. In store proprietor, C.L. White's, telling of the story afterward, Clayton gave the robbers a shocked 'shit-eating grin' as though saying, "Ok, game's over now... give me back my gun." The bandits however, weren't playing. They cuffed and wrestled the hapless lawman into the backseat of his own car and took off through the blizzard heading east on Highway Two.

The benighted robbers were undone by their own poor judgment in robbing a bank during a Montana blizzard. With no option but to stay on the increasingly storm-battered highway, they ran into a waiting roadblock of cops and reservation police at Wolf Point, thirty-six miles away. My guess is they were relieved to be locked up in a warm jail cell. Clayton Vreland however, never lived down the humiliation.

I became the focus of Clayton's "policing" over a teenage stunt fueled by excess beer consumption one Fourth of July. My brother Ed took over sheep-herding duties on Fourth of July each summer so I could come to town to participate in the annual festivities. About 1:30 in the morning, after my buddies and I had polished off a case of beer, one of them dared me to set off the town siren. Used for summoning the volunteer firemen or the 9:00 p.m. curfew meant to remind kids to go home, the siren was taken seriously by the whole town—except me. When I set it off, we all scurried for home. Unfortunately, my prank did not go unnoticed. Mrs. Galgerud, who ran, and lived above the Fort Peck Café saw me.

The following evening after I was back at the sheep camp on Tomato Can creek, Vreland confronted Ed in Vick's Bar

"He's got to be punished for that Ed," Clayton said gravely.

"Well," Ed responded, "He's up on Tomato Can. You can drive on up there and try to apprehend him."

"That boy can't get away with stuff like that," Vreland admonished.

"OK," Ed replied. "But I should warn you, he's riding a pretty fast pinto horse right now and if he sees you coming, you'll never find him."

"We gotta do something," the sheriff complained.

Then Ed threw his arm over the Vreland's shoulder and said, "C'mon, Wyatt Earp. Let me buy you a drink."

Unable to resist free booze, Clayton sat down at the bar and after a few shots of whiskey with beer chasers he forgot about my "crime" and I was never bothered.

In the mid-1960s, Clayton finally wore out the town's patience. During a town council meeting, he threatened to shoot my brother Paul, then a councilman, over some dispute related to town business. Clayton was fired and disarmed, presumably while sober, and left town. What little policing Nashua required was taken over by the county sheriff's office in Glasgow.

The Keystone Cop era for Nashua was over.

"The Cornbridge Mansion"
Illustration by long-time *Groundwaters'* cartoonist, Nick DeAngelo

The Cowshit Cotillion, A True Story
By Ann Rau

The postman delivered the strange, official-looking invitation to us on that hot, humid summer day in New Hampshire. Addressed to the members of our Goose Hollow Yacht Club it read: "You are cordially invited to attend the first annual Cowshit Cotillion. The event is formal, black- tie only which will be held at Stowe, Vermont. Please R.S.V.P." Ready for a good time, our members voted unanimously to attend this unorthodox-sounding event.

We didn't have anything resembling formal wear, so we drove to Boston and ravaged thrift shops. We decided it would be wise not to mention the fact that our yacht club didn't have a flotilla of expensive, fancy yachts. Alternately, our club owned large, truck inner tubes for drifting on lakes and rivers. We were free-spirited rebels of the '70s and a socially inept group who took pleasure in showing high-society people how the other half lived. Our excitement grew, thinking that this could be an epic and unforgettable end to an otherwise bland summer.

Arriving at the parking lot, we were greeted by the sharp pungent odor emanating from the neighboring cow pasture that quickly inflamed our nostrils. Astutely, we understood the connection between the name of the cotillion and the neighboring bovines. As we started walking toward the event, we heard a strange noise off in the distance which got louder by the minute. Finally the noisemaker appeared crossing over a mountain range. A helicopter seemed to be heading right toward us. The noise became deafening and suddenly it was apparent that it would be landing in the parking lot next to us! Covering our ears to the noise, the helicopter landed and nearly blew us over when a well-dressed, silver-haired woman jumped out and walked nonchalantly toward the nearby building. Then the helicopter, black against the silver sky, rose up and vanished back over the mountain.

Standing there in disbelief, we struggled to manage our new bird's-nest-looking hair styles and brushed off the sandy dust. Now we felt ready to meet the enemy!

The piercingly loud, live music emanating from the event could be heard in the next county. The dance floor was packed with gyrating people, fueled by too much booze, who were trying to stay vertical. At first glance we noticed people wearing everything from formal wear to jeans and tee-shirts. But one young man stood out in the crowd. Apparently he read the 'black tie only' part of the invitation and he just wore a black tie, along with a skimpy little Speedo of course!

Sometime around two a.m., the large, double doors of the place flew open and a man on his Harley-Davidson motorcycle appeared in the doorway wearing his tattered leathers. He seemed tentative like a place-kicker warming up for a field goal. Looking poker-faced, he rocked his neck from side to side while revving the engine, then he goosed it and roared onto the dance floor, scattering a snaking conga line of dancers as they ran screaming, looking like ants escaping fire. After he made a few passes around the dance floor, he stopped; a woman approached, gathered up her expensive gown and got on the back of his motorcycle. She threw her long string of pearls over his head melding the two together and then they disappeared out the door and into the night in a cloud of exhaust! Revelers looked stunned until the band jolted them back to life with a Latin song and someone yelled, "How low can you go, let's limbo!"

On and on it went, long into the early haze of the morning hours. Around five a.m. with adrenaline coursing through our bodies, but feeling as bubbly as a five-dollar box of sparkling wine, we decided to catch an hour of sleep in our cars before meeting at the local diner. With crippling hangovers, our debriefing session began when someone volunteered, "We've been duped!"

Clearly there were no debutantes dressed in virginal white ball gowns ready to be socially introduced to Stowe's heady social scene. We realized that the cotillion was intended to mock the social elite of the place and it had absolutely nothing to do with cows. The kinship we developed with this sufficiently demented group felt enormously gratifying.

As we pulled out of the diner's driveway with Don McLean's song, "Bye-Bye American Pie" blaring on the radio, I wondered aloud:

"Do you think there will be a second annual Cowshit Cotillion?"

Cruisin' Down the In'erstate

Cruisin' down the in'erstate
no let-up yet in sight,
this fully-loaded loggin' truck
starts passin' on the right.

Then when we're runnin'
side by side
I'm blinded by his spray
an' curse the unrelentin' rain
that's hounded me all day.

My pickup holds the road alright,
but strug'lin' hard to see
I visu'lize the grinnin' reaper
sneakin' up on me.

Yet, when the driver pulls ahead
my world is good once more
an' thoughts are turned to memories
of yesterdays b'fore.

In time, with need to resupply
I stop at Sam's Café
to grab a burger, fries n' Coke
an' then get on my way.

But sittin' there's this loggin' truck
a-loaded to the brim,

an' guessin' he's what passed me by
I gotta speak to him.

I go inside an' order up
prepared to wait a spell,
then lookin' to catch up with him
I scan the clientele.

Direc'ly, there's this han'some couple
strollin' down the aisle,
so, bored as bread I flag 'em down
an' quiz 'em for awhile.

They say they love the open road
an' trav'lin' side by side,
one behind the steerin' wheel
an' one content to ride.

Then, small-talk done an' patience thin
we're headin' for the door
intent on gettin' to our rigs
an' rollin' as b'fore.

We separate, an' as we walk
there just ain't no mistakin'
where they're goin' an' what's the one
they're gonna be a-takin'.

They board that muddy loggin' truck,
an' when they get inside
she's the one behind the wheel...
an' he's the one who rides.

Discomfited, I reco'nize
my etiquette miscue,
but nothin' disrespec'ful said,
ain't nothin' to undo.

Yet, learned I did, an' swear I do
to nevermore assume!
I'd rather stand a sightless mute
than be a fool buffoon.

Sure, lotsa things once done by men
today are shared with ladies,
but cows'll fly an' pigs lay bricks
when guys start birthin' babies.

~ Wayne Westfall

An Eight-Second Ride

You'll rub on the rosin to make your glove stick
The luck of the draw is a chance that you'll risk

Behind the chutes, you'll work out your own plan
Another bronc rider has told how he'll land

Takes time and effort to keep out of a rut
Your hat never turned to dump out your luck

A bronc throws a fit in the Chevrolet chute
We check all the riggin' and find no excuse

Out through the gate with incredible force
How smart can it be to ride a wild horse

Spurs to his shoulders, front hooves to the ground
A proper mark out to start the countdown

He'll spin and kick and pitch a good fit
A suitcase handle is hard to stick with

He'll squeal when he bucks or grunt with each jump
You'll feel your head whip to the back of his rump

At times you'll feel like you're losing your grip
And then you'll remember the pain when you hit

You'll take some abuse that's kept to yourself
You'll carry this pain that's not often felt

Some special techniques may get you hung up
The way your hand fits could spell some bad luck

A cowboy's best effort may lead to defeat"
By a raunchy old bronc and unstable seat

Your vision gets blurred with the bronc's final fight
A turn for the worse to threaten your life

A cowboy may fall and the crowd will all stand
Horses are careless where they choose to land

Full speed or slow motion, he'd like to score high
But he took his last chance on an eight second ride

~ Dana Graves

The Boys and I

To be among the bison,
Is to go back to another time.
I've grown to love The Boys so much,
Sometimes I think they're mine.

I've fed them hay and tended them,
In driving wind and rains.
I've closed my eyes and seen millions of them,
Stampeding o'er the plains.

I've heard them roar like lions,
And been among them on the prong.
I've seen them go all out,
They let me ride along.

I've had a one ton bull,
Just inches from my face.
I looked him in the eye,
And he put me in my place.

I've held a new born calf,
Still wet all red and alert.
And I rubbed an old cows nose,
While she lay dying in the dirt.

They don't know how to steal,
Nor could ever tell a lie.
Still leaves me chilled to see the boys,
Agin the evening sky.

Civilization is closing in on us,
At a frightening, steady pace.
I wish they'd all just up and leave,
'Cause The Boys and I need our space.

I pray that when my time has come,
And I've spoken my last word.
The good Lord see
it fit,
To leave me with
the herd.

In Memorium
~ Michael J Barker

Canine *Semper Fidelis*
By Frances Burns

On July 13, 2021, Isobel, a devoted and beloved Welch Corgi with a long tale (either way you spell it), fell in the cold McKenzie River and drowned. A kind neighbor, living just past the Goodpasture Bridge, saw her body floating by, jumped into his rowboat, grabbed her tan, short-legged, 39-lb. body and made a phone call to a neighbor to determine her owners. Then, thanks to Marcia, delivered her to our door.

With endless tears and a flower in her grave, we buried Isobel in a newly-planted lilac bed beside the uphill driveway that we trekked up to the McKenzie Highway daily to retrieve our mail and daily newspaper from their delivery boxes. Coming down the driveway on the return to the house, I'd shout, "Let's go home, Isobel!" and down the drive she would scamper toward the house—Little Miss Flutter-Butt—as fast as her

Isobel on her first ride home

stubby, short legs and husky little body with a long waggy tail could go—homeward bound! Once I'd collapse into my easy chair with the paper, Isobel would settle herself just so in her bed on the hearth.

Her history, before I selected her from a dog rescue outfit in Sweet Home, Oregon, is vague. She had been found wandering the streets, freshly spayed after producing a litter for someone who wanted puppies, but not the mother. She was a survivor, lived on vegetation, mice, and vermin she caught, until picked up by the dog catcher, and taken to the pound. We cheerfully paid the $75 fee to the Humane Society before putting her in the back seat

of the car, and headed home, some 70 miles away. She rode unperturbed in the back seat of the car, calmly viewing the scenery out the window as if she knew she was heading to her a forever home. She was so regal, it was a shame she wasn't trained to give the "royal wave" that Queen Elizabeth uses when riding through the streets of London. On the spot I named her Queen Isobel.

Because she was potty-trained on the concrete floors of the shelter, to my dismay, she forever pooped on the concrete patio outside our home's living/dining area—discreet firm little blobs easily removed with the hose. The roses planted below the patio were ever so grateful—never look a gift horse in the mouth, I say. She was nicknamed "my appendage" because she wanted to be where I was, inside or outside.

She especially loved being in the garden while I sat on a bench savoring the rhododendrons and hostas in the shady areas to the tune of the McKenzie River rippling along over the rapids. She counted on licking my dish clean after a meal. Said dish might look clean enough to have gone back in the cupboard, however, I kept faith with future guests—and my grandmother watching from above—and, as always, stuck it in in the dishwasher instead.

Our two black cats, Gigi and Jadore, adored Isobel, rubbing heads with her frequently. Lukewarm about their affection, as dog/cat DNA requires, she endured their head rubs with stoicism, not wishing to appear either too keen or too cold on sharing the love! Giving her a treat was risky. If one weren't savvy, she would grab finger and all with an iron grip, so consumed was she to gobble down the treat—her clench always drew forth a chilling "DAG NAB IT!" from me.

Oh, God, how I will miss her. With no idea how old she was—possibly 8 or 10—I can hardly get my mind around the fact that my 'appendage' is gone forever on this planet. It has always been my hope that my lifetime collection of beloved dogs will all be waiting for me—and a few cats, too—when I reach St Peter's gate in the heavens above. What a romping reunion we shall have!

I have heard it said that the best way to get over losing a dog is to get a puppy. That I would love, but at 95, using a cane, a walker, and other accoutrements of old age, it does not appear in a crystal ball too smart to get a pet that will outlive me. The three adored dogs I have left will have to do. Finding second homes for grown pets is risky—it is not likely the second-hand pet will be as loved as much as its original owner loved it. So, possibly they give it away, beginning a grim cycle of 'giving it away.' Not all folks share the same ardor for pets that original owner did, especially if the second owner rehomes an adult dog again. Fortunately, this was not the case with Isobel, though she wasn't overtly delighted to see us for a while. Isobel's little scarf from her last trip to the groomer sits on the dining room table. I pat it every time I go by, wishing it were she, in person, lapping up the love it evokes.

Farewell, my beloved appendage...

By and By

Little by little
In moments stolen from the sun
Or granted by a generous rose
We are made whole

~ Rachel Rich

Yesterday

When experts forecast sun or snow...
or windstorms on the way,
geezers want as well to know
what happened yesterday!

~ Wayne Westfall

Bless This House at King's View Farm

Bless Michael and Amber's House, built with love
It was presented to them by God above

It was a dream of Michael's for his Lady Fair
The cost seemed to be more than they could bear

The community stepped up, with friends far and
   near
The message they sent was more than clear

Each amount added showed love and care
It was amazing what people would share

Now this home sits on the side of the hill
It warms your heart and gives you a thrill

It's a perfect setting for God to paint the sky
Bless This House and its owners is our cry

Written with love
~ Mildred "Millie" Thacker Graves

The home the community built for Michael and Amber

The Mysterious Case of the Disappearing Dog
By Bill McConochie

This is a true story... or is it a tale?... or about a missing tail?... or about an entire dog that went missing? I'll let you decide.

A friend had two dogs—dogs who had been with them for years. They were sweet little lap dogs—the kind that love sitting on your lap and being petted. She could tell how much she was missed by the way they wagged their tails and jumped for joy when she come back home after being away for an hour... or when she'd been gone on a weekend trip or a two-week vacation.

One day while visiting, she told us a story about one of them—Murphy.

"We came back from a weekend away, and the dog-sitter was wringing her hands when we opened the door. She was frantic. She and her 8-year-old daughter had stayed at our house overnight and had fed and walked the dogs for us. She said they'd left the dogs in the house that afternoon while they went for a walk around the block to the corner drugstore for a prescription. When they returned, only one of our two dogs was in the house. They were both certain that the other one, Murphy, had been in the house when they left.

"'We can't find Murphy anywhere!' she said.

"We looked at her 8-year-old daughter, who simply stuck out both hands from her sides, palms up, and said, 'I looked everywhere,' and then looked at her mother for confirmation.

"Her mother nodded her head and said, 'We've been searching ever since we got back.'

"'Upstairs and down?' we asked.

"'Upstairs and down!' the mother assured us.

"'In the backyard? Could Murphy have slipped out to pee?'

"'We looked in the yard, but we hadn't let them out while we were gone,' she replied.

"'And the windows were closed?'

"'Yes.'

"We all sat down, stumped. Silent.

"Then the little girl said, 'I thought I heard Murphy panting.'

"'Panting?' I asked.

"'Yes.'

"'When?'

"'After we looked everywhere.'

"'And where were you when you heard the panting?'

"'Over there.' She pointed to the den, through a double door off the living room.

"We all walked into the den, looking around, standing still, listening... no sounds were evident.

"'Where was the panting coming from?' we asked the girl.

"She looked around, then back at us, and said, 'I don't know. I was standing here.' She took a couple of steps closer to the old blue couch... the one that folds open to make a double bed for guests.

"We slowly stepped over to the couch, then George and I glanced at each other. We reached to the back of the seat cushion and slowly lifted it to the bed position.

"And there was Murphy! He had fallen behind the cushion to the space under the couch! He was fine. Not scared at all!

"We cried out 'Murphy!' and picked him up and hugged him. He wagged his tail and licked our hands and faces, happy to see us!

"Where, oh where, had our Murphy dog gone? No where! He was right there all the time! We all smiled. We all felt happy."

Is there a moral to this story? A lesson, such as... Don't ever leave your pets with others when you're away from home?... or, Don't ever leave home without taking your dogs with you?... or, Put a bell on your pet's collar so you can hear where the pet is?... or, Get a prison ankle band as a collar, so you can locate your pet with your cell phone if he or she gets lost?

Are there other lessons from this tale? I'll let you decide.

Let's Pretend
By Judy Dellar

Cream of Wheat is so good to eat yes, we have it every day. We sing this song, 'It will make us strong' and it makes us shout HOORAY!—Let's Pretend opening theme.

In 1943 when I was five-years-old, Saturday morning didn't begin until *Let's Pretend* came on the small Zenith radio next to my white junior-size bed. For thirty minutes I was transported from the mundane realities of my small world in the Great Lakes city of Erie, Pennsylvania, to far away fantasy lands of make-believe. I suspended disbelief and joined the child actors portraying whimsical fairy tale characters without reservation.

I was a few years older when I was exposed to "adult entertainment" via the CBS Sunday night line-up. I giggled listening to the antics of Baby Snooks, the poster child for mischief-making. She was followed by Jack Benny, star of the eponymous program who was defined by his miserliness and imaginary violin prowess as evidenced by his screeching rendition of *Love in Bloom*.

Fred Allen was also part of the wealth of comic talent on the air waves. The highlight of his show was the Allen's Alley segment in which he interviewed various recurring comic characters such as Mrs. Nussbaum who tickled the audience with her Yiddish accent and malapropisms; Titus Moody who parodied a taciturn New Englander; and the Southern political wind-bag, Senator Cleghorne, who, it is said, "wouldn't drink anything unless it was in a Dixie cup," and that "his compass only pointed in one direction—south."

I was fascinated by the ventriloquist Edgar Bergen and his precocious wooden dummy, Charlie McCarthy. Although the medium of radio didn't permit us to actually see Bergen's lips not moving, we had no doubt that they weren't. Some of us even saw impressive photographs of Charlie dressed to the teeth in a top hat and wearing a monocle.

When I was allowed to stay up even later, I bestowed my rapt attention on such week night entertainments as *The Lone Ranger, The Cisco Kid, Jack Armstrong All-American Boy,* and *Sergeant Preston of the Yukon* with his stalwart dog, King. I was especially fond of *Mr. Keene, Tracer of Lost Persons,* later to be lampooned by the comedy duo of Bob and Ray as *Mr. Trace, Keener Than Most Persons.*

Unfortunately, there were no heroines to serve as role models, so by default King was the character I admired most. We girls had no role models for smart, independent, capable women. We listened to *Ma Perkins* who dispensed home spun philosophy and advice to her dysfunctional family and anyone else within earshot. She was analogous to Mary Worth, America's favorite busybody of comic strip fame.

Our Gal Sunday, The Romance of Helen Trent, Mary Noble, Backstage Wife, and others were tear-jerking representations of women held in the thrall of unavailable or otherwise preoccupied idealized men. These characters were universally dedicated to getting or keeping a mate amid melodramatic plot twists and turns. These were the media role models for girls in the 1940s and it took decades for us to get over them.

My entertainment world wasn't limited merely to the pleasures of radio. Courtesy of "Uncle" Walt Disney, we children of the early forties were treated to horror films created just for us. Their lurid plots involved such child unfriendly topics as murder and mayhem, kidnapping, bullying, poisonings, and natural disasters.

In 1942, the children of America were treated to the spectacle of *Bambi*, a terrifying tale in which the mother of a fawn named Bambi is murdered by hunters, and as if that wasn't enough to traumatize the young audience, Bambi himself is wounded. Just for good measure, Bambi is caught in a forest fire. I watched the all-consuming flames on the screen with my little hands covering my eyes leaving just enough space between my fingers to peek at the bright red and orange sky signifying Bambi's world literally going up in flames.

Another scary Disney opus for little kids was *Dumbo*, the story of a young circus elephant with ultra-large floppy ears who was ridiculed for their size and made an outcast by the circus community. To make his situation even worse, *Dumbo* became a virtual orphan when his mother was locked up in a cage by the cruel ringmaster. Somehow, Disney slipped up and Dumbo had a happy ending when the little elephant discovers his large ears can enable him to fly and he becomes the star of the circus. The happy turn of events allowed me to dry my tears and prepare for the next tale of woe.

The tale of *Pinocchio* presented a wooden puppet who came to life, was kidnapped by villains and forced to become a law-breaker. To add to his misery, he had the unfortunate curse of dissembling which caused his nose to grow longer with each falsehood he told. Instead of cautioning against prevarication, the take-away from the "entertainment" was that lying can be cute.

The most terrifying of all the kiddie entertainment Disney concocted was the harrowing tale of *Snow White* whose wicked stepmother commissioned a woodsman to murder her in the forest. When his attempt failed, she poisoned poor Snow White with a toxic apple. For the remainder of the movie, Snow White languished in a glass coffin only to awaken after being kissed by a handsome prince. The presence of adorable dwarves didn't compensate for the scariness of the homicidal tale.

Just in case any children failed to get the message that the world was a dangerous place and that our sense of security could be ripped from us in any number of terrifying ways, the grainy black and white newsreels that preceded the feature films made the point.

I looked on with horror at the sight of starving Chinese peasants and babies left on the roadside to die. "Famine" was a new vocabulary word we learned at the movies. Next up might be military battles featuring bombed out cities, exhausted looking soldiers, and vast convoys of mud-caked military vehicles. At the end there would usually be an upbeat human-interest segment about the Miss America contest or Frank Sinatra surrounded by swooning teenage girls uniformly shod in bobby socks and saddle shoes.

The fearsome images and messages presented to little children cannot be unseen or unheard, and they remain in my memory. How refreshing it would be to once again be transported to the carefree radio land of make believe that was *Let's Pretend*.

Creative Mystery

The blank paper --
My friend.
My foe.

I have pledged to you,
To seek you out each day.
Let you stare at me.
Who will look away first?

Perhaps today I win.
26 words already on the white page.

I wonder,
Is this how musicians roll?
One note at a time, squeezed onto the page.
Or whole melodies, in clusters
Blossoming onto the page?
Finding their way into the musician's ink
Flowing, as sometimes my sentences do?

Creative mystery.
What a perplexing thing.
What a joy,
And yet a conundrum.

~ Kathryn Fisher

A Party In My Plants!
By Jennifer Dalen Wolfe

Just two short seasons ago, I was looking at the yard through my kitchen window. The last of the autumn leaves were falling from the trees. The sky was a light grey from the low-hanging fog. Would it burn away?... or would it just hang overhead, wrapping its coolness around my day.

The garden border winds its way through the yard looking lonely with no ferns hanging over the edges, almost as if it feels the same way I do—waiting for the warmer days that seem to take their time getting here.

Grabbing a cup of coffee and my blanket, I sit in my chair, relaxed. I slowly begin to fall asleep, thinking of the spring and summer soon to come... of flowers, vegetables and fruits—anticipating the smells and flavors.

I am swept into slumber by the cool but gentle breeze as I dream of my garden. There are colors—so many colors. They are like a party in my garden. What a way to dream! I smell the flowers that are blooming as they bob and sway in the bright but mild sunlight. Each scent wraps its gentle arms around me, bringing back memories from the past.

In my dream, music plays and many friendly folks are strolling or sitting, quietly conversing and enjoying what I have grown. The music is festive and happy, just like the flowers that are showing off their bright red, pink, orange, yellow, purple, blue and white blossoms.

Butterflies and bees join in the festivities, fluttering, buzzing and nuzzling the nectar and pollen. Snails, slugs, beetles and worms scoot their way around, enjoying the cool earth.

I sit under a tree, running my hand over the cool green blades of grass, enjoying each little bit of colors, smells and sounds. Birds begin to introduce their song along with the music. It feels so nice.

I hear the doorbell and I am suddenly awake. Hold that dream! Hold on to that dream...

Two seasons have passed and my garden is now blooming, the party is going to start, and I know how it will end... just like in my dream.

I am having a party in my plants!

Fingers and Toes

This
has
happened
more
times
than
I can
count...
21

~ Kris Bluth

My Color
By Dale Dickson (In Memoriam)

As a tribute of remembrance for my loving husband, Dale Dickson. He passed away of COVID-19 September 2020. He was a retired Captain of almost 30 years as a firefighter for the City of Los Angeles. One of his greatest enjoyments was creative writing. The following is just one of many of his stories he enjoyed writing that reflects his wonderful sense of humor.

When I was a kid I wondered why some grownups called me "Red;" then I guessed it was because I had red hair. My best dog, ever, was named Rusty, but she also answered to the name "Red." There are a lot of red things in this world, but there is one red thing I am sure all people dread to see. Read on...

I was toodling down the Beltline about 10:00 at night—not much traffic—when I saw it in my rear-view mirror: a flashing red light.

Oh, no, I thought. The fuzz. What did I do? Am I speeding? Or going too slowly? Did I make an unsafe lane change? Or not signal for a lane change? Tailgating? But there is no other traffic. What did I do wrong? What am I doing wrong. This can't be happening to me. I'm the safest driver on the road. And I obey ALL the speed laws. Darn, a traffic citation will cost me at least $125 dollars... at least. And my insurance rate will have about $100 a year for two years tacked on it. I can't afford it. It means I can't get my latest electronic toy. Darn! Stinking red lights. Flashing. Getting closer. Do I have my license, registration, and insurance papers? And are they current? Yes, they are, I'm sure.

I start to pucker up. I have a sudden surge in my heartbeat. I start to tremble... and sweat. Wow! My armpits are drooling. My brow is pouring out the salty fluid, just like when I was on a working fire. My palms are so wet it is hard to control the steering wheel. Ratzel-fratzel!

I slowly pull to the right side of the freeway, as far off the road as is feasible and safe.

What can I tell the police officer? Shall I let him do the first talking, telling me what my violation is, or try to smooth talk him? I hope he doesn't see all my sweat. Where is my handkerchief?

Darn red lights.

I know; I'll flash my retired Fire Department ID at him and he might just give me a professional break, seeing as how we both are public safety guys and all. Just don't act so nervous.

Rats! Darn RED lights! Gadzooks, I hate them!

Getting closer. Almost on me. Holy Moly!

And then they pass me. It's a fire engine!

Hey, the good guys! Way to go! Keep safe, you people.

It instantly brings back hundreds of memories of days long gone. And, as my excitement and angst leave me, I realize that RED is good. I like red lights... really do.

A Novel Approach: War and Research
By Jeanette-Marie Mirich

For me writing involves examining things with a magnifying glass of words.

Currently Ethiopia is on my radar as I finish rewriting a WWII novel. Did the war actually begin with Germany's invasion of Poland? Or was it when Italy invaded Ethiopia in 1935, and no one interfered. As a member of the League of Nations, Ethiopia should have been protected by the signers of the Charter. However, the nation of Ethiopia was left to her own devises, but an embargo of arms was placed on her. So, a story winds through my brain.

I want readers to experience life with all its textures and cultural nuances. Writing of the thunder of Tisisat Falls as it cascades into the ravine, the gooey texture of a chocolate truffle, and the scent of jasmine wafting through a Kenyan garden gives me joy. I prefer to do my location research in situ. Sitting at a sidewalk café in Addis Ababa and indulging in the sour pancake injera with friends is how I learn. Experiencing the ripe scent of unwashed bodies in Mombasa harbor and the cough of a lion on the prowl infuses my work with reality. In my imagination, I'm up to my eyeballs in desert sand. Having lived on the end of the Mohave and experiencing a haboob or two, I can draw on my familiarity of chasing sand around when cleaning and attempting to spit out grit in a lady-like manner.

I've dealt with a few things in life—a swat team on my roof firing at a kidnapping suspect—yes; bullets flying from a Regina Aeronautica's Caproni Ca 101—no. I've never had to contend with bombs. I do not think I need to experience being a target of an air raid to write about it.

It must be terrifying reading the accounts of the survivors of the London Blitz. What can I draw from to communicate the fear people had? The light slowly dawns. We live with fear from too much information about

skullduggery, pandemics and shortages. In a culture that has news at the touch of a finger, we are riveted by the latest outrage. When our minds are whiplashed by irate opinion-sharers, we become like the people Absalom chatted up at the city gate—easily troubled.

I am challenged to think about an appropriate passage in the Bible: 'What is true, what is honorable, whatever is just, whatever is pure, whatever is lovely, whatever is commendable, if there is any excellence, if there is anything worthy of praise, think on these things.' *Philippians 4:8-9*.

During this season I'm fleeing the whispers and seeking the peace that I glean from His word.

Life on the Hill, Close to the Mill
By Mildred "Millie" Thacker Graves

Vernonia was a mill town. It was the location of Oregon American Lumber Company, the largest inland mill in the world at the time it was built in 1923 and 1924.

The company provided housing for some of its employees and the rent was unbelievably low. In 1956, a two-bedroom house rented for $16 per month ($4 per room, not counting the bathroom). The electricity was very inexpensive, as well (three cents per kilowatt-hour during the 1950s), and was furnished by the company. They also had their own water system, and the water was free and plentiful for the renters. As an added benefit, the company also employed their own carpenters, plumbers and electricians to maintain the houses. Lest this sound too good to be true, keep in mind that wages in the early 1950s at the mill were not much over $1.00 per hour. So you can see there were many advantages to living in a company house which were very much in demand. It was enjoyable living there. The houses were very close, and the neighbors developed a closeness also, almost a feeling of family, as everyone knew "everyone else's business" as well as their comings and goings.

The mill was the glue that kept us all secluded and shrouded in the fog and the rains of the coastal mountains in and around Vernonia, Oregon. Everyone's life revolved around the mill and its time-frame. The mill whistle was a very invasive presence, although at the time, we never thought of it in that manner. To us, it was just a reminder that kept us informed as to when we should be doing certain activities. After a while, it became a very comforting presence. The whistle blew with two short sounds at 7:45 a.m. as a warning; then, one long

Oregon American Lumber Company, 1929
From the Gerald W. Williams Collection

whistle at 8:00 a.m., letting everyone know that it was time to begin work. At 12:00 noon, there would be another whistle to signal that it was time for a one-hour lunch break. The whistle blew again with a 'two-short' warning at 12:45 p.m. and was followed later with a 'one-long' whistle which meant workers should be on the job at 1:00 p.m. Most people carried their lunches with them in metal lunch boxes—a 'lunch pail'—with room at the top for a Thermos bottle filled with coffee. These people ate their lunches on the job, usually in the lunchroom. The lunches varied as much as the economic situation of the worker and his family. One employee who had recently moved to Vernonia from Mississippi and had grown up amid hard times, always had about a half inch of molasses poured into the bottom of his lunch pail for 'dipping' with several baking powder biscuits thrown in on top for his lunch. That was the extent of his lunch along with some coffee. If he were feeling particularly wealthy, the molasses was replaced by honey. It was not long until he had a new car and money jingling in his pockets, since during all the years he worked there, rich or poor, his lunch never changed.

Some men carried a very sumptuous fare, similar to what you would take on a Sunday picnic in the park or to some favorite spot next to the Nehalem River or Rock Creek, the two streams that ran through Vernonia and the area surrounding it. Most of the lunches were somewhere in between the two extremes. A few of the men who lived in company housing or whose houses were nearby, walked home for lunch. There were some, but very few, who drove their cars home for lunch. The whistle blew again at 1:00 p.m., which meant it was time to get back to work. Then at 5:00 p.m. the whistle would sound another time, signaling the end of the working day, only to begin the routine all over again the following day for five days during the week. On weekends the whistle was silent.

The maintenance crews worked on the weekends to get the mill ready to operate for the week ahead. Not content for the mill to be in control of the time issue, the city chose to sound a siren at 9:00 p.m., as a curfew for young people and those who 'went to bed with the chickens.' Those times when the whistle did not blow during weekdays were considered the 'sad times'—the times of strikes—the time when the mill began running out of the huge "old growth" timber for which this mill had been constructed. Ultimately, it was the time of the final 'shutting down' of the mill after the last load of logs steamed its way into Vernonia on Locomotive 105 from Camp McGregor in 1957. It bore a hand-lettered sign someone had attached below the Oregon American Company logo on the train, stating,

Ain't No More.

Drawing by Jonathan Dugger, age 10
(Millie Graves' great-grandson)

Millie Graves' Family Contributions

The Seven Devils Hide Out
By Cooper Moss (Age 14)

Last year on my Dad's 40th birthday in mid-July, we went hiking in the Seven Devils Mountains in Central Idaho, so he did not have to endure the torture of a surprise birthday party. We got to the trailhead later than we expected. We couldn't go on the trail that we wanted to go on because of snow, so we went a different way. We got to Camp #1 about 30-45 minutes later.

Early the next morning, we packed up camp and headed out. About 6 hours later we made it to Shelf Lake which was Camp #2. The thing I liked the most was that the lake which was clear so you could see all of the fish in the lake. Later that night we tried to catch some fish, but no luck. So the next morning we tried a different spot and caught lots of fish. After we caught our bag limit, we headed back. We had to cross a log to get to Camp #3. Then we left early the next morning, we stopped at Camp #1 to eat breakfast. Then we drove down to Riggins and had one of the best burgers of all time. I would recommended hiking the Seven Devils because of it views.

* * *

Pancake
By Finley St. John (age 7)

This is a story about Pancake. Pancake was born with all the other Longhorns close to my Grandma's house in a big pasture. He could not drink from his Mom so he came to Grandma's house and lived in a dog kennel on her porch. Papa brought him up to my house. He ran and played. I named him Pancake.

***

Blake's Rapid
By Blake Moss (age 12)

One time my family was rafting on the Grand Ronde on a very hot summer day. I was filling a squirt gun near a rapid and I fell in. My dad reached back and grabbed my life jacket before I was sucked under. We named that rapid Blake's Rapid because I fell in. My dad said it was like the time he dropped his hat in the river.

Then five miles down the river he found his hat. My dad belongs to the Search and Rescue so these were two rescues he could have fun on.

***

The Lord

The Lord is always right by my side,
But He also leads me so you could say He's my guide.

He paints, by hand, every sunset
So beautiful, your expectations are met

But when you think the Lord can do more,
He has lots and lots and lots more in store

He has healed the sick, made the blind see
Jesus died on the cross for you and me

God is like the Potter and we are the clay
He slowly shapes us every day.

~ *Carson Moss (age 12)*

"Spring Flowers" by Josslyn Belding, age 7

* * *

The Time Janae Fell Off Hank, The Mule
By Allie Moss (age 9)

One day Janae, Finley and I were riding horses. Janae was riding Hank, Scott's mule, Finn was riding Cloud, Leroy's horse, and I was riding Moe. We went on a trail ride. When we got back to the barn, Papa showed up and we were talking to him. Moe and Hank got too close to each other, then Moe bit Hank. Hank started to buck, Janae tried to pull his head up so he would stop bucking. Hank would not stop bucking. Then Janae fell off Hank. We all stayed away from each other after that. We will from now on stay away from each other.

Three Days and Bad Blood - The Bay Horse
By Brian Palmer

He walked diagonally from the post office to the saloon, from the southeast end of the street to the northwest. In that 150 yards he decided he would go ahead and buy the carbine his brother was selling. It was a scratched-all-to-hell Winchester that still shot straight and his brother wanted $70 for it, but Bill Hitt knew Nathan would take $50. He knew because Nathan had lost $50 in a poker game up in Clyde and didn't have the money to pay back Mike Winzel. Nathan, the elder of the two brothers, had borrowed $50 from Winzel to buy two traps and a new lariat. Nathan didn't know that Bill was aware of the poker game.

Bill really didn't have a use for the rifle; he owned a perfectly good one already that didn't look like it had been raked over with a mesquite limb. He told June he would just hang onto it for a while, maybe let their son shoot it a little. Clint was 14 and would enjoy it. Then, in a year or so when Nathan wanted it back, Bill would sell it to him. For a change he and June had enough put away that he could spend the money without worrying her.

It was cold enough for a coat, but not gloves. The red clay dirt swirled into little clouds up and down the street with bits of paper and debris dancing and running from one end of the street to the other. Winter was around the corner and Bill wished he had painted the front of the house before now. It would wait for spring, unless June got to griping about it.

Hitt walked up the five steps of the Iron Bar Y Saloon. The Nolans had built the place years ago and named it for their brand. They sold beef and corn and had made a run at the casino business for a couple years, but that particular venture never panned out. Bill knew one of the daughters, AnnaMae, and she thought they probably hired crooked dealers. Bill figured it was the old man that drank too much and spent an awful lot of time in Ft. Worth, even for a cattle buyer. Either way, they gave up on cards and dice and went back to decent whisky and beer. The gal in back cooked well enough. Folks said she learned to cook in a woman's prison back east, but Hitt never asked. He thought her name might be Alice but he wasn't even sure of that. He might ask AnnaMae next time he saw her.

Off to his right, two youngsters playing with a broom caught his attention for a moment. Next door to the saloon was Miss Pretty's Dress and Sewing Shop. The two establishments shared a long hitching post and between the two boys and Hitt a stout bay horse was tied. It was a tall animal and had white lashes over one eye. It was a pretty unique damned horse.

Hitt walked closer to the horse and looked at the saddle. On the back of the cantle were the initials JMW, and on the fender closest to him was some sort of a shield design sewn in, similar to what a Roman soldier might use, he thought. He had never seen the saddle before and didn't know who JMW was, but he damn sure knew the horse. He had owned Jack for six years before the horse turned up missing at a rodeo in Anson that Bill and June had gone to.

He and June had stayed in town for a couple days thinking some drunk rodeo bum had ridden the horse back to camp by accident and would bring him back when the hangover and embarrassment wore off. But no rodeo bum ever showed up and Hitt had purchased a little mare to ride back home. Hitt had never had a horse stolen from him before and if he hadn't had a good extra mount back at the house he would have been in a helluva spot. That was nearly two years ago.

Staring at the animal, Hitt could feel himself tensing. He could shake the tunnel vision, but not the anger. He had been tied in knots six ways from Sunday for a month after the horse was stolen and June had been afraid that he might do something rash. His temper had gotten away from him before and she knew their little place in the country couldn't run itself if he were laid up in jail.

He thought about untying the horse and simply riding it back to his own back at the post office, but the animal was in clear view of the saloon and he feared catching an axe handle or worse in the back. He could walk back to the post office and retrieve his own horse and return for Jack, but he may have been seen by the thief from inside the saloon. He would have to go inside.

Turning, he walked the few steps back and entered the Bar Y.

A dozen or so men sat, stood and leaned around the room. It was the middle of the day and all the curtains were pulled open, he could see the room pretty well. The moment he walked in he chided himself for not wearing his shooter. He had had no intention of being in town any length of time at all when he left the house so he had left it in the kitchen.

He let his eyes finish adjusting before going completely inside and walking past a pool table that no one was paying any attention to. On his right at a table he could see two younger men he recognized. One hovered over a beer, the other had something stronger in his grip. They were hands out at Hodges' place. He couldn't remember their names, but he had run into them before. They were decent boys.

Approaching them, they nodded in recognition.

"Hey fellas, how y'all making it today? Hodges know y'all are in here getting soused?"

"Well sir, he knows we're in town, but at the rate we're drinking it's gonna take us a week to get soused." They grinned back at Hitt.

"Yea, I'll bet. Either one of you see who tied up that bay yonder by the dress shop?" Hitt asked them with a slight turn of his head. He didn't want to give any sign that he was looking outside.

"I believe it was the fella in that buffalo hat and bandana."

The smaller of the two was looking past Bill at a man at the end of the bar. He was leaned over the bar, talking to the bartender.

Hitt turned enough to see who was being described. Medium build, gray hair. The man was wearing a coat, so Hitt couldn't see if he was wearing a firearm. He had to figure the man was. He looked back at the two.

"Thanks, boys. Tell Hodges I said hey. What's he paying y'all, anyhow?"

"Twelve dollars a week, but we're set to get a raise."

"That sounds fair. Don't spend it all in here," he said with a quick wink. "And don't go to sleep for the next ten minutes, either."

They both said, "No sir" and he turned away. He closed the distance between himself and the man in the buffalo hat with six steps. When he was close enough to speak, the man turned away from the bartender and spoke first.

"You need something, mister?"

Hitt looked closely at the man's face and hands. He hadn't turned enough for Hitt to see if he was wearing a gun or not.

"Well, yeah, I might. What do... Winzel? Mike Winzel?"

"Maybe. You asking me or telling me?"

Bill was caught off guard completely. He was the Mike Winzel that Nathan owed money to. When Winzel spoke his words were clear enough, but his eyes were not. They had the sheen of booze.

Hitt had never cared one way or the other for Winzel. The two of them met by accident at a fish fry a few years past. Hitt heard that Winzel had lost a son in a fire a while back. Nathan said he started drinking pretty heavy after that.

"Sorry about your boy. That was a real shame."

Without skipping a beat Winzel answered, "Yer right, it was. Who are you?"

"Bill Hitt. You've had some dealings with my brother Nathan. Ring a bell?"

"Yeah it does. What might you need?"

The bartender backed away from the two. He felt the tension and would give them room.

"I need to know where you got that bay horse out yonder."

Winzel looked squarely back and took a long second to answer.

"If I thought you needed to know Hitt, I would have looked you up when I got here."

He had shifted just enough that the rig on his right hip left a print under the jacket that Bill could see. Gun.

Now their conversation was the centerpiece of the room. Nobody was behind Winzel, the bartender had moved several feet away and the other closest man took a step towards the door.

"That might have been a good idea, Winzel. In fact, it would have been a real good idea. You ever been to the Anson rodeo? You might enjoy it. They sell lots of horses up there. 'Course, some of them ain't for sale, neither."

Winzel laughed a small laugh and looked down. It was the motion of someone preparing to move quickly.

"Sounds like you're trying to say a mouthful, Hitt." He turned slightly and spoke over his right shoulder.

"Is that how it sounds to you, fellas? Sounds like…

That was when Hitt smoothly, but quickly, pulled the pool ball out of his coat pocket and threw it at Winzel. Unnoticed, he had picked it up from the table when he entered the room. He threw it hard and hit Winzel on his exposed collarbone. The thud and the crack of bone were hard to tell apart and Winzel staggered, grunted and nearly fell. Hitt stepped to his own left and adjusted his feet to kick with all he had. Winzel tried to draw his pistol, but his broken collarbone hurt like a bastard and

wouldn't let his arm completely make the motion. He got the thing pulled, but only part way. At the sight of the gun, Hitt kicked, but struck Winzel in the hip, not the revolver. The roar that followed deafened Hitt, but didn't freeze him. He rushed Winzel, pinning him to the bar. He managed to get both hands on the big Colt and Winzel didn't have the strength in his arm to keep Hitt from wrenching the weapon away. He threw the gun and stuffed Winzel's Adam's apple into the crook of his right elbow and slammed him backwards onto the floor. Two fast right fists into Winzel's face ended the fracas.

Breathing hard, Hitt stood up and said out loud to the room, "I still got the papers on that horse in my sock drawer."

Hodges' two men kept watch on Winzel and helped to steady Hitt. The bartender handed him a beer and said, "I never liked that SOB, he just kinda struck me funny."

The sheriff showed up and asked a few questions, the last of which was, "With a cue ball? Hit him with a damned cue ball? I guess that would do the trick, although I wouldn't necessarily recommend it."

When the dust had settled and the sheriff had taken Winzel out the back door to avoid a scene in the street, one of Hodges' men spoke to Hitt.

"That was something, Mr. Hitt. My wife will get a kick out of it. Sorry about your horse an' all. What are the odds?"

"I know. Pretty damn lucky finding him here. He's a good horse, I use him for cutting. Glad to get him back."

"What? No sir, I mean I'm really sorry about your horse. That sumbitch missed you but shot your horse deader than a hammer. Shot him right through the neck it looks like.

He's lying out there deader than hell."

Stunned, Hitt went outside and stood over Jack.

"Well I'll be a… Of all the damned things. And on my birthday on top of that."

N ick DeAngelo was 15 years old and a student at Elmira High School when he submitted his first story for the *Groundwaters* literary journal in 2007. In the April 2008 issue, he sent us the first of many cartoon strips that we published. This imaginative, talented young man went on to design our *Groundwaters*' masthead and logo and for our last anthology, he sent us two new strips and a drawing that are included on other pages in this book. Welcome back, Nick and thank you for all of your support! Pat and Jen

Nick DeAngelo has dedicated his life to writing the tragic events of himself in comics, all of which should be left alone to avoid any misery, grief, or bad stomach pains.

During his journeys to most clearly and accurately depict the terrible events in his own life, Nick DeAngelo has had to battle lions, face angry mobs, and escape from caves quickly filling with deadly fungus. Many times, Nick has been presumed dead, all times inaccurately.

As I wrote before, it would be most recommended to avoid reading the comics of Nick DeAngelo, as they contain such tragic things as pictures, words, and voice bubbles.

Right now, Nick is in hiding, as he is being sued by Lemony Snicket for copyright violations.

Chasing the Darkness
By Jennifer Chambers

While visiting her family farm, cookie baker and small-town green witch, Amelia Walks-Among-the-Stars Walker, is stalked by a supernatural wolf ("In the Gloaming," GW 2020). We rejoin her the next day at her cookie shop trying to make sense of things.

"Amelia Walks Among the Stars," she wrote on the top of the fresh, new front cover of her notebook with a black, fine-point Sharpie., and opened to the first page. She loved to write her whole name on her daily planners. It made her feel silly, like a kid, but strong. "Wheesh," she sighed, and raised her hands all the way up to the sky and threw them down to get the blood going. It was time to get to regular work in order to pay the electric bill.

She wrote "*TO DO,*" with a regular pen, and immediately wrote "*FIND OUT ABOUT WOLF SPIRITS.*" Brushing the remains of her granola breakfast cookie strewn among the items on her worktable in the back room, she perched on her carved wooden stool. A shadow cut through the early-morning sun and she started, looking around quickly left to right.

"Anyone there?"

There was no response, but the shadow moved away. She muttered under her breath and picked up a lit cedar incense smudge stick, rising to surround the room with the smoke. "There." The smoke was cleansing and rid the space of negative energy. She couldn't be too careful.

Moving the notebook over so as not to nudge her mug of strong tea, she considered the day's plan. It was near Imbolc, the beginning of February, a time to celebrate the very beginning of the return to the light time of the year, halfway between the winter and spring solstice. She felt both sides of her, the Native American side and the Celtic side, were well-represented by her art and her business. Preparations for the season would center her, she thought, and allow her to think more deeply about the wolf experience the day before at her parent's farm. It had been so difficult to sleep. The smoke and the other protective spells she had placed on her business and home should protect her. It didn't make sense. She shook her head. Things seemed to be going on that she couldn't understand. Her estrangement from her magical parts of her family didn't help. At least she had her friends and co-workers in her coven, but they couldn't always be around. She needed to build her own defenses.

Also, she had to make money to support herself and there was no way she would let her workers down. The trinkets she made sold well alongside her cookies and other decorative goods, and she needed to get this wolf out of her head to organize her supplies as well as her thoughts. "Moss," she wrote, followed by "Orange Slices," and "Cedar/Pine Bundles." Creaks sounded from outside. She mentally checked the locks: yes, they'd all been locked with regular deadbolts as well as the magic enhancement spells. She would not let anything frighten her in her own business.

A stack of four-sided, braided Bridgit's Crosses lay before her on the table, each with slightly different decorations of dried white flowers, greenery, and stones tucked into it at intervals. One had bright green knotted ribbon interwoven in the cross, and the ribbon matched accents on the pile of small straw dolls that sat beside the crosses on the table. She wrote several more items on the list: "feathers, holly, pinecones." Rain started to pour down on the cottage's tin roof. Oh, great. Now her sense of sound would be dulled out.

Sighing, she set the notebook aside and took the already done decorations to the front room. A long wooden bar separated the back third of what had originally been the living room of her small, two story cottage business from the entrance to the rooms beyond. It made a good spot for cookie and accessory sales. Four small tables lined the front room, with sturdy wooden chairs, and a long thin bench ran the length of the room on the left under a shallow bay window. It only took a few minutes to add the dolls to spots in the window and around the tables and on the tables set with cheerfully mismatched crockery. Empty nails on the walls were perfect places to hang the crosses so they were visible amid rustic grapevine wreaths and folk art of local Pacific northwest forest scenes, animals, and evening landscapes. The plum-colored curtains were drawn but some morning light was visible above them.

A door painted with iris and roses was ajar on to the right of the doorway to the house, and Amelia went to flick on the light to make sure the customer bathroom didn't need attention.

She poked in her head and switched the light with a touch, then scanned the window tops for any more shadows.

Back to the worktable, she thought, with a quick glance at the clock. 8:00 a.m. Still two hours until opening. As if triggered by the thought, a timer went off and she rushed to the kitchen to wash her hands and retrieve the morning's cookies. Once they were on the large industrial cooling rack, she put the remaining batches in the large commercial ovens and passed over the glossy finish of the largest one with a rag soaked in bleach water, taking extra care to make sure the name "Marge" painted in Old English, tattoo style script on the pink oven door was clean.

"Oh, good," she said aloud. The lavender lemon sugar cookies she had baked earlier were cool and ready to be frosted. Carefully, she placed two dozen on each of two racks and readied the thin lemon glaze. She saw with a satisfying sniff that the light color of the powdered sugar glaze was flecked with zest and smelled pungently lemony. Once each cookie had been covered in glaze, she reached for the small bowl of dried lavender buds waiting on the work surface and sprinkled a few artfully on each sweet-tart cookie, moving counterclockwise and whispering blessings.

"There."

"Talking to yourself again?"

Her bare feet thumped after she jumped off the ground. "How did you get in?"

The man behind her was thin and tall with a bald head and a thin build, his narrow, black-clad shoulders squeezed into her kitchen but faded into nothing at the waist. "I'm not here," he purred, "not really. There's a window you forgot. I just slipped my projection inside to have a little chat."

His evil smile showed grey teeth and a split tongue. "I'm here to warn you. My mother is very angry at you. My brother is too. You need to stop trying to find your family."

Amelia mentally spun through the catalog of spirits she knew. This looked like something nasty, for sure. His form trailed off into black tendrils that looked alive, almost like tentacles, and the split in his tongue almost seemed sharp on the edges like twin knives. A thorny celtic three-part braid tattoo circled his neck. "Dother!" she pointed a finger at him. She had finally remembered it.

Leaning heavily on the counter, she shifted to face the demon. "Dother. I know you. You, your mother, Carman, and your brothers, you're evil for no reason. You have no power here. Leave!"

Heart pounding, she dipped her fingers into the salt bowl on the table and flung a handful at him.

His image wavered, then went out slowly, his face the last thing to dissolve, as he said, "Sssooon. Sssooon we will ssseee you again."

Once he was completely gone, Amelia grabbed a walking stick from the side of the counter and went to check the bathroom as fast as she could. He was right. She shut the window and sprayed the small bottle of moon water mixed with black salt over the seal. "Only those who wish me well, may go through this window sill." Not a great spell, but it would do. Her breath was calmer now.

Back in the kitchen, she washed her hands and stacked the baked goods on the cart to put in front. When the room looked ready for customers, she went behind the counter to sit on her stool and pulled out her phone. She sat a little straighter. She wasn't alone, not really. Time to rally the troops, otherwise known as her friends and coven-mates. Time to chase the darkness.

"Shaniko, Oregon; Ghost Town"
Photo by Riley Chambers

"Understanding Stocks" by Nick DeAngelo

"Bubbles, the Axolotl"
Drawn by Keira Chambers

Miss Octavia
By Randall Luce

...She kept her hands in her lap. "Whites own it now," she said. "It was such a sweet land. It smelled like leaves, and fish and bone and offal. Some of it was marly—sandy clay. Uncle Paul said you could bury your hands in it clear up to your elbows. The one time I returned..."

She fell quiet. She began to play again, and presently began again to speak.

"Grandfather cleared that first piece of land himself, him and his boys. That was one of the hardest parts, because that work paid him no money. He'd be careful about what he spent on food and such—he'd parcel out the money from his box. Every night, he'd count that money, and recount it, and he'd recalculate the figures—because his life depended on it, and his family's.

"Grandmother was with child that year, and gave birth to a perfect little baby, but it wasn't but months before that baby caught a fever. Grandmother tried every cure she knew. Then she asked Grandfather to carry them to a doctor. My Uncle Paul—he told us he was just thirteen—he heard them arguing, and two days later he took that baby himself, in the middle of the night—he'd find a doctor. Come morning, Grandfather went after them with his horse and wagon. He found them that night in a clearing in the wilderness. He saw my uncle's camp fire. He found him digging a hole with a stick he'd sharpened. My grandfather put the baby in the back of the wagon and sat down on the ground next to his son. He told him, you can stop that now.

"My uncle kept on digging.

"Grandfather patted the ground. He told his son to study this land. He told his son this was a sweet land, but it was also a hard land, and unforgiving, and all about us were the white men and the world they'd built. That world had no room for colored people like us. It wouldn't have had any room for that little baby either. So we had to be hard too. We had to plow a straight row, we had to keep our eyes up with every step, that's the only way you can plow a furrow straight. You can't look down at whatever rocks might come up. You can't lay down or cry.

"My grandfather told him, 'It's too far to travel, that baby wouldn't have made it, you can see that now. Whatever doctor—that doctor'd be white—he wouldn't save our baby. He'd take our money, but he wouldn't save our baby.'

"Grandfather said he had a plan, about how much more land it would take for us to really have something, and how much money it would take to buy it, and he'd worked out the money they'd make when they started farming and the money they'd need from what he already had. There was no room for a doctor in that plan.

"My uncle kept on digging."

Miss Octavia closed her eyes. Her fingers skimmed the tops of the keys. There was no sound—or was there? Elon listened closer, he leaned his head toward the upright box. Miss Octavia's hand came still and one note whispered. She breathed deep, her fingers to the keys.

"Then my grandfather told him how, when he was searching for their first piece of land, how he'd listen to the nighttime, to the sounds all around him that came up from the plants and the trees, and the wind through them rustling and from the animals too. Once he got to know those sounds he'd say his name, he'd whisper it at first, and then a little louder. He was trying to slip the sound of his name in there to see how it fit. And he'd bend down and smell the ground and put it to his lips, and he'd rub the blackened leaves on his palms, and put them to his face and smell them, and ask himself, 'Is this a smell I know?'

"Grandfather told him, 'I wasn't *me* until the day I claimed my box.'

"Grandfather told him there was a gap in time that was his slave days, and before that gap there were our African ancestors, our unknown ancestors, but grandfather knew they were farmers. This was not told knowledge, not anything he'd heard. He said this was a deep-down certainty he had, that before and after slavery his people and he were a people of the land, their land, and they knew the smell of it, its taste, and the sound of it, and the sound of their names—the names themselves and how they said them, whether their voices were high or low, or gruff or smooth. The sound of their names had to fit into place with the sounds of their land. So, this was a long line of long lives lived that my grandfather was taking up again.

"He told his son, 'I would tell you everything about our ancestors if I could, but nothing, not a word, about that gap there in between. I'll buy from any white man, I'll sell to any white man, but I'll never work for a white man again. I'll never, ever, be a slave, not as long as I have my land and my box, and the money I put in it. There's just enough to keep us free, but not enough for any doctor.'

"By then my uncle stopped digging. They found their way home and the family buried their baby."

Miss Octavia drew her hands to her lap.

"When my uncle told that story he never called that baby's name, or even said he or she. He'd just say, 'the baby.' But one day I found her grave. It was a little wooden cross, weatherworn. I could barely trace the letters of the name burned into the wood... Cecelia. I asked my uncle. He said they called her Cee-Cee."

Miss Octavia paused, and drew a finger underneath her eye. She whispered, "All along, I knew that baby was a girl."

She turned to Elon. She wanted to explain.

"By the time—in my time, we owned so much land. Grandfather had bought over three hundred acres by then. It was good land, in my time it was all cleared by then. We had ourselves our own cotton gin. We sold our cotton directly to the factors and they bid for it like they did the whites'. And we built a church and we held our school in it. We hired a schoolteacher and we supported a preacher one Sunday every month. We did for ourselves. We asked for nothing. We were under nobody's thumb. That'd been my grandfather's plan. And it came to fruition. He made it so."

She started to play again, and stopped.

"I never saw my grandfather and I never saw his box, but they were the testaments—they were the Messiah and the Arc of the Covenant by which my family lived."

She put her hands back on the keys and played.

"When he was searching for his first piece of land, he knew it—he knew that when he'd finally hear those sounds fitting all together, it would be something he was remembering, even on that very first time. Because those sounds together were already inside him, waiting for him to hear them and remember. Then he would know that he and his family were truly at home, and that their days of wandering were over."

Miss Octavia drew her hands down from the piano to her lap.

"Whatever might have made me doubt him, I've always known that this was true: He *had* spoken his name in the night. He *had* listened to the sounds and smelled the land and tasted it. He *had* searched for those sounds and smells and tastes that would wake up within him something that he knew he would know, but had not yet heard or tasted or smelled. Because that was the way it was for me and this music. My first night at that piano—no, when I had first pressed my fingers on the keys that Sunday after church—I knew. It was a sound I had known but had never heard before—the sound of *my* making. It was an unknown part of *me,* not ever lost but still found, and it beckoned me forward to be me, to be every part of me.

"I never saw my grandfather... But he was me."

Elon had no sisters and he had no brothers. No grandparents. No uncles and no aunts. His mother and he, they just had each other. At night, when he'd burrow into bed, he'd listen to the night sounds, how their house would come alive at night—the creak and groan of wood and nail—and the wind outside, and sometimes a wagon passing by, or a worrisome dog. And he'd listen carefully for any sounds from his mother's room—whether she was crying or not. It had been a long time since she had. Still, he'd listen. Through the years, he never stopped listening. He was her night watchman, though he knew his listening never did her any good.

But it was the only thing he could do for her.

Back when she was crying, he had listened to every sob, a feat of concentration because he was only a small child back then, and he'd think of what he'd do to whoever it was who had made her cry, until she finally fell asleep and the night had its sounds to itself again—the wind, a dog, the house's creak and groan.

But she hadn't cried for years now. She was probably past it. But Elon wasn't, even now at seventeen, and he felt he owed her his watchman's duty. He'd listen until he couldn't anymore, as her silence slid seamlessly into his sleep.

Once he was old enough, Elon had asked her several times, "Which white man had it been? Did he still live in town? Is he still alive?" She never told him.

She never told anyone. Nobody knew. "It wouldn't do you any good to know," his mother told him. "It would only bring you trouble."

Elon would ask her, "Why do you protect him?"

"Does he know about me?"

His mother never said.

Miss Octavia sat and played at her piano.

"My father and uncle took their wives from the Hills. Hardly any colored folks owned land in the Delta. Most of them that came here, they worked for the white man on some new plantation. And when you worked for a white man, when you needed something, the white man gave it to you. My grandfather said that made you soft-minded. It made you a slave. He said, no white man would want a hard-minded man, because a hard-minded man wouldn't fit in a white man's pocket. Now, everything that white man gave you, he'd write it in his book, and take it out of your share once the cotton was in—there wasn't any free ride. But to my grandfather, it was still too easy. So Grandfather didn't want any relations with the coloreds who worked for the white man. When we joined with families in marriage, Grandfather had his sons marry women from the Hills, from where he had come, from hard-minded, land-owning families, like ours. My uncle and my father married sisters.

"They had no choice in it.

"When I became of age, my father and uncle arranged my marriage to a nephew of their wives. I first heard about it when they told me. I knew the man. He was all right. We would've had our courtship—we could've taken our time to grow accustomed to what our lives would be.

"But I told them no.

"They told me he was a good man, a hard-working man. I said I knew that, and he had always been respectful to me.

"But he wasn't my man. He wasn't my choice. So, I told them no.

"They were surprised to hear that. 'Did I have another man in mind?' They were willing to hear me out.

"I told them no.

"And this, they didn't understand. They said the way I was acting was a disgrace to my grandfather. If I had any respect for my family, I'd marry this man."

Miss Octavia stopped her playing and turned to Elon. "But Grandfather lived his life to be free. I wanted that same freedom, Elon."

Then she resumed. A gospel song.

"That night I snuck out to the church. I thought about my grandfather and I thought about his box. It seemed to me that freedom—it can't be given out on one day and locked away the next. I played and I dreamed and I wished I had a box like my grandfather's. And it was funny—I realized I wasn't listening to what I was playing. So, I listened. I didn't try to play any tune, I just played … and what I played was beautiful. And that was when I realized: I do have a box.

"I knew what I had to do. It was too late that night, so I waited all the next day and left after everybody'd gone to bed.

"I hopped a train for New Orleans."

Miss Octavia laughed, and played a boogie-woogie.

"Just me. And a matchbox for my clothes."

~*~*~

From *The Dark Tree* by Randall Luce; an unpublished manuscript.

Maybe I Too Can Be a Poet

I want to turn everything I do and see
into poetry.

Can you help me? Can you laugh when you want
    to criticize or distain?
Can you lend me your best images and phrases?
Or, will you hoard them
and only let them out when you want to impress?

Let's try it together
Let's vow to see beauty in the ugly and
the ugly in beauty.

My granddaughter taught me that.
She did it with visual art

She made a drawing with
black slashes and scotch tape flowers.

She called it
"Beauty in Ugliness, and Ugliness in Beauty"

How does she know so much about the human
    heart?
With her as my Guide, maybe I too can be a poet.

~ Lois Angela Czyzewski

Riding On
By Mary Lee Radka

The morning sky was mostly blue, combed through with fluffy clouds. A slip of a moon still loitered behind the trees. Sunlight broke through so that the young leaves, rippling in the wind, shone like foil.

Hilltops became gold against the sunrise, and windows reflecting its light were so orange, you could imagine a fire blazing.

Later, while waiting for a break in the rain—for after all, this is Oregon—I saw a crow with its head bowed, its feathers so wet they shone like tar.

As I rode my bicycle, I was surprised by how much there was to see—if only I had known to look.

Stopping at a tree swing, wide enough to hold three, I slowly swung in the chilled light, pouring like water from above. Looking across the Willamette River, I saw flashes of yellow, pink and blue as the river floaters swirled across the choppy white water.

It was exhilarating to be swiftly passing other bikers, walkers and skaters, especially on hills, with my electric bike. Everyone was the same, yet also unique, as if this was the dilemma of being human.

It is as if all my life I have been waiting to start really noticing the varied highways and byways to heaven.

Softly pedaling with a steady rhythm.
Feeling the sun, wind, and sometimes a light rain
misting on my face.
Watching a red-tailed hawk soaring overhead,
Or stopping to watch a muskrat and his ratty tail
Navigate the murky water, with a great grey
heron silently poised behind,
Feet lifting and falling.

The Poetry of Place
By Terah Van Dusen

After waiting a full five minutes for the lodge's hot water to kick on in the shower, I wash my hair twice with 2-in-1 shampoo and conditioner. Autumn sits on the shower floor, folding and unfolding a damp washcloth. We are on a girl's trip to track down Dad, who lives off-grid in Northern California. Dad has no telephone, so it is often hard to reach him. I don't mind the adventure in tracking Dad down. I like that he isn't like all the others, but sometimes it is hard—the not knowing.

We tried watching TV, but turned it down to hear the creek outside—Patrick Creek—a tributary to the Smith. Now I bounce Autumn, trying to soothe her toddler boredom, and somehow keep my pen to paper, too. I'd say she can't sit still, but the same would have to be true for me, too. (*Proof:* I couldn't stay put on the farm near Eugene this weekend. I simply woke with the urge to ramble home.)

I told myself it was justified to see Dad. Autumn's dad gave us his blessing, and then tried to suggest routes and game-plans. But I already had it mapped out in my mind; we'd get a hotel room closest to home. Hiouchi Motel or Patrick Creek Lodge. No one knew this stretch of highway better than me.

The rooms at Patrick Creek Lodge have mission-style furniture and vaulted redwood ceilings. In the past I would have camped in the van or in a tent or on my best friend's couch in Crescent City. But parenting, and then the pandemic, has changed everything.

Driving south on the I-5, the words "Do whatever you have to do to feel alive" came to mind. So maybe that's what this is really about. More than seeing Dad, it's about feeling alive. I'd forgotten how, when we travel, it upsets Autumn's natural rhythm. She gets antsy and angsty and now she sits across from me, Indian-style, on the white '70s-style bedspread. "Let's talk," she says. So we talk about what's outside the window—bushes, trees, lights, leaves.

There are no other cars in the parking lot and I am uncertain if there is an overnight watch person or not. The friendly fellow who checked us in said he was "locking up and heading home for the night."

A couple and a lady stumbled out of the bar around 7:30 p.m., piled into a full-sized pickup and drove south toward Gasquet (pronounced *gas-gee*). Other than that, crickets... metaphorically, of course, because it's winter in these woods. The temperature registered at 34 degrees, but it had been sunny and t-shirt weather all day. Of course we only got out at a rest stop somewhere near Riddle, Oregon.

Pacific madrone and redwoods—that's what I came for—other than to connect with Dad, the man who raised me—Pacific madrone with its smooth, chopstick bark, the redwood groves already shooting up toward the sky, just seven or ten miles into California.

When the sun set, we decided it would be best to surprise Dad first thing in the morning, rather than an hour or two after dusk. Dad, like me, is better in the morning... freshest and sharpest and most optimistic. We both like to have our coffee, too.

When I was a girl, Dad took me to this very lodge once for breakfast. The waitress seated us by a window where we could watch Patrick Creek flow by. A small porcelain ramekin held strawberry and grape jelly packets. I chose grape jelly to smear on my sourdough toast, not because I liked grape best, but because there were just two choices: grape or strawberry. I knew that a better family, one that would come in next, would have a little girl or boy who would prefer strawberry, and that kids from better families always got what they wanted because of people like us. I knew that my going without kept everything in balance.

The grape jelly kind of tasted like the liquid cough syrup Dad sometimes had to force down my throat. He'd either pin me down on the cabin floor, knees holding down my kid-arms, or convince me that if I plugged my nose I couldn't taste it, so then I'd just drink it myself. I hoped that kid enjoyed his strawberry jam, whoever he was. I was in heaven just with the butter alone and the creek flowing by.

Dad sometimes liked to elbow his way in to a class above our own—the ski lodge at Mt. Bachelor in Oregon, riding elevators in the business district in San Francisco, the fine dining restaurant in The Wharf where we just ordered appetizers, then sheepishly paid and left. Dad had a penchant for experiences he couldn't quite afford, and if I am being honest, sometimes I do too. But at least it's a penchant for experiences, not a penchant for things.

"What are we going to do tomorrow, mama?" Autumn asked me.

"Well, we are going to get up…"

"Use the restroom?"

"Yes, use the restroom."

"And then what?"

"And then we are going to make mama some coffee and Autumn some breakfast."

"Coffee? Brickfest?"

"Yep. And then we're going to take a walk down to the creek… Patrick Creek."

In my mind's eye, I can see the dirt path leading from the lodge, then along Patrick Creek, and under a bridge to where the creek forms a confluence with the middle fork of the Smith River. The middle fork of the river meanders southeast through mossy canyon walls until it intersects with the south fork of the river. You head up the south fork, and that's where I'm from. I was raised in a single-room cabin that burned down in a fire in 2010. Now Dad lives in a fifth-wheel his ex-girlfriend gave him.

"And then?" Autumn asks.

"And then, after our walk, we are going to see Grandpa Rob!"

"See Grandpa Rob?" Autumn repeats, in her high-pitched voice. It's as if the higher pitched her voice, the more likely she will get an answer she's satisfied with.

"Yup. "

"Oh."

We haven't seen Grandpa Rob since Father's Day—five months ago—when we met up with him halfway between his home and our home and ate salmon bagel sandwiches on the bank of the Umpqua River. He didn't eat much that day, and it worried me. But I am always worried about Dad: worried about him driving distracted, worried about him choosing nutritious over junk food, worried about the steel parts collecting on his property, worried about his future. But mainly, I'm worried that he's sad, and that I could have done something to prevent that sadness.

Autumn is snoring now. She is lying on her back, mouth slightly open, arms and legs splayed, sleeping off the day. Today was a big day. She said the word "California" and dealt with her mother's impulsive need to "connect with her roots," enduring what turned into a 4-hour drive. She kept asking for "Nana" and "Grandpa Norm," her father's folks who she is more acquainted with than Grandpa Rob. Dodging fallen granite from rock slides in the road, and maneuvering corners I haven't seen since Aunt Dort's memorial in March, 2018, I tried to explain, "No, honey, this is mama's family. Mama has family too."

"No, I wan' see Nana."

I don't know what to expect in the morning. That's the thing about mama's family. It's the reason we pulled back at dusk, instead of gunning it forward. In the past, I slept on riverbanks or friends' couches, desperate to connect with Dad, but not willing to endure his lifestyle off-the-grid, which due to his disability and a variety of other factors, has degraded some through the years. A leaky chimney and no refrigeration. Rodents. Simply limitations that often come with poverty. No news to me. But my soft place to land has always been these hills, fog hanging in the treetops like ghosts, white fingers wrapped around the branches of the evergreens. This place hasn't moved an inch since I left home. Oh, but I have. I'll be lucky if I can still recognize myself in the mirrored reflection on the surface of the river water.

I close my journal, place my writing pen beside it on the nightstand, and open up a new *Sun Magazine*. Barbara Kingsolver's essay "The Only Real Story" jumps off the page:

A world is looking over my shoulder as I write these words; my censors are bobcats and mountains. I have a place from which to tell my stories. So do you, I expect. We sing the song of our home because we are animals, and an animal is no better or wiser or safer than its habitat. Among the greatest of all gifts is to know our place.

I didn't know what to expect in the morning.

I didn't know that we would arrive just in time for coffee, and that Dad would pour me two steaming cups, before hitting the trails just outside the doorframe.

I didn't know that Dad would be fine, and not sad at all.

I didn't know that we would hike the land of my youth until noon, Dad with Autumn on his shoulders.

I didn't know that we would crouch by the rivers and streams and say our blessings.

I didn't know that I would harvest bay laurel and Dad would find a field of matsutake mushrooms.

I didn't know that, when no one was looking, I would press my forehead into the earth, addicted to the feeling of the damp soil crushing into my third eye.

I didn't know that Dad would go on and on about God, as he always does, and I would just gesture at the nature all around us as if to say,

"Yeah, but... *this*."

I didn't know that it would all be intact—the land and Dad—just as I'd left them.

But one thing I did know is just how *alive* I'd feel when we left.

Destination - Rock Springs, Wyoming
By Elizabeth Orton

Several years ago I had the opportunity to live in a small Wyoming town. For approximately eight months, my customary surroundings existed only in dream land. The barren landscape I journeyed, gave way to large quantities of learning—learning to accept and, eventually, embrace this adventure, came at a snail's pace. Maneuvering myself through the wild, cold, winds of a Wyoming winter produced challenge.

Discovering secrets beyond what looked like a sterile desert, began to intrigue my senses. Veiled treasures enticed my curiosity. Embracing the rough–empty–outer layer, of what appeared to be nothing more than a barren landscape, required letting loose of stereotypes and embracing new thought.

When I let go, life unleashed a treasure-trove of surprises...

Openness - From the majestic royal blue firmament, given as a daily greeting, with brightness attaching itself to a chilled earth. A blessing, above and below.

Quiet - Unhurried and undisturbed, with a modest approach of pride and pleasure in the fulfillment of a days work.

Duty - Garnered with slices of knowledge, skill and frivolity brought forward thinking, with occasional backward doing. Celebrating both.

Freshness - Chilling the body, warming the mind. Chilling the mind, warming the body. Providing simplicity in tangled opportunities.

Rock Springs, Wyoming - Gives attention to the hidden. An adventure stored in secrecy. Beauty awaits for those who search. Murmured joy gives way when least expected. You are energy, born in my heart. You are stillness, igniting my thought. I am thankful for your openness, for secrets unveiled, for caution in presentation.

Will I return? Not a chance!

Hero for a Day
By Demetri Liontos

On our last visit to the Bay Area to see family there, the conversation after dinner turned to heroes and superheroes. My grandsons, fifteen and twelve, both avid readers, had read tons of stories featuring these superhumans and could recite many a feat. I chortled and said that sounded "super," but of course it was fiction. Real life heroes took a different form, used less glamorous transportation to get around, and sometimes were pretty ordinary Joes just doing extraordinary things.

That sounded like a cue for the twelve-year-old to beam, "How about you, Papou, were you ever a hero?"

Having never thought of myself in those terms, I was about to laugh off his question when a flash of memory struck me: "...an ordinary Joe doing something a bit extraordinary"—something out of the comfort zone. And so I cobbled together the story of Rufus on our Washington, D.C. trip.

Last spring my wife and I were on a weeklong trip to D.C. with a group of friends from Eugene, primarily to see the sights. One morning, between sights, we stopped into a Starbucks for coffee and pastry. This was one of the crowded Starbucks, located strategically across from the White House, with a throng of visitors waiting to get in and wrapping around the corner.

We got our order and settled in to enjoy it when the door swung open and in strode a terrifying-looking man—disheveled gray hair, greasy khaki shirt, filthy frayed jeans, and glassy bug-eyes that looked about to pop out of their sockets. But it was the yelling that we all noticed first, slurred yet deafening, and with a faintly Southern drawl.

"I told 'em... I told 'em she done it!" he shouted. "He got 'er money... but she got 'im! Right 'tween the eyes, man!" We were in the middle of a story and our teller had everyone's attention.

"Yeah, right 'tween the eyes wit 'er sweet Colt 45," he continued, shuffling from table to table. "Cops t'ought it wuz me, da basta'ds! But I tol' 'em and tol' 'em. Buttah woodna melt 'ner mout' but she dun it, f'sure!"

With arms flailing and eyes gleaming, the wild man stumbled from one table to another, clearly frightening most of the patrons, who cowered when he approached. The litany was repeated over and over, without adding more to the story.

It occurred to me that none of the Starbucks staff, who could see the whole spectacle, weren't stopping him or asking him to leave. They were too busy making lattes and warming croissants for the mid-morning D.C. crowd. Appalled by this, I suddenly had the feeling we were all our own with this guy.

Soon he was at our table, all smelly and reeking of booze. He bellowed the story on as if it was the first time he was telling it. I sensed my wife cringing, as his spittle shot across our table. I wanted to crush him, stop his blabbering and kick him literally out of the shop. Instead, I did something I didn't think about nor expect that I would do. I stood up.

"Excuse me, but do you know you're scaring everyone?" I said in an even, moderate tone. "Is that what you want to do?" The man looked at me with insane eyes. Before he could repeat his story, I started in. "You look like a nice guy to me," I said calmly. "What's your name?"

He mumbled that it was Rufus.

"Now, you wouldn't want to hurt anyone here, would you, Rufus?"

He looked at me quite perplexed and muttered, "Guess not." Then he did something I hadn't expected. I worried he might lash out indignantly, but instead he shrugged, shook his horrid mane of greasy gray hair and slowly turned away. Soon he was out the door and a hush fell over Starbucks. I sat down, inwardly happy I hadn't been stabbed, and heard a clap... then another, and another. Soon there was a collective sigh of relief rolled into an applause that was almost embarrassing .

My wife smiled at me. "Nice going, Dee," she said, squeezing my arm. "No telling what that guy was going to do."

We finished our coffees and resumed museum hopping along the National Mall. It was a beautiful sunny day and people on the Mall were enjoying it. Soon I didn't think much about the encounter and felt my usual "ordinary Joe" self.

Later, when telling the story to my grandsons, I still didn't think I acted especially heroic, just doing what I thought was necessary. It was an unscripted occurrence which turned out okay—but also might not have.

And perhaps that's where "heroism" lies... in not knowing.

fringe of famous

salivating dogs
with notepads
trying to increase
the narrative
criteria inherited
from nomads
only their decision
is imperative

no one can dissuade them
many do complain
how can you deride them
when everyone's to blame

on the fringe of famous
mock you if you cry
everyone's in a hurry
to get their slice of pie

~ C. Steven Blue

Night Lines

The daylight is fading now
the lines and boxes
that keep my mind contained
are softening
melting like butter
swirling and mixing
blending into dark rainbow whorls
of forbidden thoughts
and creative imaginings
tired of being bound
they wander outside propriety
breaking house rules
ignoring social norms
and violating ancient taboos
they become wild archetypal dreams
of love and power
of lust and rage and conquest
where brilliant inspirations
mingle with the smell of sex and fire
and images of naked imps
jumping from rooftops with
gossamer wings flapping
in the cool evening air as
they learn to fly

No wonder some fear the dark
it is not a squared and measured place
and for those who need the boxes
it doesn't make sense
at least not in a linear way
the curves are softer than the lines
they don't hold you up
or tell you where to go
they fold themselves around you
and carry you into a current
unbound by imagination
sometimes frightening
sometimes dangerous
always exhilarating
so breathe deeply
make a few notes if you must
but mostly pay attention
and remember
the curves are where the treasures lie
the curves are the magic

~ Marv Himme

Grandstands

By William Crutchfield

As Doyle pulled into the long gravel road leading to the parking lot, he was shocked to see the skeletal remains of the old neighborhood ball stadium. It had served the community well for so long, and its history was legendary throughout the county, but especially so in Doyle's memory.

A rusty chain link fencing still cordoned off the asphalt parking lot, and tall weeds had overtaken the orderly rows of white lines and numbered parking spots. The steps and concourses were covered with debris and dead moss. The green wooden bleachers, what few were even left intact, were bleached a dull white by the sun, like the ghostly ribs of a whale stranded on the beach.

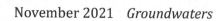

Doyle was dismayed at the sight of the abandoned facility, and his first inclination was just to pass on by and let the glory days fade away, but at the same time he was drawn to explore what had happened to the grand 'ol girl. It was one of those bittersweet moments, and he was apprehensive at the thought of what he might find.

As Doyle surveyed the structure, he grimaced as he looked up at the roof's columns and girders. They were massive, rough-sawn, and hewn from the county's old-growth timbers. They were checked and split from base to top. The deep-veined pitch pockets oozed sap, filling the voids in the rugged bark with amber-colored nectar. The stout Douglas Fir rafters had sagged under their own ponderous weight. Multiple layers of shakes and shingles were ragged and missing, their edges ripped and torn, turned up against the wind, and would offer little protection against the coming fall rains.

Blackberry vines and morning glory ran rampant, trailing up and over the stadium walls, overrun with desiccated ivy. It choked the faded siding, a spider web of dead vines etching and staining them black like the shriveled veins of a corpse.

Scheduled for demolition but delayed by countless protests, indecision and bureaucratic red tape, the venerable old stadium was suffering an inglorious death. Sadly past its prime, it patiently awaited the wrecking ball as soon as local politics gave sway.

"The sooner the better," Doyle muttered. "Get it over with and put her out of her misery."

It had been built in the late thirties, as part of the Civilian Conservation Corps projects. It was part of the noble plan to provide honest work for the masses of unemployed, depression-era tradesmen. Carpenters, masons, roofers, painters and laborers all lent their talents to fashion what came to be regarded as a community treasure.

Local farmers, bridge-builders and roughnecks clamored for a chance to get involved, no matter how small the task, and despite the meager pay, they all were proud of their work and grateful for the jobs. If you had boots and a lunch pail, you were welcomed aboard. Many didn't, but were hired on anyway. Doyle had briefly worked as a handyman, and could vividly imagine himself on that job, helping to set the beams and raise the roof, building some stairs or installing the bleachers. He envied the skill and satisfaction those tradesmen must have felt on opening day. He had always regretted not being there to join in their efforts, but that was a long time ago—way before his time.

As the stadium took shape, the entire community had been involved, hosting bake sales, bazaars, and bingo tournaments—all held to help raise funds, supplementing the government costs. It was to become a community icon. Eventually it was widely recognized as such by the baseball farm teams across the western division, not to mention to the legion of hometown fans.

It became home to the developmental leagues—the minors, as they were known. The teams were officially part of the 'Triple A' system, the sanctioned proving grounds for aspiring young players with their eyes set on a chance to play in *The Bigs*.

But really, it was much more than that. Its hallowed grounds had played host to high school sporting events, graduations, car shows, weddings and even on occasion, rodeos. Old-fashioned carnivals and Fourth of July firework displays brought throngs into the stands, much to the consternation of the fire marshal and law enforcement officials who kept constant watch, lest vagrants or hooligans set the place ablaze. In fact, it had happened once before and the charred remains of supply lockers still smelled of cinder and ash. Doyle had read sporadic newspaper accounts of such incidents, but he could remember no serious threats to the structure, even after the stadium had been shuttered.

Despite occasional attempts at upgrades, the cost and maintenance of an adequate fire suppression system always thwarted the obvious safety concerns. The steady turnover of maintenance workers and groundskeepers served as testament to the frustrations of trying to combat the ravages of time, weather, and political agendas.

Doyle had seen the newscast stories and newspaper reports, and felt that some organization should rally to save the ballpark, but knew that it hadn't a chance. The structure was unsound, and the land was regarded by "investors" as too valuable to "waste it on a baseball field."

Climbing out of his truck, Doyle was mindful of these sad facts. He stood before the chain link gate and for a moment gripped the top rail. His shoulders sagged as he lifted his feet off the ground, momentarily suspended. Letting loose, he dropped back on the ground and examined the fence line, searching for a chink in the rusty mesh. He was not surprised to find a small gap between two steel rails leading down to one of the entry tunnels. Pulling out his cell phone camera, he reeled off a few shots of the stadium exterior before deciding to venture inside. He ducked in between the rails and entered the low tunnel. Creeping through the long dark passage, he grasped the flaking metal handrail as he went. Stopping every few steps, he looked back, expecting to be apprehended as a trespasser. The tunnel led down a set of steps and accessed the dugout along the third base line. A faded plaque hung over the mid-rail, indicating this was the visiting teams' dugout. The concrete floor was filthy, littered with broken wine bottles, trash, and spider webs . Old scorecards, cigarette butts, and abandoned clothing lay strewn under the bench among the traces of mouse and bird droppings. The warren of dilapidated bat racks was festooned not with a quiver of classic Louisville Sluggers, but cobwebs and rat nests.

Doyle's heart sank at the sight of such neglect. He moved to the top step of the dugout, propping one knee up on the field as coaches and anxious teammates had done, hundreds of innings before. His eyes swept the infield, but long gone was the pitchers mound and toeing rubber, as was home plate and the padded bases. The hash marks, batters' box, and baselines were all erased, filled in with tall stalks of dandelions and crabgrass.

Totally dejected, Doyle took one more look at the field. Just as he turned to head back to the truck, his eyes were drawn toward the centerfield fence where the antique wooden scoreboard still stood—weatherworn, but still there. It had never been fitted with electricity, and the game tallies; the scores, the outs, the ball and strike counts, had once been displayed on painted wooden squares-- propped up into the appropriate holes, cut out of the plywood backboard. Posted by neighborhood youngsters under the watchful eyes of a home team player or manager, the scores were tallied and placed into view, scrawled in white chalk, often with comic results. Games were often 'interrupted' by time-outs to correct errant scoreboard information, much to the amusement of players and fans alike. Six runs suddenly became nine, and an upside down seven was prelude to chaos and concern— especially for the leading team. Such ''time outs' were actually appreciated; affording an opportunity for conversation, camaraderie, and breaks for refreshments. Beer and popcorn vendors scurried to serve customers before the action resumed, secretly wishing for more time to complete their rounds—a little bonus along with the traditional 'seventh inning stretch.'

The stadium field lights were shorn of their globes, and the few naked bulbs were caked with dirt, dangling by bare wires, their bright lights extinguished years ago. Doyle couldn't bring himself to take any more photos, and was resigned to accepting just fond memories of the simple past. "Time to let it go, a bygone era," he mused. "Just savor the past for what it was."

Turning to go, he glanced across the diamond towards the first base line. Squinting into the late afternoon sun, he was alarmed to see thin wisps of smoke drifting up towards the roofline. For just a moment, his heart raced, thinking something was on fire. He made out the slight silhouette of a person sitting about three rows up. It was an old man, adjusting an old green and grey ball cap covering a shock of wispy white hair. The figure nearly blended into the rows of seats that surrounded him.

The man was intently scribbling in a wire-bound notebook, a journal or ledger of some sort. He would gaze out towards the scoreboard and then bend his head to his ledger, almost puncturing the paper with his pen. He wore a well-worn cotton or flannel jersey, faded grey with green piping frayed along the seams. Doyle thought it looked as if something one might find at the second-hand store.

The man stood, waving his cap in Doyle's direction, summoning him over. As Doyle moved towards the first base seats, he could smell the rich aroma of cigar—the old man was smoking a long, regal looking brand, a Maduro or Prima Dominica—the same kind Doyle's father used to smoke. The aroma immediately took Doyle back to fishing trips, camp-outs, and just like here, out to the ballpark.

Doyle inhaled deeply, savoring that memory, and looked higher up into the empty stands, seeing nothing but starlings and pigeons flitting back and forth.

At first Doyle was hesitant to walk across the diamond, surprised to see anyone else in the abandoned stadium seats, let alone being waved over by some phantom sports fan. But the memory of long evenings spent here allayed any fears, and Doyle walked reverently around behind the vestige of home plate as he moved towards the first base line.

His mind quickly conjured a scene from the past. Doyle's father held reserve seats in just about the same spot—along the first base line, about half way between home plate and the bag—the perfect spot for snagging pop fouls tipped off by impatient young batters. Doyle's Pop would wave the beverage guy over, and treat him to sodas, popcorn, a hotdog, or some roasted peanuts. The old-time refrain of *Beer here—cold beer here* ensured that the tray of snacks was nearby as it echoed through the crowds.

Occasionally, Doyle would slip down to the edge of the retaining wall, careful to avoid the discarded gum and tobacco juice splattered on the sides of the concrete steps. His Pop would have a beer or two, shelling peanuts and sunflower seeds, spitting them into any empty cup. Some of the old-timers chewed harsh plugs of tobacco.

With routine precision, they would pluck a 'dip' from the round 'chew tins,' tucking the little wad up against their lower lip, inside their gum line. Doyle thought this a rather nasty habit, but as a youngster, he would watch the players do the same thing, spitting the excess on the fields with abandon. He remembered stuffing wads of pink chewing gum in his mouth, emulating the habit of the big leaguers, but without the 'yuk' factor.

As Doyle approached the short retaining wall surrounding the seats, the old man tipped his hat. "Howdy young man," he smiled, nodding towards the outfield. "How you like the game so far?" Doyle was intrigued by old man's serious tone of voice.

"Well, to be honest, Doyle answered, "it looks pretty slow right about now," thinking perhaps the old man was kidding.

The man just looked up, squinted out at the diamond, as he tugged on the brim of his hat. He turned his attention back to the ledger balanced across his lap. Spinning a chewed up pen between his teeth, he deftly flipped the ledger over, examining some tiny script covering the back cover. "Ahh sport, you just 'aint payin close enough attention, this is a tight one." Shaking his head, the old man leaned back, stretching out his arms, "Sonny boy, we got us a ballgame here!"

He flipped the ledger back over, regarding it with obvious enthusiasm. Not taking his eyes off the ledger sheet, his voice began the rundown. "See here, take a look," he said, clearing his throat, his voice suddenly shifting into a deeper register. "Bottom of the ninth, runners at first 'n third. Two down, count at three and two. Lord have mercy, this guy's gonna walk and load 'em up," he said, frustration hanging in his voice.

Doyle was intrigued by the old man's concentration, and decided to play along.

"So who ya rootin for here? Doyle nodded towards the field. The man cleared his throat, spitting out a cheek full of sunflower seed shells, saying, "Don't matter much, I just like me a good game." Doyle gestured towards the ledger.

"So whatcha ya got there, new scouting report or something?" The scorekeeper scanned the infield, answering "Nope, box score. Never watch a game without one. The old man smiled and tipped his cap towards Doyle, giving him a wink, "A true fan fills 'em out in ink! You'll know one when you see one, I guarantee."

Doyle peered over the sheet and indeed, it was filled in with neatly drawn columns and line-by-line tiny squares, numbers inserted in each one—a miniature scoreboard crowded with the arcane data specific to statisticians and obsessive fans

The fan interrupted Doyle's surveillance, "Next one's gonna be low and away and the batter's gonna foul it off."

Doyle leaned in, waiting for the outcome.

"There it is," the fan gestured, continuing his broadcast, "fouled off—a high pop up—drifting out behind first aaaand... whoa, just out of reach! Second baseman over to cover, but it's drifted away. So the batter stays alive. Count remains three and two."

Doyle instinctively looked back over his shoulder, half expecting to see the ball ricochet across the bleachers. Hoping to get some perspective on the old guy's gambit, Doyle tossed him a meatball question. "So, you get out to see many games these days?"

The fan tilted his cap back on his head, leveling his eyes on Doyle. "Yep," he proudly announced, "almost ever day, all season long—spring trainin', All-Star break, playoffs, then the Series... it don't matter—I'm there. Even the farm team games."

Doyle nodded out of respect. "So you played pro ball? What position?"

The fan leaned back and studied his hands, turning them over with fingers splayed wide, as if he was gripping a bat or stretching out a glove. "Sonny, I played 'em all. I played infield, outfield, even pitched a few... did everything but pinch runner and catcher. Knees weren't up to all the hard slides n' home plate collisions. I'm a finesse guy—not no fullback."

Doyle had to smile at this, owing to the fan's long slender frame. He could almost see the old man pedaling back to the centerfield wall, leaping up, arm outstretched, up high, the glove just clearing the top of the backboard, robbing a hitter of a sure home run. He could hear the crack of the bat and the long, slow-motion silence following the ball as it soared out towards the wall. The cheer of the crowd echoed in his ears, some erupting in celebration and some hushed, disappointed at the fielders' heroic snag.

The old man continued, "Wasn't no slouch at the plate, neither. Had me a lifetime average .292! They used me to pinch hit alot too. I used that P-72 Louisville Slugger or the H&B thirty-seven. Sweet spot was huge. They don't make 'em anymore."

The man's brief reverie was suddenly broken as he snapped to attention, then announced, 'Uh oh, looks like we got us a pitching change here. Christ! Are they gonna put number twelve on the mound? I don't believe it! He's gonna put this guy on—give up an intentional walk—load up the bases? What are they thinking? If this guy walks, we're one batter away from top 'o the order. I can't stand to watch" He tugged at the brim of his cap, twisting it left and right, removing it to wipe his brow, then clapping it back on, only to jam it down, almost covering his brow.

The fan fidgeted, flipping the score sheet over and over, nervously chawing at the butt end of the pen as if it were a new Maduro clenched between his teeth.

Doyle too strained to catch the action as the next pitch was thrown. The fan stood, pacing back and forth, just a few steps in each direction. He resumed his narration, all the while intently watching the pitcher's mound. "Ok, here it is, the three and two pitch, and it's low and inside. Yep, the batter walks to first and now the bases are loaded." The fan shook his head, slumping on the bench, muttering under his breath.

Doyle watched the fan intently. The fan's voice continued, louder now, booming throughout the vacant stands as if from a concealed loudspeaker, " Well here we are fans, tie game, bottom of the ninth. We have the bases loaded two down, and the number nine hitter, batting .187, the shortstop Angelo Del Sorto coming to the plate."

Doyle sat down on the bench patting the splinter-covered boards beside him, gesturing for the fan to sit.

"Heeere we go, " intoned the fan," here comes the wind up and first pitch!" Jumping to his feet, the fan's voice exploded with excitement, "Look out, it's a low fastball, swung on, hit hard... a tricky hop to the right, aaand, the second baseman moving to scoop it up, and... he... he... he bobbles the ball! There's no throw. The runner is safe, at first. The winning run scores!" The old man exhaling loudly, as if exhausted, "Whoa Nelly, that's the game folks."

Both Doyle and the fan slumped back on the tattered bench. The fan made one final entry in the ledger, then carefully folded up the score sheet and deftly placed it in his pocket, whispering to himself, "Well, so much for this one."

His eyes were cast out towards the ragged scoreboard, as if peering up at an oracle. All Doyle could think to say was to offer a feeble, "Oh brother, that was quite the inning, right?" He stood still for a moment, respecting the silence, and then moved to shake the old man's hand. "Thanks for the game sir, I really enjoyed it. It's been a long time."

The fan laughed quietly, and pulled another scorecard from his hip pocket. "What'cha mean son? It ain't over yet; today's the double header. We got one more." The fan began scribbling on the new card, nodding with satisfaction, "Here now, take your place, we still got the best seats in the house."

The air stilled for a moment, and the old man fished in his pocket for another cigar, offering it to Doyle. Doyle shook his head, politely refusing the offer. He looked at his watch and hesitated. Gazing up at the scoreboard, he smiled wistfully and took one last quick photo. A slight breeze now swirled across the infield, raising puffs of dust and the faint aroma of the new cigar. Doyle took a long, deep breath and sat back down, nodded to the old man, saying, "Yeah I guess I got time."

Then, after a moment, he stood up, cupping his hands around his mouth and hollered out towards centerfield, "Ok boys, play ball!"

Pedal Thyme

Alone—riding the Willamette River trail down to
   the depths.
I've risen up having given up the expectations.
Borders pass like dreams noted.
Vanished memories resurface.
The swing, benches, turtles on a log, water fowl,
   butterflies.
Life, one pedal at a thyme.

~ Mary Lee Radka

Military Time

If midnight is the zero hour,
and logic leads to certainty,
'noon' and 'twelve' may co-occur
but 'twenty-four' is fantasy.

~ Wayne Westfall

Journey of a Spectator

I enter the ballpark, with no money left in my
   pocket,
for peanuts – popcorn – Cracker Jacks.
The bus ride and game ticket wiped out every
   cent,
gone my savings for this day of excitement.

Girl-Pals looking sporty,
caps donned, cutoff jeans, white T-shirts and
   white converse tennis shoes.
Wow what a look! - As we position ourselves
   along 3rd base line.
Preparing our softball mitts, in hopes of catching
   a foul ball.

With the crack of the bat, balls fly through a blue
   cloudless sky,
while mob-like enthusiasm pulsates with the beat
   of a sweltering sun.
Clean white uniforms gather dust as the game
   advances.
Odors of earth and perspiration, mix with the
   aroma of, peanuts - popcorn - Cracker Jacks.

Baseball in the heat of summer
sweet and sweaty, riveting yet relaxing.
Sounds of cheers, jeers, moans, applause, fill the
   stadium and streets beyond.
Passers-by give pause to the sounds, with a smile
   or nod to the noisy crowd.

The ballpark continues to
   beckon me
with that old familiar song,
"Take Me Out to the Ball
   Game."
Forever, a spectator-fan of the
   All American game.

Familiar the sights and sounds,
noticeable the enticing smells.
"Peanuts?——— Popcorn?——— Cracker
   Jacks?"
No thank you – I'll have a beer and a dog!

~ Elizabeth Orton

Big Mouths in Little League
By Bill Sarnoff

You're only given a little spark of madness and you mustn't lose it. My madness thrust itself on me when I was asked to coach a little league team of 7- and 8-year-olds. It was in West Covina, 18 miles east of Los Angeles, where heat waves belly dance over Interstate 10 during the summer playing season. Our ball field was well-maintained and even boasted a dugout, night lights and a snack stand that had been serving the community 40 years before I took on this invitation. Neatly trimmed palm trees bordered the playing field when evening breezes shuffled and clicked the swaying leaves like playing cards. We were pleased to have selected West Covina, where good schools, athletic activities and community services were well-established and welcoming.

I was somewhat surprised to learn that when you coach a little league team, what you often witness is the imposition of boorishness and the twilight of manners. My son Bret had shown impressive coordination and alertness as a first baseman the year prior and was eager to rejoin his "Lions" teammates. My wife had staffed the snack stand and was amenable to serving another year, so it became a family affair.

The league manager was an insurance actuary specialist with twin sons on the same team. He was a short man who walked tall, had a starchy textbook quality and used statistics as a drunk man would a lamp post... for support. But he shared his enthusiasm on the potential of our team winning the city-wide league. A sucker for logic, I was hooked... no, coerced into participating in this all-American frenzy. I figured it gets kids out of the house and beats gluing popsicle sticks together. However, I was not prepared to encounter the broad range of emotions and comments unfettered by such inhibiting factors as manners. My focus was to build a collection of high strivers who would carry on my inspiration on the importance of teamwork. I thus enthusiastically applied myself to building a little league team of all-stars. The players' energy, enthusiasm and uniqueness were apparent everywhere and I was energized to give it my best.

My first chore was to interview this collection of 7- and 8 year olds—each with an expectant mom or dad and sometimes both, watching my every move. Selections were made and the practice schedule announced and that's when Alvin entered my world of sports management. Alvin was nearing 8, and I was certain he was destined for a law career with his inherent penchant for asking questions.

After our first practice session, Alvin asked, "Why does the pitcher raise one leg when he pitches?"

The best I could respond was, "If he raised both, he'd fall down."

The first thing you do during little league practice is field ground balls to your players. The way to properly field a ground ball, I explained, is to stand in front of the ball as it's rolling toward you. That way, if the ball takes a short hop over your glove, you can still block it with your body. So, fielding ground balls involves a lot of fast-moving baseballs smacking you in the chest or face or scrotum. My kids were amazed to learn that rubbing Crest toothpaste on those bruises soothes the pain. Other team managers didn't know that and I felt proud to have added a dimension to the world of little league baseball.

On our second practice session, I discussed that when you are on first base, look for any opportunity to steal second base, but you have to run very, very fast when you do steal a base. After nine times up to bat and a score of 16 to 11, Alvin managed to hit a single. Once on base and heeding my earlier advice, he raced over to second base, grabbed it and ran home.

Another of my players, Sylvan, was not an underachiever, he simply lacked any identifiable eye-hand coordination. I set him aside to practice tossing the ball and striking it with his bat while I strolled off to coach others. Returning a couple minutes later, I observed him tossing the ball, missing it and calling out, "Strike one." Missing again, he yelled, "Strike two;" and again "Strike three."

"How ya doin' Sylvan?" I asked.

"I ain't a very good batter, but I'm a real good pitcher," he enthusiastically answered.

Curtis was a cookie-cutter stereotype kid... the kind that rates high with grandparents, but with a whole different perspective on the game. To give my players an opportunity to play various positions, I told him, "You're gonna play left field today, Curtis."

"What's that?"

I walked him to the position and on the way he asked, "Do I get a snow cone later?"

"Sure you do, everybody gets a snow cone."

"Lemon flavor is creepy; it looks like pee. Can I have cherry instead?"

"Sure you can, sport."

"Do I get a snow cone if I only play half a game?"

"Of course."

"Then I'd like to play half a game, ok?"

At our first coach meeting, the league manager discussed the matter of hecklers. "People like this make it difficult for the kids and spectators to have fun. Sure, we teach teamwork and good sportsmanship, but that's the entire point of little league, when you boil it all down."

It all came to mind once in the middle of a game when I called an 8-year-old aside and asked, "Do you understand what sportsmanship is?"

"Sure, coach," he replied.

"Do you understand what matters is that we play together as a team to the best of our ability?"

The boy nodded in the affirmative. "So," I continued, "I'm sure you know, when an out is called, you shouldn't argue, curse, attack the umpire or call him a pecker head, dick head or asshole. Do you understand all that?"

Again the kid nodded in the affirmative. "All right," I continued, "and when I take you out of the game so that another lad gets a chance to play, its not good sportsmanship to call your coach a dumb ass or shithead, is it?"

"No, Coach."

"Good" I said. "Now go over there and explain it all to your grandmother!"

On Top of Mt. Pisgah

There is no haze on the horizon
    but clean air and panoramic clear vision.
The late afternoon sun casts its shadows
    from passing clouds on the foothills towards
Pleasant Hill.

The fields are still lush and green from the
    spring rains instead of brown and brittle like
last summer's drought when they were
    burning up in the noonday heat.

From where I stand on top of Mt. Pisgah,
    overlooking the valley, I hear
only the roar of the cleansing wind as I look down
    towards the river below.

Patches of snow can be seen on the Middle Sister
    to the east and the sunrays cast
a faint glow through the rain clouds
    to the west over Mary's Peak.

Another layer of darker clouds form
    above the coast range
and lighter clouds drift over the tree-lined ridge
    of Spencer's Butte.

An afternoon shower falls from the cool gray
    skies and a hawk flies overhead
into patches of blue.

Then the sun breaks through as it sinks into
    a sea of violet red.

~ Thomas Avery

A One-Deer Drive
By Vicki Graves Doughty

There have been times in my life when I almost get hit on the head with a message. One of those experiences happened some years ago when I was traveling home between Crow and Noti after leaving my parents' house. I had this ritual of calling Mom and Dad to let them know I was safe and sound after arriving home. I usually reported that I had a 1– 2– 3 deer drive, etc. to indicate the number of deer I encountered along the way home. That particular night, it was dark and misty, and I had just passed through the old company logging town of Vaughn when a deer ran out in front of my Mazda pickup. Because the road was damp, I gently touched the brakes, but wasn't able to slow down enough to miss the deer—instead, I hit it dead center against my grill. I stopped quickly, pulled over, then sat there looking as something small had been thrown up on the hood of my pickup. I was reluctant to see the damage, but grabbed a flashlight, took a quick look at the grill, then started looking for an injured deer. I couldn't find any sign of it, not even a trace of blood on the ground. I started looking up in the brush on the bank, but still no sign of a deer. Next, I went back to my pickup, looked at the grill again (no noticeable damage to my vehicle), then grabbed what had landed on the hood of my pickup. It was a small piece of plastic and as I turned it over and shined the light on it, it had "Save a Life" printed on it. It was part of my license plate holder that I had received from donating blood. That was the only damage I could see, and the remaining part of my license plate holder was still intact, being held on by a screw on each side. This remaining part, still attached, said, "Give Blood," with Lane Blood Center printed on it. At the time, I wondered if the deer was what the "save a life" message was all about, but I didn't think it was.

At few years later, on Friday, July 13, 2012, we were in the hayfield. My husband was baling hay and my not-yet son-in-law, Michael, was underneath, working on his bale wagon. He mentioned that he needed a piece of baling twine, so I walked several feet away, grabbed a piece of twine and as I was walking back, the bale wagon kicked into gear and backed over the top of Michael's chest and ribs. I was able to call 911, and Michael was able to give me info to relay to the dispatcher. While we waited for help, the Lorane Fire Department arrived in only 6 minutes. The Cottage Grove paramedics and Life Flight arrived in 16 minutes from my emergency call, and they were able to transport Michael to Riverbend and help save his life.

Michael had an excruciatingly painful recovery, but was eventually able to return to work. I sometimes think of what might have happened if I had not been there when Michael's accident happened (He calls it his 'crushing'), as no one else was near him at that time. Before Michael mentioned that he needed some twine, I was getting ready to go get some new twine packages from his car a couple miles away.

I feel what I did for Michael was one of the most important things I have done in my life, and it changed me forever. Often, we wonder if we have made a difference by being here on earth. I think I have. I helped give Michael and my daughter, Amber, the best gift I could have given them—more time together.

How to Fish
By Michael Matchulat

"There's trout up there bigger than ten pounds. Wanna go?"

That's all a 12-year old boy with a bright smile and a fishing rod combo older than himself needed to hear. My dad never fished, and although his abstinence was likely fueled by the lack of catching in the sport coupled with the endless want to leave the fishing part behind and engage in a productive activity rather than twiddle your thumbs and pontificate about the upcoming revolution. It seemed like a waste of time. Through my adolescence the quotes about teaching someone to fish became more about learning how to fish through life and not catch things every outing rang truer and truer each season. How was I to know my abstinent father wouldn't be breathing air in another 3 years? Fishing solves a lot of life's problems.

The giant "High Lakes" region of the state lends itself to the person who loves desert canyon vistas with sagebrush and puny toothpick pine trees rather than my native scrub brush and Douglas fir. Up there, it always looks like part of the view is clouded by a patch of wildfire in the distance during summer months, fueled by ignorance and mismanaged emotions surrounding our natural resources. At 12, I was none the wiser to the social issues now demanding the forefront of my thoughts, but that's only when I'm not fishing for solutions. Back then, we could cut the top front part off of a plastic milk jug, fill it with water, and catch 6-8" trout all day off the bridge at Perry's with the same 20 yards of line which was on the reel since before dad bought it for the garage sale deal it truly was. As a youth, women loved me and fish feared me. It didn't depend how many fillets I brought back home to the family after a day or weekend adventure with a fishing family— Dad was never convinced with the logistics of budgeting regarding fishing. He's right, it never paid off, but it's not all for the birds.

Most of the high lakes have at least three things in common, the first being that they're all on the verge of freezing over. It's a temperature which according to beef-jerky-fueled youthful endeavor is warm enough to enter with a dive, but not by wading. The temperature is a point in frigidity where atmospheric conditions must align with the vistas surrounding the lake to create more of a desire to swim than is natural. The water temperature, high altitude, snow-covered cliffs and mandatory brushes with wildlife allowed us to swim for a solid twenty minutes before it was time for mandatory rewarming.

After exiting the water, mosquito avoidance was the next item on the menu. In the war over territory manned by a tiny, eerie, cello-string-whining gnat and *homosapiens,* we should just stay inside. The bugs always won. We used it all—special soaps, candles, sprays, and goos which on the labels guaranteed success against the striped blood suckers. None of the flashily-labeled sauces worked against bugs so large we routinely strapped a mini-saddle onto them and watched them take their prey for a ride. In my personal experience, only two things work against the hitchhiking vampires: DEET and chemotherapy. It's argued that the DEET causes the cancer which requires treatment with chemotherapy but, either way, I'm covered for bug control. We were always coached so carefully to apply the rich man's one-ounce spray bottle antidote only to clothing and never into our eyes, nose, or mouth if the bugs were thick enough to impede respiration.

The third thing all the high lakes have in common is algae blooms. Chemically putrid, but visually-stunning pea soup saturates otherwise crystal-clear water. The blooms coincide with warmer summer temperatures and tourists, and they take over the lake with government vigor. Signs regarding unsafe swimming conditions always teased us as we sat lakeside, sweating over the fact that our lines weren't going to tighten. We knew that fish who couldn't breathe in the choking algae, let alone sense a pebble of power-bait in a sea of tiny green moss, wouldn't have the urge to snack. The algae blooms created a different kind of fishing trip.

During these times, instead of swimming and fishing, intent on catching, the days consisted of sampling each roadside tackle shop for deals on special local lures and sugary snacks. I hardly ever drank soda unless I was on expedition. In one related story on one such trip, my adolescent body consumed all but three slices of two medium-sized pizzas, with room to spare. In those stores, I realized the value of shopping lures with the intent of catching the eye of fisherman, not the fish. Flashy, top-shelf baits beckoned to us instead of the budget-friendly fish snaggers beside them. It was about the year of the bird when we started to learn how to tie our own flies and build our own lures.

When you're in a drift boat with two other people, etiquette is ether in vogue or thrown out the window. For us, it was a free-for-all of flatulence, fireworks and topics of discussion off-limits at school. When you're in a sixteen-foot long glorified metal bathtub on a lake big enough to hydro-power the cities below it, the value of tolerance is quickly learned depending on who's casting beside you. Adrift like that, being prepared for emergency circumstances is paramount. Strategic places of the vessel were for life jackets or one extra of everything which could catastrophically fail. After that, it seemed like every other stashing space on the boat was filled with crinkly bags of sweet, salty, savory or crunchy snacking apparati, especially when we tried to fish during the algae bloom days when the fish weren't there. On algae bloom weekends, the focus was on the view and conversations, not the monsters fighting to breathe below the boat. The diversity of life in the world became apparent in every sensory encounter.

Nothing was more stunning than the ashy colors in the skies as migratory birds hovered in to land, many times beside the boat. The birds, meaty enough for eating, knew that summer time is when they are off limits for hunting, so their actions bordered on arrogance toward a species which would normally wring their necks. They knew the rules, and so did we. There must be nothing more frustrating to a father than explaining to two gung-ho hunting youths why a delicious goose can only be bothered for a few months a year and is otherwise completely illegal to molest. Sometimes the tweety-style birds would land on the gunnels and show off their squawks and plumage. It was amazing to be immersed in a culture of nature which is missed by anyone who remains on the dock. The birds also knew about the onboard snacking stash, so they were naturally drawn to us. One day, I got to experience the wrath of feeding the birds.

In one corner of a finger of the lake, there are a series of petrified trees which make a line of exposed limbs above the water. Anchoring a little boat steadily on a lake that size in the wind is difficult, so we would use the trees to tie the bow and anchor the stern. The solitude was so vast we would set out baits and let them rot as we drifted into sunny dreamland while the water patted the sides of the boat. The problem with anchoring to the trees is catching one to tie onto. The wind gets big up there, so logistics of avoiding a scenario where ramming speeds are engaged is difficult. I was usually the kid on the bow of the boat trying to catch a limb. On that particular day, it wasn't a routine catch. I poised myself to embrace a branch, reached out, and came face to face with a hole in a crotch of the tree just below eye level. As we boisterously neared the edge of the hole, it became apparent only from my vantage that it contained a bird. We neared the creature, and

I came to the realization that it was a bird so large it wouldn't easily fit into the space of the hole.

The web-footed, sharp-beaked falcon-imitator emerged and I reclused back from the beast as the sharp point of the bow jammed straight into what we immediately recognized as a nest. The bow of the boat was set to completely smash the nest of a bird who had my face imprinted in its brain as the one responsible. The devil bird was not happy about our sudden appearance, so we smashed harshly into the limb and left a dent in the boat. We pin-balled to the next branch, leaving the nest obviously destroyed and the bird taking to the skies to voice its disapproval. And it did. The bird obviously knew it stood no chance against three humans, but it also knew we couldn't fly and it had sharp claws and a curved beak. It turns out there isn't much anyone can stow while adrift to prepare for persistent dive-bombing by a pissed off mother. Even if it was hunting season, there was no way we had enough firepower to keep up with the insults she was throwing at us. I tied a big knot to the tree just prior to her taking to the skies to punish us, and she was now guarding the rope so I couldn't go near it to disembark. She was successfully implementing her battle plan. I waived out wildly to stave off attacks and eventually she stole my hat and dumped it into the water vastly out of our reach.

I was almost fully-disarmed. After the frenzy of barrages left me in the fetal position on the bottom of the boat and laughter rang through the air, she realized she had another offensive maneuver to sling at me. She perched herself on a limb just out of my reach at an angle just perfect to have her constantly visible in my upward line of sight while sitting forward. She perched facing away from me and did something I've never witnessed a creature publicly do again. She flared her vent in a way that evoked fear and wrinkled my hatless face every few seconds for the next several hours.

If I made a motion to the rope, she would dive bomb. If I sat down to relax, she would perch above me. She pulsed her butthole in my face with a cadence which left me helpless. She released a few attempts of fecal-focused blows but her aim was slightly askew. After most of the afternoon being tethered to the tree waiting for imminent attack, my twelve-year-old wisdom decided the sunburn from having no hat outweighed the risk of injury by bird bomb. I mustered the courage, risked imminent death, and quickly untied the boat and pushed away from my bothered friend. One last time I gazed up to the branch where my recent overlord kept me prisoner and locked eyes for one last time with the mama whose offspring I'd certainly destroyed. She took aim once more and delivered an eye-for-an-eye blow so accurate it was certainly fate. She sprayed a white concrete fish and berry spackle of paste across my face and into my open mouth which left me unable to balance on the small shelf in the front of the boat. I fell into the water and the bird retreated back to the branch it formerly called a nest.

After I was hoisted back into the boat and assured I was no longer the target of attack, I cowered into the small front section to warm up and eventually rolled back to my seat searching for a source to clean my face other than the putrid pea soup water beside me. It turns out we didn't routinely pack beach towels on the fishing boat. Nature has a specific way of punishing us if we don't treat it the right way. As for that day, I certainly learned the intended lesson behind interacting with assholes. Usually, the more gently we approach a problem in front of us instead of blazing forward at ramming speeds, the more gentle the response pushed back upon us. I know there are certainly parts of the memory of this story my brain has purposely embellished for me over time, but I went on every trip from then on and never caught a 10-pounder fishing out of those lakes, either.

Johnny Bluesky
By Dave Polhamus

As a college freshman, I'd come straight off the reservation. In growing up, our family sometimes spoke in our local Athabascan tongue. It was probably an effort to help preserve our heritage. However, I felt a little backward because I knew we weren't mainstream America.

My aunts sometimes talked of how handsome I was. My favorite female cousin said I looked like the Indian on the flip-side of the buffalo-head nickel. Her older brother said I just looked like the buffalo. I guess I am whatever I am.

I'd done well in high school and was curious about things in the 'outside world.' I wanted to study my own heritage more, as well as others, too. It was exciting to think about going to the university. As time drew closer, I became nervous—scared and mildly optimistic.

Some of the elders had gotten together to give me a little send-off. In the dim light of the underground sweat lodge we'd talked about my studies and school.

"You'll need to stick with the program," someone had said. "Be tough."

"But, whatever, we're proud of you," another offered.

Last thing before I left, they'd prayed to Grandfather that I would succeed in a strange land and a strange place—the University.
"I'm not sure I'll be accepted there," I said. "It's different than here."

"You'll do okay. Just listen. You have a good mind," I was told. It was nice to know that I had support of the tribal elders.

Once there, I was enrolled in one of those freshman seminar classes where the instructor—often a graduate assistant—lectures to a bowl arena of newbies just out of high school. That was it. Except this class—something like History of Western Civilization—was taught by a full professor.

His sharp tone of voice reflected arrogance as he looked down his nose at us. As he assured us that half the students would fail this class, I began to dread a whole term of this guy.

The second day he whined, "Everybody should be in the proper class by now; if you aren't, it's time to hit the road. I'm going to call roll—not alphabetically, but at random. I'll explain some about your family name, based on my... uh... extensive knowledge of culture, linguistics and studies in race and heritage." O-kay. He informed us that he had written a text on the origin of people's surnames and made sure we knew that the university bookstore offered his volume at the modest price of $39.97... well worth the money.

He began with Ellen Harwood. "Ah, yes," He says. "Harwood, a good English title; probably Middle English. Harwood. A literal translation might be rabbit forest. Har being hare, or rabbit, and wood meaning forest. Ah, yes, thank you." Then it was Judy Jansma in the spotlight; she reacted by looking away. It was explained that the name Jansma is Dutch and that an American version might be Johnson. Next was a guy named McMullan—his family name suggested that he was the son of a bald man, a Scottish bald man. And so it went; "Fenstermacher means window maker in the Germanic tongue. Ogata is Japanese, and Vasquez is Hispanic. Robetelli. Robetelli is an Italian name. Many Italian names end with the letter 'O' or the letter 'I.' Safstrom is a Swedish name, probably meaning rushing river." The Safstrom guy appeared surprised. Others seemed irritated, as it went along.

The instructor droned on. "Oulette is French, originating from an early French settlement at the current city of Quebec, Canada. Carpenter is English, meaning, of course, someone who works with wood." This all seemed curious just in order to find out if everybody was present. There were glances left and right. Some were flippant in answering the roll.

He said that the name Gatov is of East European heritage, no doubt Russian. He went on. "Cosmo. All those Americans named Cosmo have had relatives who once lived in a small village named Cosmo in the country of Denmark. Strannigan is Scottish, and Delgado is Basque—Spanish Basque. The name refers to someone who is thin or slender." We couldn't help but notice that, in answering roll, Ms. Delgado was neither thin nor slender. He failed to apologize, but plowed ahead: "Tozlosky is Polish and Graf means prince in the German language. The name Gilliam is English, as is Ward." I was next. "*Blu-e-skie*," he said, breaking the word into three syllables and pronouncing the "e" as in the word echo. "Bluesky is also Polish."

"Uh, sir, it's Native American." I raised my hand tentatively. "My name is Johnny Bluesky. Uh, blue as in the color blue, and sky as in the space above us," I said modestly. By now, I realized that all eyes in the room were on me and for several moments, the entire universe was silent. Confused, I remembered my earlier concerns of being accepted. Then, several began clapping, some hooted. There were murmurings and hissing. The instructor's face darkened as he pulled off his glasses and massaged his temples.

"Uhh, uhh," he managed as he backed into the chalkboard and knocked the eraser onto the floor. He stuffed his hands in and out of his pants pockets. After several minutes, he composed himself. Roll call stopped with that. The rest of that term, we never heard anything more about name sleuthing or his book.

The next day I was invited to join a fraternity—a more social situation. None of the guys mispronounced my name. It felt great to be accepted.

Janine

We were born 15 months apart—you in February
   '45, and I in May '46,
but for years we were like twins–
or at least people thought we were.

We spent every day together, such an idyllic
   childhood in Shamokin
wandering the hills, meadows and orchards
   behind our house

We buried our colorful, recently deceased chicks
   in those hills,
as well as our worn-out teddy bears, giving them
   all proper funeral rites

We ate bitter and peppery weeds in those fields
   of tall, willowly grass,
and collected multi-colored soft stones to grind
   into powder for art projects

In the attic of our big, sprawling old house, we
   played crucifixion –
do you want to be Christ or the Roman soldier
   pounding the nails?

Our older sister, Carol, had us play school, using
   the broad stone steps
that climbed the steep hill beside our house; each
   step was a grade.
We had to answer her questions right to advance
   to the next one
She also dressed us in make-shift nun's outfits
   using robes and blankets for habits

In the evening you and I would take a bath
   together in the same huge tub.
Always kind and attentive, you would wash my
   back. Did I also do yours?

When you went to kindergarten, I walked you to
   school, because you feared the big dogs who
   roamed freely along the way.
I, being too young and naive, had no fear of them,
   and let them climb on my shoulders and lick my
   face.
When I returned to meet you, when school was
   almost out,
I'd stare into the the window of your classroom,
   watching you and your classmates enjoy
   cookies and milk.

I was jealous, but thought my turn too would come. It never did.

On Saturdays, among the lilacs and cherry tree of our big backyard we played "Life of Riley" and accurately repeated the script lines of the two main characters from the previous night's TV show. Was I Riley or Gillis? Maybe we took turns.
When our parents abruptly moved us to a foreign land – Maryland –
other kids laughed at our Shamokin accent and our odd name – Czyzewskl.
We stuck even more closely together for support and friendship

Our new school was so small that our classes were combined in the same room
Together we studied math, grammar and religion for 3 years in that same small space.

We hated our atrocious uniforms; sometimes I rebelled and conveniently forgot
to wear my dark green clip-on bow tie; But you stayed steady and out of trouble ,
always compliant and ready to please.

We sang Gregorian hymns in the choir together, marched in May processions,
dressed in blue and white; and had the same Confirmation Day.
We shared a bedroom in that crowded flat, plastering our walls with pictures of Elvis (pre-1960) of course!
When I couldn't sleep, you'd sing me lullabies, such as the Bonny Banks O' Loch Lomen and Tura Lura Lura; and you'd gently scratch my back until my nerves calmed.

In high school, we were finally in separate classrooms and began separate friendships
We sometimes "double-dated" as they say,
but you were the more gracious and popular one – our Homecoming Queen.

The highlight of those high school years was seeing you perform as Helen Keller in the *Miracle Worker.*
You had people in tears by the end, and received a 5 minute standing ovation.
I knew all those years of playing Life of Riley and crucifixion weren't completely for naught.

Our differences started to emerge by your senior year. Your heroes were Jane Austen and George Eliot, mine were Karl Marx and Camus.

After high school, we didn't spend as much time together – you were in Greensburg at Seton Hill and I was in Nebraska, then Baltimore.
But we did spend one glorious vacation in Newport, Rhode Island, in 1967
at the home of your college roommate.
We had always been jazz lovers (Elvis was passé after the army years!)
How many times must we have listened to Time Out and Blue Rondo ala Turk?
But our favorites were Stan Getz and Gerry Mulligan, whom we had met at that '67 concert.

After college, I moved West, but you stayed in Maryland and got a teaching job.
Your majors in European History and French were utilized, but they exploited you by piling on so many other courses; Special Ed, PE and who knows what else.
I sometimes feel that all that stress and hard work may have contributed to you getting ill.

When I visited you and Jim in Darlington, the family would sometimes play games.
But if it was Password, you and I played partners and always won, because we could almost read each others minds or send telepathic messages – we were still that close.

Now it has been almost 23 years since you left us.
All those who knew you – family, friends, colleagues, students, neighbors -- were crushed with grief at your untimely death at age 51.
We know that life is not typically "fair," but this cosmic blunder is more than the mind can comprehend.

The shining light, at the end of this dark and painful thought tunnel, comes when we see your children and your beautiful grandchildren, who like you, are actors, linguists, writers, joy-bringers and loving souls, who give truth, humor, and laughter to those around them.
Janine, we love you, we miss you always, you are still here with us.

~ *Lois Angela Czyzewski*

The Man With Good Intentions

Strolling down the avenue
a most unlikely pair –
I in shiny leather shoes
and he with none to spare –
I sense with subtle certainty
there's reason we are paired,
so, as we walk I wait to see
what priv'leged things are shared.

Gray his hair, bowed his back
and rather slow his gait,
this man commences to unpack
a life he seems to hate.
He claims 'twas cruel, callous luck
and too much on his plate
that caused his plans to run amok
and finally seal his fate.

A PhD at Harvard earned
he likened to a win,
but spurning friends, he later learned,
was tantamount to sin.
A mountain once he planned to climb
with comrades, friends and kin
but never seemed to have the time
or driving force within.

He once was moved to settle down
and love a lady fair,
but never seemed to get around
to learning how to care.
And, yes, he speaks of private lore
I'm most surprised he'd share:
Snippets of a life-long war
and shameful love affair.

Fresh aboard to cruise afar
across the ocean blue,
he quickly found the vessel's bar
and ordered just a brew.
But soon it was, as oft before,
he crossed the line he drew,
disgraced by what he stoutly swore
he never more would do.

Draft or bottle, glass or cup
or old ceramic stein,
hopeless 'twas to cover up
his love for beer and wine

and blended cocktails tart or sweet
of which he'd not decline.
So, when desire became defeat
he couldn't uncross the line.

With this revealed I self-assess
and struggle with my thoughts.
Was I predestined to success
and he ordained a sot?
Perhaps he's just a scatterbrain
unwilling to be taught?
Or, do we share a human
stain with failure just our lot?

My bet is we are much the same:
We win, we draw, we lose.
So, if each day is like a game
and we select the moves,
to comprehend what time has brought
upon this man so bruised
I'd have to walk where he
has walked …
and do it in his shoes!

~Wayne Westfall

You and I

You and I are like…
Two ships in the night

Our destinies predetermined
Guided by the currents and winds
Of the vast ocean called life

But when they do cross paths,
Magic Happens!
The seas calm down

Long enough for us to come together
For a midnight rendezvous

Alas, the beacon in the sky shines
And it's time for us to part
Continuing onto the next destination

~ Oswald Perez

The Runner
By Martha Sargent

Only a whisper of a thump sounds as the runner's foot hits the ground. One after another barely audible thuds hint of his steady pace. He is practiced at moving with the minimum of effort, and he is a joy to watch. His strides are even, his timing perfect, his balance so controlled that he appears to glide over the dirt path.

He was destined to be a marathon competitor from the moment he left his crib and started to run. His very first step was measured, calculated, efficient, and he spent little time learning to walk. Almost immediately he ran— back and forth to the well, to the yam fields, the cattle pens, back and forth to school— everywhere, anywhere. His siblings watched him in awe and with a little jealousy. All day long he runs. He is a natural.

He is running now. The brilliant red clay of Mutumba clings briefly to his feet and then is shaken off to be replaced with new red dust. The deep green scrub bushes, the lawns and crops disappear behind him as he flies past. Children, cattle, small animals, turn to watch him vanish down the trail.

He runs alone as he speeds down cow trails so there will be no interference from cars or trucks or people. When he passes, if you are lucky, for a few seconds you witness fleeting beauty.

What a sight. His dark, dark brown skin shines with a thin layer of sweat and body oil. The African sun shatters off of him creating a spectrum of colors. Ethereal and magical, the muscles beneath his skin move in rhythm with the earth and trees and all living things, in partnership with the land he covers. He is like a thoroughbred stretching towards the finish line, or maybe like a cheetah racing for its dinner. His breathing is slow and steady. His heart is in the race. No part of him is out of sync.

He rests at night and finds his supper. One meal a day keeps him light to run. He sleeps in the trees and wakes before dawn to begin the next part of his journey. On the fourth day, he crosses from Burundi into Tanzania and runs the grasslands between the game preserves that occupy the area. Then he passes south of Lake Victoria. There are almost 900 miles to cover before he can stop.

He runs. Days and days pass. He never rests long. Each day he prays to be a little farther from his pursuers.

He stays well away from the roads now. Even the footpaths could spell trouble for him. There are many travelers, tourists of the game preserves, and the promoters who want him could easily hide among those tourists. Day after day he runs until, east of Moshi, he crosses into Kenya where he might be safer, but still, he takes precautions. He understands that his accent might draw attention. He tries to keep out of sight.

He is very thin now, and his muscles and tendons stand out against his near black skin. He has no money left in the little purse tied around his waist. Nothing remains in his small food sack. He is a beautiful and hungry running-machine.

Near the Taita Hills Wildlife Sanctuary, two English tourists witness him eyeing the food stalls. He sees them, too, and starts to run away, but the man shouts after him. Another man blocks his path.

"It's all right," shouts the Englishman. "He misunderstood. Let me handle this." The Kenyan porter backs off, and the man and his wife approach the shaken runner.

"You look starved. Let us get you some food."

"Non, non," says the runner. "I need to go home," he says in French.

"You're not headed for home. French is spoken in Burundi, and Burundi is behind you. You're running away," says the woman.

A fearful look of confirmation crosses the runner's eyes.

"Where do you need to go?" asks the white man. The runner looks down, afraid to say.

"Stay here *avec ma mari. Je trouverai quelque chose pour manger*. I'll get some food," says the wife.

Later, the runner is no longer so hungry, and a stash of sandwiches are in his carry sack. His canteen is full, and the tourists have persuaded him to go with them in their jeep. He lies down on the back seat and prays.

Faster than he could ever run, he rides down the A109 toward Mombasa. In this miracle of speed he and this man and woman drive past an abandoned bright red Coca-Cola stand, then some cattle, and then past a woman carrying wood and a gourd on her head. Then past Kenya's Tsavo National Park. The runner is sorry he told them about Mombasa and his brother, but there is nothing he can do now. He's tempted to jump from the vehicle, but he knows that would also be a mistake.

By end of day, they are at the docks in Mombasa. A well-lighted, glittering cruise ship, with its gangplanks down, stands there like a cross between a prison and a palace.

Will these people turn me and my brother in, or are they as kind as they say?

A tall black man with a huge smile appears at the top of the gangplank. He hesitates to leave the ship, so the runner leaps from the back of the jeep. Once again he is running with the perfection of all his other strides. At the top of the gangplank, he grabs his brother, and they hug and jump up and down. Then they disappear into the ship and don't come out again.

"Did we do the right thing?" asks the wife.

"I think so. He's running towards a new life."

"He doesn't seem like a criminal, but he doesn't even have a passport."

"I saw him earlier. We were north of Taita, and he was running through the grasslands. He's brilliant fast and running for the joy of it.

Then when I saw him later, I realized he was also running because it freed him. He might have stolen to eat, but he's no true criminal. I don't believe he could be."

"The way he looks; the way his brother greeted him... I agree," says the wife. "To deny a person that gifted, that beautiful, that courageous a new life... well, it would be a sin."

The Emigrant

Pack carefully
there is no coming back
whisper tender goodbyes
give hugs all 'round

Remember these people
you likely will not see them again
but they will remember
and there will be stories

A tear on your cheek
a catch in your breath
turn away now
there is no good future here

Step out
feel your heart race
the adventure begins
be brave

~ Marv Himmel

A Christmas Wish for the Whole Year Round

By Olivia Taylor-Young

The Christmas Eve my oldest child was nearly three, he refused to fall asleep until he saw Santa. We wheedled, cajoled, fed him warm milk and solemnly explained that Santa can't come until children nod off; and like free-spirited youngsters everywhere, he summarily ignored us.

So there he was, wide-awake in his crib at one in the morning, stubbornly staring out at the night sky. And there were we, his dog-tired parents, desperately waiting to assemble a tricycle and bring out the rest of Santa's bounty.

The Christmas Eve my youngest son was 8, we were on the way home from candlelight services when Santa, complete with red costume and a sack on his back, stepped into the crosswalk as we stopped at a red light. He had a round face and a little round belly; and when we cheered and waved "Merry Christmas," he sprinted to our car shouting "Ho! Ho! Ho!" and handed out candy canes all around.

"I understand you saw Santa," my sister kidded our little boy the following day… and his eyes lit up like our Christmas tree. "Yup, Aunt Margie, I saw him right there on Balboa."

Twenty years later, Santa came to our family on Christmas Eve, not in bright costume, but in the clothing of dearest friends. We'd lost that once bright-eyed little boy the week after Thanksgiving; and aside from the Emergency Room phone call which left me clutching a countertop screaming *No! No! No*, that holiday season will forever remain a blur of numbness and grief… except for Christmas Eve. On that special evening, those friends arrived bearing not only food and gifts, but their PJs and bathrobes and plans to spend the night. By the warmth and light from the fireplace and warmed by the light of their love, we had an impromptu pajama party and together watched the classic, "It's a Wonderful Life." To paraphrase thoughts from another Christmas classic, "God bless them, every one."

Like life itself, holiday memories are indefinable blendings of emotions and experiences, joy and sadness, despair and hope.

I consider myself among the lucky. Most of mine reflect happy times spent with those I hold most dear. Across the years, they also reflect life seasons, each one unique as it yields to the next. Babies who delighted at sparkling lights on a tree grew up to share that wonder with children of their own… who in turn now share it with the next generation. The grandchild who once cried on Santa's lap now owns an honorific of Doctor. And youngsters who wanted every toy in sight now donate their time and dollars to charity.

Yet our most unique Christmas experience was one my husband and I shared many miles away and totally out of context from home and friends and family.

I consider having been able to travel among the greatest gifts of my life. Since business often took my husband overseas and I was lucky enough to tag along, we had the opportunity to soak up history, visit world famous sights, call at birthplaces and graves of the great, climb ancient stairways to the tops of castles and cathedrals and even kiss the Blarney Stone.

Outstanding among our memories, however, is the year we spent December in Munich. "What an opportunity" our then twentysomething kids agreed and encouraged us to stay for Christmas after the three week class their Dad was teaching ended on the 21st. "We can get together on New Year's instead and look at all the fun you'll have shopping."

They were right. The beautiful city of Munich is now the Christmas capital of Bavaria. As if in rebuke to Hitler's madness, what was once the cradle of the Third Reich has paradoxically evolved into the gathering place of top artisans and musicians who, each December, create a delightful, fun-filled street fair called Christkindlemarkt.

Among breathtaking displays of decorations and craftspeople hawking their wares, Christkindlemarkt transforms downtown Munich into a happy, festive, freezing month-long celebration... warmed up considerably by steaming cider and mulled wine. Enthralled, I shopped there for everyone on my gift list that month. I also spent long hours gazing at and window-shopping for largess I could not afford.

At noon on December 24, my husband and I headed for Marienplatz, the quadrangle in front of City Hall, to witness Christkindlemarkt's closing ceremonies. To our surprise, we found ourselves in the midst of about 5,000 people standing bundled against the cold. We joined the joyous gathering to watch and listen while lederhosen-clad musicians played Alpine Christmas Carols from a balcony overlooking the square. The mood was enchanting. The music exquisite... if not very traditional for us auslanders. Then came the final Carol, as familiar as holly and Santa Claus and blessings of peace.

Stille Nacht. Heilege Nacht. The notes rang clear in the chill December air. *Silent Night. Holy Night.* And as often happens with well-known melodies at Christmas, everyone began to sing. We joined the chorus—in English—and from across the square we could hear others singing in English with accents different from our own. We also heard the sweet sound of French. Lilting notes in Italian and Spanish. Unfamiliar words of more than one Slavic origin. *Stille Nacht. Heilege Nacht. Silent Night. Holy Night.* A harmony of words. A melody divided by language, yet together in verse, sound and celebration.

And there, two years from the time the Berlin Wall came tumbling down, that one shining, tear-filled moment became not only our greatest Christmas gift, but the greatest gift of all our travels. Through the common bond of music we witnessed the ability of people to cross imaginary borders with good will as their only passport. It was the voice of humankind united. United in a prayer for peace

Now more than ever, may that prayer be answered every day and in every language... here at home and around the world.

I've Got to Go Back

I've got to go back to the tall timber soon,
Back where the big firs saw at the sky.
Back where I rise to the cries of a loon,
Back where the osprey and eagles still fly.
The city and its woes scare me to death,
The squalor and stench burns in my eyes.
My heart is pounding, I can't catch my breath,
To tell you the truth I'm sick of their lies.

The bells and whistles, the honking of horns,
The screeching tires, the curse and the yell.
I need to wake to clear, quiet morns,
To be stuck in some city is like living in Hell.
I'm gagging on a swill mistaken for air,
And I can't trust a soul that I see.
I'd just as soon lie in a rattlesnake's lair,
I can't live in a city, I need to be free.

I need to have my campfire at night,
I've got to be able to count my stars.
I'm blinded by the glare of the city's light,
And frozen like a deer in the eyes of their cars.
I've got to go back amid the valley and peak.
I need a good lashing from the wind and rain,
I crave the culture of a babbling creek.
I've got to get back to my mountains again.

I've not seen a smile since I looked in the mirror,
Their gaunt furrowed faces tell of their fears.
They scurry like mice amid the din and furor,
And they've all got cell phones stuck in their ears.
I gave it my best,
And I failed the test,
Now I need my rest.
I need a good lashing from the wind and rain,
I've got to go back to my mountains again.

In Memoriam
~ *Michael (Hoss) J Barker*

Christmas is a'Comin'

"Bah, Humbug!" was Grinch's first thought,
"I seem to have forgotten what I was taught."
He then retorted, to straighten up
"I should be grateful, I have full cup."

And thus, began, his poetic try
To come up with a poem, sort o' quick on the fly.
"How can I write of a Christmas 'white'
"When there ain't no snow, and the future ain't
    bright?"

He'd been kept in, with the curtains drawn
For eleven months of the Covid "post dawn,"
With ill clouds above and death fog beneath,
He cowered on holidays, could muster no
    wreath...

No wreath for Christmas, no hope for the spring,
No service on Sundays, there seemed no way to
    bring
A glimmer of hope to our grim, grinchy, grouch
The bachelor old writer, sinking deep in his couch.

But then there arose a faint rap on the door
A rap that he never had heard there before
A rap that his dog, little Fido, did hear
As he jumped to his feet and barked loud in
    Grinch ear

And Grinch slowly rose, and wobbled, then
    stood...
He took aim for the door with his cane made of
    wood
He got to the door and undid the latch
And opened the door and there stood Miss Patch.

Miss Patch, she explained, had just moved in next
    door
To the vacated house that she'd lived in before
As a child, years ago, and she hoped to move back
Since her husband had died of a bad heart attack.

And Christmas was coming, and she needed a nail
And a hammer to pound it into the rail
Of the rickety fence on her rickety deck
So, she hoped he could help, so she just came to
    check.

Well, Grinch did have a hammer and did have a
    nail
And would you wish for a happy end to this tale?
Would you wish that Miss Patch was well pleased
    with this guy,
And offered in thanks hot coffee and pie?

Well, I'm happy to say that your wish did come
    true.
Just as good things will happen to you,
As your life goes along and plots thicken and thin,
And there's hullabaloo and there's racket and din.

And sometimes when things can't get any worse
There's a twist of fate and instead of a curse
Things turn right around, and you weather the
    test
And instead of disaster, things turn out for the
    best!

So now I must leave you, I've things I must do
I must think of a poem that is catchy and true.
I must write it real quick, for the gal at the church,
    as
She needs it today, she was left in a lurch.

~ William McConochie

If I Could Cry, Would the Pain Go Away?

Mother, you're gone
You died too many years ago
and I will never hear your voice again.

Your spirit left this earth too soon
Where did it go?
Is there a heaven, an afterlife, or a netherworld
where good people go, when their breath leaves
   them
and their hearts no longer beat?

Science says "no," and religion says "yes"
to an existence beyond this life.
But no one knows the answer.
Certainly reincarnation is a ruse
But we won't go there, because it offends too
   many people,
and that's something you'd never have done.

You had not an offensive cell in your body.
To me you radiated, in your quiet way, only love,
   generosity, thoughtfulness, and self-sacrifice.

You taught me so much about how to live and care
   and behave. But it took me too long to apply
   those lessons,
long after you were gone.
Now I have no way to make up for all that lost
   time,
to tell you how much I loved you,
to act like the daughter you deserved.

I'm sorry.

I'm sorry for all the pain I must have caused you
when my wild side blinded me
to the short time we would know each other.

I came back to Maryland,
leaving my California days behind.
To be near you, when my child would be born
I thought I could finally give back
some of the love you showed me,
and maybe even learn how to be a better person.

But that was not to be.

I arrived in Maryland in April, to rent a house on a
   farm.

Little did I know that I should have stayed in the
   town,
in your town,
so we could spend more time together, so I could
   learn
how to be a better daughter.
I thought there would be time enough, but you
   were gone by July's end.
And me, nearly 8 months pregnant
torn between the joy of new life
and the tragedy of your death.
I couldn't cry.
I was in shock, and preparing to give birth in one
   month.

It didn't help that my partner, and the father of my
   child, completely lacked empathy, especially for
   my parents.
He made me leave the hospital, as you lay there
in your last bed.
He wanted to smoke a cigarette.

It was the last time I saw you.

My punishment:
To no longer see you or to hear your voice,
not to be able to atone for my negligence,
or to make amends for my folly.

I know that this is 'classic guilt,'
and it is truly deserved.

But I don't deserve to never hear your voice again.

My father owned a reel-to-reel tape recorder,
and he taped all kinds of conversations
and music that he played.
But he never taped your voice, his wife's voice; the
   person who meant so much to all her kids, and to
   him.

But when I hear your voice again,
I will finally cry, and maybe the pain will go away.

An analyst would probably say "You haven't dealt
   with your grief." And that is probably true.
But when I hear your voice again,
I will finally cry, and maybe the pain will go away.

~ Lois Angela Czyzewski

Taylor Camp
By Lee Boutell

In July 1975, I flew from Oregon to Maui to visit my girlfriend who, for weeks, had sent me steamy love letters about how much she missed me. After finishing up business in Eugene I arrived on Maui only to find she already had a new boyfriend. I couldn't really blame Keith for being with Paige, but I lost respect for her over what she did. She could have told me about Keith before I flew out to visit. Crushed, I left on a hiking/camping adventure for a few days.

Since I didn't know anyone else and didn't know what to do until my return flight, I talked with Keith who knew the islands well. He seemed like a good guy and I liked him. He said I could stay for free on the island of Kauai.

"It's the 'Garden Isle', even more beautiful than Maui, you'll love it!" he said. "You can stay in my friend Diane's house. She's away for a while and lets me stay there when she's gone." I did like the sound of that. He continued, "The coolest thing is—it's a tree house in a hippie community right on the beach."

"Sounds incredible! You sure it's okay if I stay there?"

"I know she's cool with it; we're good friends. She built this beautiful tree house with tons of windows, a kitchen, house plants and bookshelves. It's like a regular house and it's the best one there."

Intrigued, I believed my next adventure had just dropped in my lap, thanks to Keith. Yeah, he wanted to get rid of me, but I didn't have anything better to do.

He told me the story of Taylor Camp—how, in 1969, Elizabeth Taylor's brother bought beach property to build a home on the north shore of Kauai at the end of the road. State authorities wouldn't let him build because they wanted the acreage for a park. Angry, he went to the jail and bailed out 13 surfers and hippies who'd been arrested for vagrancy for unauthorized beach camping. Taylor drove them to his property and told them they could live there for free without getting hassled. The surfers, Vietnam veterans and hippies gladly moved onto the property and set up camp. Eventually they built a tree house community of over a hundred people.

Keith drew a detailed map for me to find Diane's tree house and told me her full name in case anybody asked. I caught the next flight to Kauai.

After landing at Lihue Airport, I hitchhiked north to Hanalei Bay, a picture-perfect spot on the wonderfully scenic Kauai north shore. I bought supplies, had lunch and learned from fishermen that the iconic 1958 movie, "South Pacific," had been filmed on the beach at Hanalei. I marveled at the backdrop of beautiful spires of volcanic mountains that made me think of the song "Puff the Magic Dragon" who lived in the enchanted land of Honah Lee. It truly looked like a magical place.

I explored the quaint village and then followed Keith's map, walking west on the narrow coastal highway, eventually catching a ride the remaining miles to the end of the road. There, at the base of a mountain, I checked out a mysterious wet cave and thought, maybe this is the cave where Puff once lived. My map told me I'd made it to the right area.

As late afternoon shadows grew longer, I followed a path toward the beach into a grove of ironwood trees. I walked past a vegetable garden where a couple women picked vegetables for their evening meal. Around me I saw tree houses of all shapes and sizes, most with wooden pane windows and ladders leading up to living areas. The size, craftsmanship and artistry of the dwellings amazed me. These were not hastily thrown together shacks.

As teenagers in Kansas, a buddy and I built a pretty decent simple tree house. The experience of building that partly influenced me to attend architecture school in college. But, at Taylor Camp, I found multi-level tree houses of amazing creativity. Supported on trees and wooden posts, all were enclosed, roofed and protected from rain and wind and had lots of windows. Many had friendly-looking, shaded sitting areas below the structure. Potted plants, lawn furniture and outdoor art sculptures gave the tree house community an almost suburban feel, but the pleasant sound of waves breaking on the beach made it feel more like a resort.

A small clear stream ran through the grove and out to sea. I saw young kids playing in the stream and adults doing chores or bathing. Other people swam offshore, and one guy was paddling out on the blue waters with a surfboard to catch a wave.

Keith's map took me to a large, two-level tree house right at the edge of the beach, with a panoramic view of the ocean less than a hundred yards away. On both levels, the house had rows of recycled multi-pane wooden windows facing the ocean. It had balconies with railings, several hanging flower pots and a window flower box at the upper level loft. It was the most beautiful tree house I'd ever seen on one of the most incredible beach scenes I could possibly imagine. I thought, this must be what Heaven on Earth looks like. I couldn't believe my good fortune to be staying at this place.

I went to the ladder-like steps of Diane's house and went up to see inside. The first level had a pleasant living area with bookshelves, kerosene lamps, framed art, comfy low chairs and rugs on the floor. A well-lighted, spacious kitchen had windows on three sides, counters, shelves, a four-burner gas stove, a wok and all kinds of pots and pans. It looked like almost any kitchen, only without a refrigerator, sink or appliances. Diane had stocked the shelves with dishes, cups, kitchen implements and a nice assortment of herbs. She cooked and could eat well—right from the community garden.

The house had two sleep... the main floor and one above in th... had indoor plants, pillows and mats on the flo... covered with patterned sheets and colorful India-like tapestry cloths. I saw no blankets or sources of heat in the house—such things are unnecessary on Kauai.

The view outside every window of the house amazed me—ironwood trees, a volcanic mountain, the beach, the blue ocean, a clear stream cutting through white sand, a next door tree house and the dark forest grove.

I looked through the collection of books on Diane's shelves—an eclectic selection of fiction, nutrition and health, philosophy and spirituality. Many of these books I had on my own bookshelf, such as the seminal 1971 classic *Be Here Now* by Ram Das. I felt right at home in this idyllic, restful place. I threw away my cares, breathed deeply and completely relaxed.

After darkness fell, I laid my sleeping bag down on the floor mat of the downstairs bedroom and listened to the gentle rhythm of waves breaking on the beach just beyond my window. That night I slept better than I had in years.

The next morning I awoke to brightness shining through the bank of wood pane windows next to me. I gazed out beyond her hanging mobile of little white seagulls and the variegated green leaves of potted Dieffenbachia plants in front of me—looking out to a view of the majestic spired Na Poli Coast mountains, a white sand beach and the deep blue Pacific.

Lying there, I felt amazement at being in this special place. Seeing the unique environment around me and realizing all the loving work, thought, and great care it took to create this tree house masterpiece, I felt like I got to know Diane even though we'd never met. I loved her books, her art, her sense of style and her sensibilities. I wondered if she might be an old girlfriend of Keith's or whether they were just friends. But at some level, I felt Diane and I were connected. I vowed to leave my name on a thank you note, for whatever it's worth.

I went down to the beach and found a group of fellow hippies doing yoga—both men and women. I joined them going through movements of the sun salutation—a series of flowing deep stretches, poses and breathing exercises. I hadn't done that much yoga, but I did know this one. Though I didn't know any person at Taylor Camp, I got a smile of acknowledgment and felt welcomed joining in.

After ten minutes with fellow tree house dwellers on the beach doing silent yoga and hearing only the gentle sound of the ocean, I felt both deeply relaxed and energized as people slowly started wandering off.

The vibe of the moment felt to me like I experienced after a deep meditation and becoming completely centered within. I had the urge to connect with others, to talk with the residents, but at the same I time did not wish to disturb the deep feeling of peace we had achieved. I sensed others felt the same way. I knew the residents likely had more than their share of visitors and transients passing through, and I did not want to create any waves.

Some of the men had looked at me a little skeptically. Hippies always had to be on the lookout for narcs or FBI agents posing as one of them, so I didn't blame anybody for being stand-offish. Later I overheard a story about drunk townspeople that came through the camp at night, shouting and acting threateningly. None of the residents wanted violence of any kind. Several of the guys had fought in Vietnam and only wanted peace.

The resident doctor had been a flight surgeon in Nam and came to the community to heal and learn how to smile again. He began healing himself by helping others to heal themselves, both physically and emotionally. Over the years he served as counselor, took care of minor medical issues and helped deliver several babies at Taylor Camp.

Other residents were refugees of other kinds—escaping oppressive families, a dangerous city or horrible relationship. Some faced alcoholism or drug addiction, and some just wanted to get high and surf the waves. But above all, everybody sought a life of peace and freedom. All wanted to live in a positive, cooperative environment with nobody in charge, nobody making rules, and everyone respecting others as equals. Everyone shared and money didn't rule their lives.

Taylor Camp residents built a place of worship. They also had a water system and a latrine where a normal-looking porcelain toilet sat on a wooden deck built around a cluster of banana trees. It had a sink but no walls. Privacy at Taylor Camp was never an issue. I used the toilet when I needed to and didn't feel particularly weird about it, as everybody gave you personal space and nobody cared anyway because they had to use it, too. Clothing was optional at the camp and seeing nude people walking together or swimming was normal. On most evenings, residents played nude beach volleyball.

After a couple days, I started running out of food and went to the Taylor Camp Coop in the grove. They created the store for acquiring food and supplies without the hassle of going to town. This community to me was just ideal—peaceful, free, loving and generous people living together in cooperation and mutual respect—and at the edge of paradise.

While staying in Diane's tree house, I toured Kauai to see the fantastic 'Grand Canyon of the Pacific' and hiked the cliffs along the Napali Coast trail beginning near Taylor Camp. The jungle trail, high above the blue Pacific, crossed several streams emerging from creases in the rugged green mountain formations. I hiked into jungles, up stream valleys and found trees filled with breadfruit, guavas, star fruit and mountain apples. Further into the jungle, up one stream, I encountered the dramatic, secluded Hanakoa waterfall. It fell several hundred feet over mountain rocks into a crystal clear pool—a perfect spot to cool off while hiking in the July sun. I floated on my back and took in the beautiful jungle waterfall scene. I felt a little like Tarzan.

I stayed in Diane's tree house for several days and wish I could have remained and become friends with the residents, but my return flight to Oregon awaited. I took one last look at my beautiful, temporary home, left a thank you note and sadly departed from the utopian tree house paradise. Someday I'd like to meet Diane and thank her in person for allowing me this unforgettable experience.

Taylor Camp existed for a brief moment during a special time, and it's not likely that anything like it could exist today. Authorities condemned it, forced out the residents and, in 1977, burned Taylor Camp down. It is now Haena State Park—still at the end of the road.

The Lighthouse at Cattle Pass

From my vantage point
on this rocky spit
this miniature headland
I watch
it is my duty to watch
and to warn the unwary during
nighttime passings or
winter's fog and storm
to send out the light
to sound the horn
and alert the danger
while during the summer months
I pose for the noisy powerboats
the elegant sloops and skittering kayaks
giving them my best whitewashed sides
and jaunty red cap for their cameras

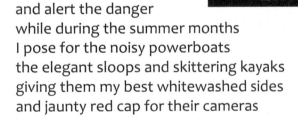

A sentinel to casual sailors
and the local fishing fleet
I watch as they maneuver through the
slit between the islands at Cattle Pass

where the tide picks up speed
pulsing and spinning and surging
as it powers through the channel

Wise sailors time their passage to slack tide
when the great lungs of the sea pause for a moment
between inhaling and exhaling
when the whirlpools and currents slacken
and it is safe and you are not so likely
to be thrown about

But not for the novice this passage
a mere one hundred yards in length
what could be so difficult
"Watch this!" commands the confident initiate
and I do–
I always watch
it is my duty
I have watched countless gleaming
watercraft charge into the chaos
only to be caught and flung into spins
and gyrations and wild over-corrections
as they are pushed and swung and bullied
toward the nearby shoals and beckoning rocks

And if they do come safely through
I have watched these bold young captains
excuse themselves and hurry below
hands shaking
knees trembling
to change their wet pants
and repair their injured bravado
no longer novices to Cattle Pass

I am a sentinel
it is my duty to watch
and remember the passing
of time and creatures
of the wind and water
and of the convulsions beneath me
I sit here adjacent to this ocean
I note everything that passes

I am a sentinel
I am the lighthouse at Cattle Pass

~ Marv Himmel

Roughing it in the Klondike
By Mary Lee Radka

In August 1976, I was 32 years old and working as an RN at St. Elizabeth's Hospital. I kept getting into trouble for my habit of telling my patients that MD did not stand for Medical Deity. The Director of Nurses suggested that I take a few days off to consider my priorities and attitudes. As fate would have it, about that time, my good friend from Anchorage, Alaska, came to visit me and my two small children in Yakima, Washington.

Kathy Parker and I met when we were both flight attendants for different airlines, and I had "snuck" her a drink during a "Do not serve alcohol over Washington State on a Sunday." She was on her way to visit her mom in Walla Walla, Washington. We had kept in touch over the years since. During her visit, she suggested that I come up to Anchorage and stay with her during my imposed days off. Kathy was then in the manufacturing business and was making interesting curios for tourists. I still have a pair of her shellacked moose turd earrings.

My mom, Del, who was also visiting me at the time, was invited to go to Alaska too. Mom, Kathy, and I had previously gone on a fun, beer-drinking trip to Mexico City a few years earlier when we were all 'footloose and fancy-free,' so, we knew that we would have fun wherever we went. My two kids were happy to be staying with their paternal grandmother and great-grandmother and Kathy's husband was taking care of her son.

The day after we flew into Anchorage, we were on the road in Kathy's Ford Bronco. We headed up the main highway to Mt. McKinley and took a short detour into Talkeetna, where we met a friend of Kathy's named Ray Genet. Genet was often referred to by the nickname 'Pirate' and was a Swiss-born American mountaineer. He was the first guide on North America's highest mountain, Alaska's Denali (aka Mt. McKinley). By that time, he had made 25 successful climbs to the summit of Denali including the first winter ascent with three other climbers. Sadly, a few years after meeting him, he froze to death in his sleeping bag on the descent of Mt. Everest, and is still entombed on that side of that mountain in Nepal to this day. There is a memorial to Ray Genet, on the slopes of Mt. Everest reading: *July 25, 1931-October 2, 1979. Let all who read this know that this man never said 'I quit' to the summit.* I remember him as being very fascinating and a bit of a flirt.

On our trip, the three of us stopped at Mt. McKinley Park headquarters. Old trains cars that housed guests and tourists were parked on the original train tracks from Anchorage to Mt. McKinley. We also saw the only bar in a National Park, the famous Golden Spike Saloon which was in one of the railroad cars.

From the park, we drove to Fairbanks, where Kathy had made arrangements to sleep at a friend's new condo. While in Fairbanks, we saw the Malamute Saloon which was really a turn-of-the-century place with sawdust and peanut shells on the floor. Fairbanks was also the home of Mining Valley in Pioneer Park, Bartlett Plaza, Bonanza Creek Long-Term Ecological Research program, the Fairbanks Gold Rush Town, an Alaskan wildlife park and native villages.

The Fairbanks Gold Rush Town holds an interesting true story. From Memorial Day to Labor Day each year, you can go through the Kitty Hensley House. The house dates back to the early 1900s and originally had two small rooms with a shed outside that was used by Kitty as a summer kitchen. Kitty fell about four years after moving into her remodeled home and broke her hip. While she was in the hospital 'the good women of Alaska' decided to clean her house… mainly out of curiosity. When Kitty heard of this, she left the hospital, without aid, to go home and guard her massive collection of boxes and cans.

Kitty forever-after blamed those women for being crippled and for the loss of a fortune in money and valuables. She died in her sleep in 1932. They say that Captain Smtyhe went through every inch of the house looking for money and jewelry he thought she had, but most of it was thrown away when the good women literally "cleaned house."

Fairbanks was still a frontier town in 1976 with few sidewalks. It was mostly just muddy. It boomed during the Gold Rush days, and again with the discovery of 'black gold'—oil. They still had a bar on every corner and a regular red-light district. I remember that people were very friendly, full of information, and a lot of fun.

The next day, we started for Circle which is 50 miles from the Arctic Circle, and as close as we could get by car. The early settlers who founded Circle thought they were at the Arctic Circle. The Steele Highway follows the old prospector's road and it is 161 miles from Fairbanks to Circle and we passed several miles of 'tailings'—or mining waste.

The area yielded millions of dollars in gold in its day, and piles of rock and gravel—tailings— still lie wherever the dredge dropped them. The country is arid and flat, and I remember a carpet of wildflowers and blueberries. We detoured to Circle Hot Springs and had a blissful soak in its Olympic-sized pool. It was late when we left the Circle Hot Springs and headed south to Valdez. One of the headlights had shorted out, and gravel took the other one out, leaving us in the dark. In those days, law enforcement officers were few and far between—one for every 50 square miles, but who should drive up, was an officer who happened to be looking for his horse. He led us to a rest station while he finished his hunt. At this point, we had an excellent chance to look over the largest suspension bridge in Alaska, built to hold the pipeline. When the officer returned, he escorted us to the next town of Delta Junction. He made arrangements for us to stay in a nice hotel—we thought. The rooms were clean and located over a bar. We didn't realize until the next morning that it was a brothel. We didn't get much sleep, with the music blaring up from the bar until 4:00 a.m., and the knocking on doors up and down the hall. So, after a restless night, we again headed south and stopped at Sourdough, an old restaurant whose owners boasted of their then-79-year-old sourdough bread starter.

Continuing towards Anchorage we went through the rugged big game area of Alaska, past many lakes and rivers. Because of the permafrost, the trees were stunted. Along the coast line of Anchorage, the trees are normal growth where the ocean has melted the permafrost.

On our last day of travel, Kathy took my mom and I to see Portage Glacier. Del described it as 'like soap suds that had too much bluing in them' as we watched the big hunks fall off, pass by us and go down to the sound.

That day, we had lunch at the Alyeska Ski Lodge overlooking the chairlift and we stopped to see the spawning salmon as we traveled toward Seward. The town of Seward is surrounded by big tress and is a typical seacoast town nestled in among 16 bars— that we counted—and a couple of curio shops selling California macrame' and plants. Many salmon fishing boats were anchored in the harbor.

When Mom and I got back to Seattle, we both felt that the hospitality, open arms, hearts, and homes of the friendly people we saw and met would be with us for a long-time.

I give thinks for the journal that I kept during that wonderful Alaskan adventure.

Dear Neighbor
By Michael Foster

Dear Neighbor,

When we visit over the fence, we share. Fresh vegetables go one way, a loaned tool or advice goes the other. There's usually some humor. But more importantly, we solve problems in our neighborhood. There's the elderly widower we take meals to. We water each other's plants. We watch out for each other. We're human—that's what people do. We have each other's back even though we may have voted differently.

Margaret Mead, after giving a lecture on cultural anthropology, was asked by a reporter, "When did civilization begin?" The reporter was surprised by her reply. Instead of answering about the use of tools or planting of crops, Mead answered, "A broken femur." Mead went on to explain, "Human skeletal remains about 15,000 years old were found in a cave. The femur had been broken and healed. In the animal world, if an animal breaks a leg, they're finished. They can no longer hunt and feed. That broken bone implies that the person was carried to safety, fed and cared for. That was the beginning of human civilization."

The fence we visit over is a metaphor, a symbol of what's wrong with our humanity. Ownership implies violence. Signs reading 'Trespassers will be shot!' are far too familiar. All of us live on this beautiful, blue planet. The very things that give us life, the air, the water, the land are shared resources.

Garrett Hardin, an American ecologist, illustrated two truths. One was the notion titled *The Tragedy of the Commons*. When a few individuals monopolize the resources needed by all to survive, there's inequality. The other truth is that exponential population growth within a finite biosphere can only lead to collapse.

Where does it say in the American Dream that we should take more than we need? Kim Stanley Robinson said it best. "Enough is as good as a feast." The Cherokee said it best. "We don't have rights, we have obligations."

Challenge yourself for a day and try using pronouns differently. Instead of saying I and me, say we and us. When talking about other living things like, trees, rivers or rocks, use gender pronouns like he or she. When referring to a fir tree and knowing that she is your kin like a sister you love and not just a resource, your thinking will change. The Sioux say *Mitákuye Oyás'iŋ*. "All are related."

Most of Earth's religion have some version of the Golden Rule in their teachings. Prophets, writers and sages from our past have long given us sayings, rules and warnings about how to get along, survive—be human. It's the little things we do; acts of kindness, recycling, living small and thinking big, that will save us. When just one person takes a shorter shower or picks up another's candy wrapper, the effect is miniscule. But, when billions do it, the change in our attitude will be reflected in the world.

Howard Zinn said it best. "To be hopeful in bad times is not just foolishly romantic. It is based on the fact that human history is a history not only of cruelty, but also of compassion, sacrifice, courage and kindness. And if we do act, in however small a way, we don't have to wait for some grand utopian future. The future is an infinite succession of presents, and to live now as we think human beings should live, in defiance of all that is bad around us, is itself a marvelous victory."

So neighbor, please wear the T-shirt with me that says:

Birthplace – Earth. Race – Human. Politics – Freedom. Religion – Love.

Your neighbor,
Michael Foster

The Mystery of Mister X; A True Story
By Demetri Liontos

"Please be aware that the Guest Apartment will be occupied by Mr. X for 4 days, starting this Friday evening." The cryptic note was from Lao Sun An, the Foreign Staff Director of my college in Chongqing, western China. His frequent notes ranged from announcing power and water cuts for the week to new curfew restrictions to extra buses for our weekly Saturday shopping downtown. They were always unpredictable, and it was usually a downer to come home and find one waiting on opening my apartment door.

It was warm and sunny May in Sichuan province, where I'd come to teach and plan curriculum for English classes at Chongqing's prestigious Sichuan Foreign Language Institute. I had been there since late August the previous year and my contract would end with the school year in early July. One of thousands of teachers in China from the English-speaking world, I had gone through all the expected cultural shocks and joys to arrive at a truce between loving and hating the myriad differences with my life in Oregon. Besides, Lao Sun's downer notes had only two months to go.

The "Guest Apartment" was a paper-thin wall next to mine and it shared my front door. Upon entering Apt. 2-6, one found a cozy triangular vestibule with two other entry doors; mine was the one on left and the infrequent college guests—visiting dignitaries, politicos, journalists—entered by a door on the right. "Mister X" was the first time Lao Sun had used that designation. He either didn't know the guest's name or, more like, didn't want me to know. In any case, he always let me know when guests were arriving, probably so that I could rein in my Western penchant for partying.

When I returned to my apartment after Friday's last class, I was engulfed, not in the expected singsong Mandarin, but in a spirited outpouring of... my god, *Russian*! Now *this* was going to be different. Through their open door I spied a tall, bear-like bearded man and a shorter blond, clean shaven one, wildly gesticulating and seemingly wanting to kill each other.

"Knock, knock," I said, in my cheeriest down-home voice. "I'm Demetri from next door. Is everything alright? Do you need anything?" Silence.

Then, "Dmitri! You must to be *Rashyan*! Come in, come in!" said the blond one, reaching up to hug his long-lost brother who wasn't. Now *this* was different to bowing! I explained that, in fact, I was of Greek heritage, an Ameri-Canadian and a professor at the college. His name was Vasily Morsov, a radio/tv journalist from Radio Moscow; his bearded friend, Ivan, was the photographer assigned to their "proyect" and who spoke no English (nor anything other than Russian). So *this* was the mysterious Mister X and his sidekick. Perhaps Lao Sun didn't want to shock me, given the frigid Sino-Russo relations of the late eighties, and merely called Vasily, "X," to cloak his nationality.

After a few more pleasantries I left them to get settled and went next door to make dinner and plan the next day's classes. Throughout the evening and through the paper-thin walls, I could hear spirited discussions in Russian, the clattering of dishes, and even a set of sad songs that spoke of homesickness—or lack of vodka. I learned the next day that their project was to film and interview typical, ordinary Chinese in urban and rural areas, and to show the drastic differences of lifestyles. Chongqing was one of a half dozen sites they'd chosen. I knew the three of us would get along just fine.

On the second evening, Vasily knocked on my door to borrow the proverbial cup of sugar—something about sweetening the sweet tea that even I might enjoy. Oh, and tomorrow was his birthday, so please come over for a drink and Russian snacks. An offer hard to resist, I made him a funny birthday card and the next night went over, armed with some American canned ham and cheddar cheese remnants. When I walked in, Ivan greeted me with a bear hug while Vasily fiddled with his transistor radio to get a Russian station that played local music. Miraculously, he found a wish-wash of sound on a shortwave band, and the singing and party started.

After many songs and vodkas (the good stuff brought from home), and too little American ham and snacks, we all three vowed to be blood brothers for life. I staggered the short distance to my place and crashed with a final image of balalaikas strumming in my nine o'clock class of testy juniors.

Before Vasily and Ivan left, we exchanged addresses and I told them I would be in Moscow at the beginning of August, on the long way back to Oregon.

"Please, please, Dmitri, you mast come to visit Olga (his fiancée) and me," Vasily said. "Here is the phone for Radio Moscow. They all know me there." It was a heartfelt invitation. More hugs ensued as we said our goodbyes and I had a strong feeling that indeed we would connect in Moscow.

Three months later, I had made the seismic shift from Asian China to European Russia via a rickety Aeroflot jet. As expected, Moscow was enormous, confusing and utterly different than the year I'd just spent in China. A couple of days into my week's visit—city tour, Red Square, the Kremlin, Gem department store—I called Vasily at his Radio Moscow office and actually got him on the phone! We laughed and greeted each other like lifelong old friends, and then made plans to meet after work for drinks and dinner. When he picked me up at my hotel, we hugged and Vasily introduced me to Olga his fiancée, a pretty smiley-faced brunette who also spoke surprisingly good English. The three of us had a lively evening at a good restaurant known for its shashlik kebabs and other local specialties. It was all delicious and so different from the fare I'd had in Sichuan; I felt I was in another world.

Before saying our *dasvidanias* in my hotel lobby, Vasily said he had time off the next afternoon and had planned a picnic for us at a beautiful lakeside park just outside Moscow. It was a unique opportunity for me to experience something off the tourist track and I was excited. "Please, just phone me at eleven at my office and I will tell you when I can pick you up, okay?" Vasily said. Dutifully, I called him the next morning and a man with a dark bass voice answered.

"Vasily Morsov? No, no, he not here. No know where he is. Did not come office today," said the sinister voice. I prodded him for more possibilities but he stonewalled my questions. I hadn't known Vasily very long but I did know he was a straight-shooter, a man of his word. I hung up and called his home phone, which rang and rang until it stopped. Total silence.

Puzzled, I repeated this routine several times of calling office then home, to no avail—now no one answered either phone. My fascination with spies, KGB and CIA as portrayed in movies, only served to whip my imagination. *I'm sure there's a perfectly logical explanation here*, I said to myself over and over. But none surfaced, as I repeated the calls every day without success. Soon, I convinced myself that mild-mannered, fun-loving Vasily Morsov had been shipped to some god-forsaken Gulag in remote Siberia, for the unpardonable crime of befriending an American. At least, that's what played in my brain.

I left Moscow with mixed feelings. It was a fascinating world city with much to see and learn from. But one had the feeling that often things here weren't what they seemed. I could still hear the deep bass echoes of the monster who answered Vasily's phone at Radio Moscow, sending shivers up my spine. My plane landed in Frankfurt, the West and a more predictable journey home ahead. It would have been a dream visit to Russia had the postscript not been so dark and baffling.

Dear Vasily… poor Mister X. I thought of him often and shuddered to think that our friendship, brief and warm as it was, had caused something horrible in his life. Then again, I took comfort in the fact that since I didn't really know anything concrete about what happened, Mister X might have gone on with his everyday life. It was all a mystery.

A Close Call

A log crashed down, ten thousand pounds
A mountain wave, clearing the grounds

It rolled and rolled and would not stop
Silence was lost on the mountain top

It rolled away, no time to pray
Why did I take this chance today

I didn't think; I made a mistake
Why didn't I wait? How long could it take

I hooked it up to make it tight
It must be safe to be just right

I tickled it a bit and then--- a slip
There was no way for it to grip

It thundered down with such a sound
This could have been my trip to town

No time to move my arms away
I thought I'd bought the farm today

A face full of fear, I saw this day
As my partner watched six feet away

Imagine the imprint in four foot of snow
Might not have survived, who would know

Some broken bones of which to give
Or a chair with wheels, if I'd have lived

~ Dana Graves

Lessons of Life

I've learned many lessons in my short number of
  years
Because I'm a quick learner, not too many tears
The best place to learn, life's lessons could be
At home in the chaos of your own family
From my Dad I learned the value of a job well done
But us being kids, we were all in it for fun
The day he kicked the bucket gave us all quite a scare
The bucket almost hit me, as it sailed through the air
The barn needed cleaned, and that was our chore
The problem was, a pool table on the upper floor
The words I don't remember as my Dad came
  through the door
From the speed of the bucket, I knew there would
  be more

Growing up with brothers can be quite rough
So I learned, if they were going to be stupid, I'd
  have to be tough
After watching my sister on a short little trip
Down the hill in a wagon, as it veered ' bout to tip

As she began to get closer to the pickup parked near
The look on the boy's faces was one of great fear
The wagon zoomed under as her face hit the truck
She scraped down the side, filling her nose up with
  muck

Mom got the tweezers, and fixed her up right
I'm just very thankful, they weren't obsessed with
  flight
Living out in the country is not very handy
Once a week we'd go shopping, and stock up on
  candy
Three of us siblings would eat ours up fast
But Justin would hide his, and make it last

I learned about business from a very good source
From my brother Justin, No homework, no course
He started a business called the Rob 'em Blind Store
His siblings, his customers, he had candy galore

He marked up the prices, no competition around
And hauled in the bucks for his next trip to town

Families are forever
I've heard them say it's true
That might not be such a good thing,
The torture they've put me through

~ Kristi Graves Moss

The Player

The theater is empty
floors swept clean
curtains closed
it is resting
only ghosts are active
reliving yesterday's performances
the missed cues and bungled lines
the tepid ovations and perfunctory "Bravos"
and the dark, wondering, silence at the close
no curtain calls
no roses
just another performance
just another day

Cradling my morning cup
I ready myself
"All the world's a stage," said the Bard
so what will it be today
what role for me
the lover
the villain
perhaps the hero
nah! not likely that
more likely the fool
I have played that many times
but being well into my sixth age
most days I prefer a bit part
in the background
filling space
"signifying nothing"

But I must be ready
you never know what will be called
a tragedy perhaps
or comedy
that would be nice
but most likely a farce
most of our plays are farce
so I sip my coffee
practice my entendres
my quick steps
and soft shoe shuffles
stretch a bit
and don today's costume

It is time
the troupe has assembled
seats are filled
and theater is waiting
the curtain begins to rise
I fill my lungs
throw back my shoulders
exhale and step out
murmuring to myself

"Once more into the breach"

~ *Marv Himmel*

Garlic Chicken and the Cell Phone Plot
By Rene Tihista

So, I stop by Johnson's Farm in North Springfield after noticing their sign on Armitage Road announces they have cider—my go-to drink—for sale. No cars were in the parking lot, but the door to the large warehouse is open, so I step inside. Compared to summer, the Johnson cupboard is bare. The large flat tables contain a few boxes of vegetables, potatoes, onions, some tiny tomatoes, green beans etc. I wonder where they're getting their veggies this time of year.

I call out, "Anybody here?" No answer.

I open the freezers and note the frozen marionberries and blueberries. I walk to the back of the warehouse and peek into alcoves, look into empty rooms, but no humans are in sight; however, there is one live being in the place.

I stop and gape at a large fat Rhode Island Red hen sitting absolutely still on one of the tables, as though it's in the process of laying an egg. I stand near enough to the big hen that I could touch her. My first thought is "fake chicken." It looks too real. It's too tame. But then its eyes blink. I stare for a minute at what is a surreal tableau. Adding to the weirdness of the scene, several bulbs of fresh garlic lay behind the hen as though she has laid garlic instead of eggs. It all looks so natural. If an alien from another planet had happened on the scene, they would conclude that chickens lay garlic bulbs.

For a moment, I wonder, "Why the chicken?" All the produce and berries in the large freezers are for sale. Signs announce that the place operates on the self-service honor system. Customers are to shop for whatever they want and place cash or a check in a box with a slot where the cash register normally sits. So, what is the chicken doing there as though it's watching the place. Could it be trained—a watch chicken—that somehow is able to warn customers or to report any thieves to the owners? Could that be possible? Roman Legions used to employ geese as sentinels and as a kid, I personally experienced the angry zeal a large goose can muster when one chased me around a neighbor's farm.

I guess I was in an existential funk that day because I shrugged and left without saying goodbye to the chicken. Then at 1:30 that following morning I woke up for a bathroom run and thought, "Why didn't I take a photo of that chicken?—that scene with the garlic bulbs? Nobody will believe my story without evidence and my cell phone was in the car all along."

Lying in bed, the answer came to me—the ugly truth that I've not wanted to face, and the reason I didn't think to take the photo. I hate my cell phone, and the phone knows it. Apparently, the Android (even the name sounds sinister) has an artificial intelligence that I wasn't told about when I bought the phone and it's thwarting me at every turn.

Sometimes I receive phone calls accompanied by a ring tone. But just as often calls automatically go to voice mail. I didn't set it up to do that—Hell! I don't even know how to.

The camera doesn't cooperate. I take pictures of my foot, the table my computer sits on, my hand on the keyboard—almost anything I don't want a photo of. Then miraculously, I manage to get a photo that I actually intended to take. Just the day before this chicken episode, my friend texted me a photo that the Android decided I didn't need to see until a full day after she sent it... and, with no notification of its arrival. How does this machine get off making such decisions? Of course, I was embarrassed when my friend asked if I got the photo she texted, and she gave me a suspicious look when I tried to explain its unexpectedly late arrival.

There's some bizarre curse on the relationship between me and the Android. Last October, I signed up and paid for a class at Willamalane Center on how to use the phone. It was cancelled for reasons I no longer remember. Then I signed up for another class to start in March of this year. So what happens? A freaking pandemic comes along and cancels this class too. A pandemic, mind you! This cannot just be coincidence. Something more is going on here. I have been smugly dismissive of all the conspiracy theories currently flowing from the Internet. I've even written about them. But let's hold our horses here. My cell phone may be mixed up in something nefarious. The question is: why me? If I were paranoid this would be exciting. I'm the focus of a secret conspiracy being hatched by my Android and who knows who else. But it doesn't figure. I'm just too ordinary to be the object of any conspiracy. No, the answer is more mundane I'm sure. When the pandemic eases up, and if I live through it, I'll just sign up for another class and learn how to operate this obstinate technological crank.

Or maybe fate is telling me to throw it away and get a better cell phone. Yet a part of me hates to be defeated by a machine, even one that's smarter than me... especially one that's smarter than me. I have my pride after all—like all paranoids do. I don't know. This conspiracy stuff *is* kind of intriguing... or is all this social distancing making me squirrely?

I wonder who that chicken really is? Hmm...

For the Sake of Love
By Demetri Liontos

"Kiss me!" I said to her, with some urgency. "I... I'm not sure," she replied, in a more neutral gear.

This scenario captures the essence of my early love life. It all started in the second grade at Aberdeen School in Montreal. It is the mid-twentieth century—birth control and the sexual revolution are still a glimmer in the future—and boy-girl relations are expectedly conservative. For curious seven-year-olds, other things were on our minds.

Her name was Jane, and she and a friend had found me alone in the coat room (adjacent to our classroom) rummaging through my lunch at recess. Giggling uncontrollably, the girls approached me and the friend said, "Jane wants you to kiss her." I joined in the wild giggles.

It seemed like a reasonable request, so I said, "Sure, why not?"

Jane inched forward, pushed by her friend and, red-faced, offered her cheek. I furtively planted a peck on it that would not have registered on any Richter scale, and we all giggled our way through recess. I saw Jane daily in class, but no pecks followed, nor was I moved to ask for any. (Later I learned that something called "hormones" hadn't yet arrived and that there was nothing wrong with my budding manhood.)

Fast-forward to high school, mid-teens, and an active time in the local Boy Scout troop—knots, songs, campfires, good deeds. It all took an upturn when we had a combined Friday night dance with the local Girl Scout troop, and there she was: Cathy. A sweet-looking, plumpish brunette, she gave me a smile that said "It's okay if you ask me to dance." So I did, and we danced most of that magical evening, asking and answering questions, squeezing closer with each dance. Cathy and I saw each other often after that, and soon we fell in love, as if we had to give a name to this euphoria.

(A callous friend later dared to call it "Puppy Love" even though no canines were hurt in the process.)

Like most wondrous things, life with Cathy came to an end when MOM (hers) said we were getting too serious. Well, high school was coming to an inglorious end anyway and, though savagely crushed, I recovered enough to look to the future—night college, day job, money to spend, independence. Yay!

The working world turned out to be an embarrassment of riches where the opposite sex was concerned. My night college classes yielded only a handful of bookish females of indeterminate ages, who, as they peered above their spectacles, let me know I was out of their league. But my day job as an advertising copywriter for a leading department store brought not one but TWO attractive women into the field of play. Zita was a stablemate across the aisle who smoked incessantly but had bewitching gray eyes and black hair. Rona was a French speaker in the translation department who spoke near-perfect English, was clearly older than me and had lovely blonde hair to complement her light brown eyes. A delicious dilemma.

In time and with discretion, a sorting out had to happen and it did. Zita, an interesting but very conservative contemporary, withdrew from the running when she announced that she was returning to her home province of Saskatchewan. Could my waffling have precipitated her move? I'd never find out, because the older Rona was, in her breezy Gallic way, more fun to be with and a well-accessorized dresser. I mean, what a bonus to date a woman who could teach you about Christian Dior and French kissing all in the same evening! Suffice it to say we became lovers, a perfect blend of unserious fun and passionate lovemaking.

By then, I was in my mid-twenties, and after a couple of years with Rona, bade her farewell to fulfill a lifelong dream of going around the world. It was not an easy parting, but soon, a new world of different cultures and languages opened up and I devoured it readily. And after a number of adventures and misadventures on the road, I began to distinguish between love and lust. (I can hear my callous friend, who warned me of the difference years earlier, say "I told you so.")

And now? I maintain that in my relationships I can say that love—to some degree—figured in all of them (well, almost all). I also learned that my prime criteria of "appearance" was misleading and certainly superficial. Character and caring, loyalty and flexibility are much more important. These discoveries opened possibilities to more meaningful relationships that led to two fulfilling marriages—first with Lynn from Iowa (14 years), the second with Claudia from Southern California (21 years and counting).

After decades of amateurish "research" I've concluded that love is an ongoing process, complex and rich. And lust? Well, for one, it's a lot less complex and certainly fleeting. Hmmm.

(This is a true story with names changed to protect the innocent—and not so innocent.)

McKenzie Baptism

I plunge into the river
Like a sinner about to be reborn -
And emerge refreshed, renewed,
Glad to be alive.

Aware only of this body,
No thoughts, no worries.
Inner heat resists cold,
Feet recoil from jagged rocks.

I rise to the surface,
Stroking the water first urgently
And then with confidence -
Bathing in liquid summer.

~ Rachel Rich

My Creation

If I were someone else,
who would I choose to be?
I'm the one that I created.
I'll not give up on me.

The life I've lived was filled with joy,
Some pain, more love, more care.
Where I've fallen short of aim
Revealed a fuller share.

No cosmic force has shaped me,
Not genes, nor fate, nor scam.
For each effect there is a cause.
I chose the who I am.

There were those who prodded,
Who nudged, who led my hand.
They let me make my own mistakes
As now I understand.

Sometimes I chose to flounder
Or want a different row.
We don't select our garden space,
But choose how far we grow.

~ Gus Daum

Grow or Die
By Judy Dellar

In the mid-1970s when I was in my early thirties, I experienced a plague of deaths among many close friends and family members. Some were young and their deaths were unexpected and especially tragic. Others, such as my beloved Uncle Jack, were no spring chickens, but still seemed too young to die. I found myself feeling depressed and powerless in the face of these uncontrollable scenarios. Frustration led me to search for an opportunity to participate in the process of death and dying in a positive way.

So, I was thrilled and honored to be selected as a therapist at the Los Angeles Center for the Healing Arts—a venue designed for people with life-threatening or terminal illnesses. It was designated as the first West Coast outpost of the renowned Dr. Carl Simonton's holistic health training program. Simonton had developed an innovative approach to treating people whose diseases were usually dosed with toxic chemotherapy and radiation without addressing the needs of the whole person.

He postulated that the interaction between mind, body and spirit impacts the course and outcome of disease, general health and well-being. His theory was that beliefs, attitudes, lifestyle choices, and psychological factors influence wellness and that illness could provide a path to spiritual growth. This spiritual component could lead to prolonging survival time and improving quality of life.

The Center's mission aimed to apply his philosophy to the holistic treatment of our clients. Our intention was to blend the services of traditional healers, spiritual teachers, and therapists using various modalities. The program we devised offered individual and group psychotherapy, yoga, meditation, journaling, art and writing workshops, as well as community gatherings.

As the curriculum developed, the healing power of laughter was integrated using some of the self-healing techniques of the writer, Norman Cousins,* who conquered a near fatal collagen disease through the use of humor. He felt that the comedy of the Marx Brothers and Laurel and Hardy were particularly therapeutic, and suggested that *Hearty laughter is a good way to jog internally without having to go outside.*

The Center's founding staff were well-known and highly respected in their fields and provided credibility to our fledgling endeavor. What was I doing there among the illustrious faculty, you may wonder? It probably didn't hurt that I was a Marriage and Family Therapist with a personal and professional interest in death, dying and grief issues.

There was also the factor that, with the exception of the senior staff, we facilitators were willing to contribute our services as unpaid volunteers. Aside from the personal satisfaction of working with clients who were open to growth and change in an experimental setting, we were offered the priceless opportunity to train with senior staff members.

Our participants came from all walks of life and differed widely in their approaches to illness and death. Not surprisingly, many exhibited classic symptoms of grief and loss including fear, anger, denial, depression and anxiety. Most were receptive to the radical treatment ideas the program espoused, but there was also a minority of skeptics who challenged the concept that spirituality and positive attitudes could affect the course of their illnesses.

Staff members strongly encouraged clients to open their hearts and minds and participate in the therapeutic opportunities. Some of the therapists were so aggressively enthusiastic that many participants paradoxically demanded that they, the therapists, "grow or die," lampooning the message the therapists projected. The phrase became a motto and was a prime example of the dark humor that some who faced death developed.

As the end of life drew closer, many clients reported experiencing significant reduction of fear and anxiety; meaningful instances of spiritual comfort; a sense of personal empowerment; and acceptance of the final outcome of their illnesses as a result of the Center's approach.

A crucial aspect of the program was working with survivors of participants who had died. Many of the grieving had responses that mirrored the dying journeys of their loved ones. The more positive and accepting the participant's outlook on death, the more positive their survivor's resolution was likely to be.

Unfortunately, not everyone was able to cope with loss on a path that was headed directly toward closure. The 20-year-old granddaughter of one elderly client acted out by wearing her grandmother's clothes and moving into her apartment. A woman who had not come to terms with her husband's death transformed their home into a shrine to his memory.

Although the bereavement process was challenging and painful, through supportive grief therapy most were able to gain closure and complete the arc from death and dying to closure and peace. The process also helped me resolve the loss and grief over the epidemic of death in my own life. As they say, "Grow or die."

* *Anatomy of an Illness as Perceived by the Patient,* by Norman Cousins

I Write For Them

I write for them,
my friends who no longer know my name, nor
    my face.
For the friend who heard my written card, yet
    didn't know me.
I write for the friend, college administrator,
Who now can't recall how to write his check.
I watch him pause, not knowing whether to offer
    help or to remain silent.

I write for the friend who taught students with
    me,
Laying down her life for learners,
Helping me set up my classroom,
Bringing me mashed potatoes after knee surgery
Because she was wise enough to ask, and to hear
    what I wanted,
And who now does not recognize our memories.

I write, laboring with the words,
While I still have them.
Savoring them, rolling them around on my
    tongue.
For I understand that just as questioningly
It could be me with the blank stare,
Hearing, not recognizing.

I write for you my friends
Honoring the brilliant minds you had
And your ability to move people with words, with
    passion.
Perhaps the treasure of
    seeing and using words will
    stay with me.
Perhaps not.
I feel constrained then to
    write... for me, for
    you.

I remember your
    words.
I remember your love to me.

I still hear you.

~ Kathryn Fisher

Anchored to a Storm
By John Henry

It was the first day of another school year and Carl carried his angry attitude like a loaded gun. He had a widowed mom and four older sisters who took the fun out of summer. His sisters reveled in smothering him, the baby of the family. He knew he would be so bored again this school year. His sisters ruled his world at home which explained why Carl had fought most of the boys in his class last year and didn't get along with any of the girls. Carl would have few pleasant surprises from Miss Crumback, the sixth grade teacher, whom all his sisters also had for their sixth grade. Possibly, if there had been a talented and gifted program, but no... Carl was unchallenged and stifled and lumped in with mediocrity. He was sitting by himself at a table for two students but none of the other students wanted Carl's surly company.

Carl had his head down and was ignoring Miss Crumback's first day of school 'carrot and stick' lecture. Then a new girl walked into the room. The teacher gasped and the students snickered nervously. Carl lifted his head in time to see the new girl slam the classroom door and strut over and sit at the empty chair at his table. She examined him with narrowed baby blue eyes and softly murmured, "Mess with me and I'll beat the snot out of you."

Miss Crumback cleared her throat and stammered, "CLASS, settle down. Young lady, please introduce yourself and tell the class something about where you came from and what your father does. And please stand while addressing the class."

The new girl stood up and Carl could see she was short and skinny. She had brown hair that looked like an Afro, wore eye make-up, and had a flannel shirt and overalls on. Carl noticed she didn't smell girly at all. The new girl turned to the class and leaned on the desk.

"Hi. My friends call me Stormy because I was born on my mother's fishing boat in a hurricane. My mother is a sea captain and she claims she threw my father overboard before I was born. Our boat's in dry-dock and I'll be here until she's ready to go to Alaska."

Carl's jaw was the only one in the room not hanging open after Stormy finished. He had a grin and would have held her chair for her if she wouldn't have punched him. Stormy sat down, cracked her knuckles, and frowned at him. Carl was smitten. He knew that today and as long as Stormy was around, school would be great.

At recess, the three bullies in the sixth grade came over to see how bad Stormy really was. Carl was nearby when the toughest bully, Billy, said, "Girl or half-girl, or whatever you are, if you want to fight, you'll get more than you can handle. You're a shrimp and we'll pound you." Billy tried snarling like his older brother did to frighten her.

Stormy smiled brightly. "Do you want to fight me one at a time or all at once?"

Carl walked past Stormy and punched Billy and bloodied his nose. He swung a roundhouse right hand at a second tough and ended up wrestling him to the ground.

The playground was yelling "FIGHT, FIGHT, FIGHT..."

Stormy's assessment afterward was that, for a sixth grader, Carl had fought pretty good; but if he ever interfered in her business again, she would have to beat him to a pulp.

Carl's life was changed. He loved going to school. Every day was an adventure. Stormy's mother, the Captain, was the mom Carl had always dreamed about. The Captain smoked a pipe and drank beer out of a bottle. She talked about the sea and fishing. Her hands were like iron. The Captain took Stormy and him out shooting and she and Stormy were crack shots. Carl learned a lot about life that year. He broke the chains of his sisters. He knew a girl who was fair, smart and tough. He had found a girl who didn't play games with his head.

Stormy went off to Alaska in May of that year. Carl skipped school and went down to the docks to see her off. He helped lug the provisions on board but mostly kept out of the way. Finally the Captain told Stormy to say goodbye, they had to shove off. Stormy walked Carl off the boat. She stuck her hand out to shake and said, "OK Matey, school wasn't bad with you to cut up with. Maybe, we'll see each other sometime."

Carl looked at the sea gulls circling the bay. Then he looked into Stormy's blue eyes and knew that what he was feeling wasn't anything his twelve years had prepared him for. He heard Stormy's mother yelling for her to hurry up and the big engines on the trawler had started. Carl swallowed a big lump and wanted to look away and say something tough, but he couldn't. His eyes were leaking a little and his voice was going to shake but he only had this one opportunity before Stormy was rolling away on the high seas and probably gone forever. Carl decided he had nothing to lose. He grabbed her little calloused hand tight and got almost nose to nose with her, looking maybe for the last time into the lapis pools of her eyes. Carl whispered, "I'd go with you right now to Alaska if you and your mom would let me. I want you to be a good friend of mine no matter where you sail off to."

Captain was yelling bloody murder for Stormy to come aboard this instant. Stormy's eyes were glistening and she stayed close to Carl. Stormy spoke above the diesel engine's thumping. "OK, I'll see if it works being your friend." And she pulled away and reached in her back pocket and pulled out a paper and wrote a post office box address in Alaska on it.

"Write to me if you want." She walked back on board and the ship was cast off and with a wave they were gone.

Carl wrote semi-regularly. The next two summers, his mom knew he'd run away if he had to; so she allowed him to take a bus up to Sitka, Alaska and work on the Captain's boat.

The following year Stormy came back to school and sat by Carl while their boat was repaired. In the spring Stormy left port with the Captain for fishing off South America. Carl went to the dock to see them off. Stormy had kissed him this year and Carl knew he would miss her a lot. Stormy smiled at Carl and said, "So Carl, my soon-to-be long-distance friend again, any last words for me."

Carl flinched, but she was right that this might be the last time he saw or talked to her. Carl put his hands on her shoulders and he had shortness of breath. The Captain was yelling to stow it and get a move on. Carl just blurted it out. "I don't know about you but, me... well, I kind of love you. And I think I'd love you if you... even if you lost a leg or I never see you again. I've got another seventy years if I live as long as my Grandpa and I, sort of, ah, might like to spend some of them with you. Right now, I'm stuck here. I mean, ah, we have no choice because, uhm, ah, you're living on your boat. So my last words are ... ah, I want to be a friend, ah, you love." And he looked away hoping she wouldn't slap him or tell him to go to hell.

Stormy put her hands on his shoulders, too, and became very serious. "You know that I'll never be an easy person to be around. If I agree to let you love me, you have to accept me as I am, not like you want your girl friend to be. I think I might be more than you can handle. I'm a gypsy and a pirate and a little bastard."

Carl smiled and nodded and they squeezed each other's shoulders. She went back on board the ship and then turned around and came back to him. She smiled sadly and said, "You have to fit in my life, you know. I'll need a doctor or a lawyer when I grow up. So those might be good jobs for the seventy years you want to be my friend." And Carl watched Stormy and the Captain's ship motor away, hoping she wasn't laughing at him.

Carl got a tattoo of an anchor with Stormy written underneath it when he graduated from high school. And like a lucky penny that you lose and find just when you need it most,

Stormy came back into Carl's life again and again. He went to medical school and most of Stormy's stitches have come from Carl's needles. He now practices medicine in Sitka, Alaska and claims Stormy is his best customer. Captain Stormy often comes into port there and spends her winters with Carl.

And, Carl has delivered their two daughters who live happily with him.

Rainbow

Pine peaks awash;
chill raindrops drop
from each needle.

Dripping, dropping,
notes of wet,
steady rhythm.

Across the roof
our liquid lullaby
dances through sleepy heads,

until, from under
heavy eyelids, we see...
a muted glow.

Dare we lift the shades
to see only a foggy diffusion
of damp?

Of course we dare!
In the cloud scatter,
a bright orb awakens
our iridescent world,

sprinkling prisms across
the sky to project
on a misty screen

our rainbow arc of spring's hope
for green Umpqua,
resting among the peaks.

~ Joanne Sprott

Relax, Everybody
By David Erickson

Relax, everybody. I believe there is a light at the end of this scary tunnel, beyond our tragi-comedic blip of an existence—including the extended version wherein the last of a ragtag band of Scorched Earth Rambos put up a valiant fight, through hordes of sub-human revenants, across Biblical-level apocalyptic hellscapes, to storm their way aboard the Arc. They arrive just as the Privileged are embarking. Met with superior force, naturally, they are cast down and the Privileged depart. Cue stirring overture. Earth will adapt and create something with the horror and filth we've left in our slipstream. Look at the Fukushima tomatoes. Earth will be fine.

In no time, geologically speaking, creative, albeit catastrophic, solutions around the globe will scour out most of the deadwood. The Cascadia subduction zone and Yellowstone caldera being merely local examples of organic cleansing resources already primed and aquiver with potential. There are so many others.

Oddly enough, Styrofoam® will turn out to be all Earth really needed from us anyway. George Carlin prophesied it years ago. Cetaceans will develop flippers with opposable thumbs. Their distant progeny will find the Arc orbiting one of the Jovian moons, mostly intact. No contact will be attempted. Some history doesn't have to be written down.

But what about us?

Okay, what about us? We came. We saw. We pissed all over it and left in a huff.

Forever.

If that's not a light, what is it?

The Ergmaster 500

By Tony Hyde

Palo Alto, California, November 1964

I had decided to attend the University of Michigan. This meant returning the furniture that I had borrowed during my one year stay in Northern California. We had rented a small, two-bedroom house in Mountain View. How we managed to find room for everything, I'll never know.

I told my cousin Norman, that we were leaving. Norm was the older brother that I'd never had. Our experiences together spanned war time England, post-war high school into the '50s, and several years in Northern Canada. He had the uncanny knack of evoking in me opposing feelings of humor and warmth on the one hand and irritation on the other. It was a relationship of mixtures of love and jealousy—at least on my part.

Norm had loaned me a minor amount of household items, plus his combination washer and dryer, the Ergmaster 500. Who the manufacturer of this contraption was, I never knew. Anybody who knew Norm will attest to his persuasive powers. He had somehow acquired the Ergmaster in a deal while buying and selling houses in the Menlo Park area. Norm had no place to put it, so when I had announced that I would be open to some loaners or donations, he quickly assured me that my life would not be complete without the Ergmaster 500.

"But Norm, I don't have a gas hook-up available for the dryer portion," I reasoned with him.

"Don't worry about it," he said to me. "You just use the washer and hang the wet clothes on a clothesline to dry. After all, this IS California. They'll be dry in no time. You'll save a bundle of money by not using a coin laundry and save on the utilities too—you can't lose."

Norm proceeded to explain to me how this beast worked or would work if hooked up properly.

During the lecture, on several occasions, he mentioned that the machine had cost over $500 new and in his mind it was still as pristine as when it came off the showroom floor. In his own unique way, he was telling me that it was a highly valuable treasure that I should look after. Subtlety had never been a strong point with Norm. He completed his oration by taking out his handkerchief and polishing the knobs and saying "Now take special care of it, and don't screw it up."

I couldn't resist remarking that it really was a strange name for a washer. Norm loved it. To him ergs exemplified the way of the future, energy-defined in metric units. Norm got into full stride on the topic. Since he was teaching Physics at the college level at the time, I figured I'd let it go without argument.

The Ergmaster had sat quietly in my house for just over a year. The fact was, we needed more storage space and a round dryer drum doesn't work that well when trying to stack square boxes in to it. Without fully realizing it, we had been intimidated by this machine. Supposing this mechanical mystery had ever quit! How would we ever find someone to fix it? They'd probably have needed a Ph.D. in Physics.

Norm's schedule was always hectic, but we'd made arrangements to move the washer on a Saturday morning. Moving it was a strain for us both. Norm was 6'5", with an athletic build. I considered myself to be in reasonable shape too. We finally got it up into an old farm trailer that I had hauled down from Canada. We tied down the ends of the machine with strong cord, gave a few last test tugs on the rope and we were on our way to Menlo Park.

Several blocks from home, I had to make a left turn into Middlefield Road. Pulling into traffic required a rapid maneuver. I checked in the rear view mirror as we turned. At that moment, time went into slow motion. Through the mirror, I witnessed the maiden voyage of the Ergmaster 500. Earthly constraints were no match for it. It soared into space. While its flight was a short one, it had certain majesty about it. Norm missed the actual flight, but managed to catch the dancing, choreographed to perfection, of the various pieces that had been so much a part of the Ergmaster 500. The little knobs bounced in unison, sheet metal floated like migrating geese; pulleys, gears and springs mushroomed out of its interior. Black hoses and belts waved in such contrast past the enameled white sides, moving as if guided by the hands of a mad pianist.

Norm didn't have too much to say at this point, which was unusual for him. We both got out of the car and had to suffer the indignities of retrieving the broken pieces as motorists picked their way through the debris. Many of them saw fit to share with us how much they had enjoyed the show.

We pulled into the San Mateo county garbage dump site, where the stench of decaying vegetable matter permeated the air. A big surly individual wearing a dirty vest, a greasy Giants hat and a cigar in his mouth came over and looked in the back of the trailer. He grunted through clenched teeth, "It's gonna cost ya a buck to dump that load of crap."

A wry smile came over Norm's face. In a moment of unbridled generosity, I said "It's ok, Norm, I'll pay for it."

On Being a Woman

Women love their toenails
cleaned, trimmed, and sometimes painted.
Raspberry,
Chinese red,
Or "I eat Mainely Lobster" Pink.
Pink is my choice for today.

~ Lona Feldman

Change

There is a special moment
when I can decide
how to live my life,
and that is
each moment.

There is no moment
when I can decide
how you
shall live yours.

~ Gus Daum

Birkenstocks

I was in the midst of my "poor years"
Too long out of work, back on the job just a short while
I splurged and bought my first pair of
    Birkenstocks
I had never worn such things, they were a sign of
    change
I was starting over again, it felt good
And they felt good, those trendy leather sandals

I was driving down the highway on a warm
    summer's day
Wearing my Birkenstocks, of course
And then it happened, I passed one of those guys
You know, walking down the shoulder of the road
Shabby backpack on his back, long greasy hair,
Clothes worn a few weeks or months too long

There, on the gravel strewn shoulder
He walked … barefoot

A sudden impulse hit me.
Having already passed him, I pulled over
Took off my Birkenstocks
And dropped them on to the shoulder

I don't know if they fit him
Don't know if he'd ever wear them
But he obviously needed them more than I did
I waved and drove on knowing someday
I'd be able to get another pair

And, somehow, giving felt so much better than
    having.

~ Jim Burnett
Groundwaters Vol 7 Iss 1 (2010)

Scraps Upon the Floor

A pertinacious breed we are!
Embracing complicated chores
we strive to see our work esteemed,
and discount scraps upon the floor.

The Sculptor

The sculptor scans the uncut stone
assessing fractures, flaws and streaks
imagining what hides within
and waiting for the rock to speak.

In time the treasure trapped inside
no longer is a thing of doubt,
and so, with grinder, chisel, saw
the sculptor works to bring it out.

With overburden stripped away
the stone is valued so much more,
but worthless is the useless rubble
scattered on the workshop floor.

The Carpenter

The project more than just unique,
instructions clear and understood,
the builder and his rag-tag crew
cut and shape the gopher wood.

Though size extreme and budget nil
they stay on task a hundred years
content to focus on the work
and disregard their mocking peers.

The monster boat at last complete,
the builder looks about and smiles
knowing well the pending flood
will scatter scraps they stacked in piles.

The Inventor

A glow, a thought, a hazy dream
matures a notion to a goal
and captivates a human mind,
inflaming both the heart and soul.

For many years they tried and failed
until the point in time was right
when Edison transformed the world
with something called electric light.

Last in line of those who tried,
success was finally his to own,
and all the failures on the way
his victory would just postpone.

The Marriage

They say it's true that love is blind
and human flaws can be ignored,
so, wed we do when young and raw,
the path ahead still unexplored.

Then as we walk, there comes a change
when 'I' replaces 'we' and 'us,'
intolerance and doubts rise up,
and something ravages our trust.

But those who wake the promises
affirmed in public years before
can reconnect a broken link
and bury scraps upon the floor.

The Writer

Inspired, the writer makes some notes
to capture thoughts that come to mind,
and though prepared to process words,
still fuzzy is the story line.

But waiting for the tale to gel
would be to err 'cause writers know
that once begun, the plot matures
as time and focus make it flow.

Then when the piece is fully writ--
revisions done forevermore--
they revel in the finished work
and shred the scraps upon the
floor.

Yes, humans are a dogged sort.
Accepting of impassioned chores
we strive to see our work
admired,
content that scraps may hide the
floor.

~ Wayne Westfall

Word Quilts
By Jeanette-Marie Mirich

I'm cleaning off my cutting table so Rod can spread papers over it. Tax season approacheth. As a quilter, it is difficult to order my kaleidoscope of colors, for scraps of cotton call me to imagine how they might be used. Tiny white squares, I place in bags, red hunks into plastic bins and the blue ones in a to-do pile.

Since Rod was in medical school, I've quilted. The first quilts were for the neonatal unit at the hospital. The next were as colorful, often tied with yarn, easy to wash and for our children. When I was forcing fabric into patterns, I was also shaping words. Odd remnants of thoughts collide still and begin to form a story, a poem, or a smart remark. Pieced together they can make something.

The prose and poetry I scribbled in earlier days were serviceable but without layers of meaning. C.S. Lewis writes in his essay on Historicism, 'pre-historic poetry has perished because words before writing are winged.' As my words flitted away, lost in papers when we moved or on floppy drives that are unusable, I'm wondering what should have been saved. Tending to be practical, I long to enwrap those I love so they are embraced with quilts and poetry. For me the thoughts were not treasured like the square of fabric from my daughter's skirt or my dad's shirts that could make stuffed animals.

Like my writing, the quilts I create tell stories. There was the season of embellishments, like a gothic novel complete with overused and repetitive stitches. Or the minimalist period of quilting when I used stark colors and drama, think my terse reporter short story. My love of creating mayhem in a Kentucky small town is seen in my applique, pieced and embroidery quilts. Why does a quarter inch stitch help me to think how to hide a murder weapon? I do not know how my mind works. Neither does my indulgent spouse.

In writing I want to create beauty that reflects God's love. In the process of stitching words together, sometimes the pattern is awkward, misshapen, or confusing. Then I get to unsew words. Although necessary, editing leaves piles of words scattered around my feet like discarded threads.

Are the frayed things in my life tripping me and keeping me from walking with grace in this creative journey God has me walking?

Sounds of Work

We wage-slave in the Colorado Rockies—
an earth-fill dam.
As jackhammers cool,
my partner floats his ample belly
on the upright handle,
and imitates a tenor Johnny Cash.

In a remote Utah forest,
my uncle blades slick pitchy pine bark
off measured mine timbers,
voicing an old hymn:
"Life Is Like A Mountain Railroad."

Through Central Oregon's summer scorch
our fire "hand-crew" tent-camps in the pines.
We hose lightning strikes and wildland fires.
Riding on the sweaty crew bus, Carl warbles
love to the young ladies of the group.
His wife elbows him and giggles.

As framing carpenters
here in Green River, Wyoming,
we swing 22 ounce claw hammers.
Driving 16 penny sinkers,
our rhythm counterpoints
with the tinny radio's top 40 tunes.

A rhythm or a song—
one can't remain angry and hateful
during work.

~ Dave Polhamus

Grandma's Quilt—A Legacy of Life
By Mildred "Millie" Thacker Graves

A quilt is a wonderful thing. It warms you, it enfolds you, it shields and protects you. It comforts you!

I think of my family as a quilt, a quilt of many colors, shades and hues. Each family member is different. All are unique individuals and that is what makes life interesting and motherhood a challenge. Whether their characteristics are bold, daring, dainty, subdued, colorful or a combination of traits, it matters not. What does matter is that as each piece is necessary for the beauty of the finished quilt, each person is equally important to the completeness of the family.

Can you imagine a quilt if all the pieces were the same size and the same color? It would be a very bland, nondescript and uninteresting quilt. On the other hand, think of a quilt as a rainbow of colors, exploding into a creative design and held together by tiny stitches of love and care. Just like the pieces of a quilt are held together by tiny stitches, a family is held together by a continuous thread of life which connects us all. The thread is magical because it knows no bounds. It connects me to my family near and far, here on earth and beyond.

We need to celebrate our differences and individuality. We should not be a carbon copy of another person. Be the real thing! Develop your own style. *To thine own self be true.*

Here I am... a blend of all those persons who have gone on before me. What I am, I owe to them. I hope I can make them proud as I walk that straight line, just as the stitches in the quilt followed one another like tiny footsteps on an uncharted plain. I go forward with a goal in my mind and love in my heart. It's my legacy!

Footnote: The story behind Grandma's Quilt was a "learning lesson" for my children and other children, in the hope that each of them did not need to strive to be like their brother or sister or friend.

Like A Quilt

Life is like a pattern
Like the patches on a quilt
Some are dark, some are light–
The squares from which it's built.

The light ones are like sunshine
And the dark would be the rain
Some patterns are real pretty;
Others are very plain.

Life is just that way.
It's not always joy and cheer
Sometimes we have worries,
Sometimes we have fear.

Now, look, those pretty patches
Never would be seen,
If it were not for all those dark ones
We stitched neatly in between.

~ Rosanna Martin

The Old Quilt by Walter Langley

Dead Knife
By Brian Palmer

The black-haired teenager riding for his life on the back of the handsome thoroughbred knew the chase would be over in a mile or less. He knew he had run his horse to death and he would never live to tell anyone how far, fast and hard the animal had run. The boy was scared as hell, but his heart was pounding with pride for the animal as much as from fear for himself. The horse belonged to the company, but he could usually ask for the animal he had come to depend on. There would never be another horse like Jacob.

Their run had begun at the Kennekuk station, Kansas territory, several miles back. They were both rested and watered for the 12 miles or so to the next station, the Kickapoo. He would change mounts there and twice more before arriving at Seneca station, a little north and 60 miles further west.

He had ridden for the Express for four months and this had been his route from the beginning. He knew every inch of the terrain in both directions by heart. Every dead tree snag, every swale and creek bed, every stand of Hickory and Live Oak. He knew what prairie dog patches to avoid and what good, long flat stretches to keep to. He got a kick out of spooking pheasant or feral pigs. He laughed when the pigs scurried away in 50 directions all at once like a bunch of cockroaches.

But he wasn't laughing now.

He had picked up the Paiute raiders less than five miles from Kennekuk. He had seen them slide in behind him from the north and there were four of them. They all rode mustangs, smaller sturdy mounts that were made for rugged, uneven terrain. He had hoped they came up on him by chance, maybe while they were out hunting. But when he veered off his trail and slowed down through an oak thicket, they changed direction with him and maintained their distance of about 400 yards.

He knew that the Paiutes had killed some riders, that they were meaner than hell and if they were in fact about to try chasing him down it was going to be all he could do to stay alive. He had seen scalps on war lances before and had wondered what kind of devil could do that to a man.

As close as he could figure, he was at best halfway from the Kickapoo station. That meant six or seven miles at either a dead run or dodging and evading the riders. But as much as he wanted to bolt and run Jacob at a full gallop, he knew the horse couldn't sprint that far. They would chase him in turns like wolves and run him to ground.

He and his father had once crossed a mountain lion on a deer hunt. They had seen the big cat for a moment but it had ducked into the underbrush to get behind them. He had wanted to run for his life then, but his dad explained what they would do.

"Son, if we run that's what he wants and he'll get us in about a hundred feet. But we can't sit here all day either. When it's dark he'll catch one or both of us. We either draw him into the open for a good shot or we get out of this thicket slow and careful, but not too damn slow."

He would have to evade them while not being too damn slow about it.

At a quick, three-legged canter he began weaving his way a little further south, into stands of trees and tall grass. After what he thought was maybe a half mile, he turned back to the northwest and looked behind him. The raiders were closing the gap, they had gained a hundred yards or so. Of course, they knew where he was trying to escape to, they would have to make their move on him in three or four miles, maybe less. He checked his revolver again, making certain it was holstered but not tied down. The express riders didn't carry rifles, they were considered excess weight for the horses.

He had to cross an opening of maybe a quarter mile and he got his first good look at his pursuers. They had closed the gap again and he could see them leaning forward on their mounts and yelling back and forth at each other, planning the chase and kill.

Down and into a dry creek bed he led Jacob, the horse navigating the rocks and limbs. He stayed in the shallow bed for a few dozen yards, concealed just a bit by the embankment and overhanging Cypress and Chinkapin Oak limbs. He left the creek bed and turned west again, trying not to lose too much ground while avoiding them.

As worried as he was about escaping, part of him was riled that he had to run at all. He knew he wasn't being yellow, what he wanted was the chance to have a good fistfight with one of them and put an end to this. He was only 17 but he had been in a scrape or two and figured he could whip at least one of them. What he didn't know was that one of the four was a brave named Dead Knife. He had made many men dead with his blade and fought like a wounded animal. Dead Knife was much more of a throat cutter than a fist fighter.

Now in the open again, he spurred Jacob just a little harder, heading toward what was left of an old corn field. Settlers had abandoned the farm the field was part of, and many times he had ridden past the shack and outhouse that remained of the place. He was now pretty much back on his main route and he gathered his bearings. In a straight line he had right at four miles to safety. The Paiutes would never chase him all the way to the Kickapoo station. Daring as they were, they weren't completely reckless.

As he crossed into the corn field, he could see them again over his shoulder. Now they were damn close and riding harder. He unholstered his revolver, a Colt Paterson .36 caliber. The cylinder held five rounds and he carried the gun half cocked, the hammer over a loaded cylinder. It was a dangerous practice, as the gun could fire accidentally, but this run for his life was exactly why he carried it that way. He put the gun in his right hand and the reins in his left. He was a good shot, but knew that firing from horseback at all

was a tricky proposition at best, much less over his shoulder at four moving targets trying to kill him.

Out of the field and through another creek bed, he found himself within sight of a fairly large stand of Sycamores. He could make for the trees but knew he had to be careful not to get cornered in a briar patch or some unseen rock formation. On the run he had a chance, but if he let himself get cornered in the trees he knew he was as good as dead.

He took another look behind, 50 yards from the trees, at the same second Dead Knife cut loose with a panther scream that curdled his stomach and instantly raised every hair on his body. The brave had made his move in the corn field, out of sight of the 17-year-old Pony Express rider.

He had kicked his Mustang hard and was at a dead gallop, now 100 yards or less behind and screaming at the top of his lungs. His companions had fallen off the chase and couldn't be seen. Either they had given up or Dead Knife wanted the rider for himself. His wild mane of ebony hair and necklaces made of bones and arrow heads flew wildly all around him. He looked for all the world like a wild-eyed screaming demon flying towards the boy atop a devil horse.

The boy yanked Jacob's reins hard left and spurred him to a full gallop. The brave was too close for trying to outfox in the trees. The cat and mouse game was over, now it was a flat out run for his life. He turned and tried to take aim with his revolver, but the Paiute was now nearly flat on his Mustang and was just a sliver of a target charging at full speed. Still, the boy took a shot and cussed himself for trying at that distance. He missed by 30 feet.

Here the Express rider recognized the terrain again. He had been through here a few weeks ago, looking for a short cut. And it would have been a good one at that, shaving a couple miles off the route, if he had been delivering mail 10,000 years earlier. Since then, the Delaware river had cut a wide and deep swath of earth away from its bed and what lay 500 yards in front of the rider now was a riverbank that dropped straight down 30 feet to the water. A half mile south, the riverbed was low and gradually sloped, an easy place to cross.

He could veer south again for the easy crossing, but he would have to slow Jacob nearly to a walk through and around a huge sticker patch between the trail and the riverbank, exactly what he had to avoid. The Paiute would surely catch him there and God only knew how long he could hold his own in there until the other three joined in again.

While these thoughts were raging in his brain he blinked at an arrow whistling under his chin, coming from behind and from his left quarter. He looked in that direction and Dead Knife was galloping less than 50 feet away, nocking another arrow. He knew the savage wouldn't miss again.

He raised and fired the big Paterson twice and saw the second bullet clip the Mustang's flank. The horse flinched and slowed for a dozen strides, but the brave kicked it hard and was aiming the second arrow. He let the missile fly at the same instant the rider fired again. The bullet ripped through Dead Knife's left forearm but missed the bone completely, while the arrow cut a shallow ditch across the boy's lower back, from kidney to kidney.

The Paiute simply dropped his bow and drew his knife, as if he'd been bitten by a small dog or was quite accustomed to being shot in the arm in a gunfight. The boy could see murder in the Indian's eyes and spurred Jacob again. He knew he didn't have much choice or horse remaining.

He was looking wildly to his left, trying to gauge distances when his heart nearly stopped with fright. Two more Paiutes were coming straight at him from the sticker patch, riding fresh Paint horses. It had been an ambush all along. They were herding him to the cliff at the river just like he had helped his dad round up strays back home. He couldn't possibly get to the safe part of the river by going through all three of them.

With nothing left to do the boy spurred his fine animal a last time, knowing they would both be scalped or drowned in about two minutes. Jacob was running his lungs out and the boy knew it.

Now all three raiders were closing in and the rider took another shot at the closest one. The bullet missed but the Paiute ducked hard and pulled his animal too hard to the right in the frenzy of the melee. The animal stumbled and crashed headlong at full gallop, breaking a leg and throwing its rider into a tree stump, killing him outright.

With the remaining killers nearly close enough to touch, it was a mad sprint to the river's embankment.

The last 200 yards to the river were a blur to the 17-year-old. He knew full well the drop would likely maim or kill him. If he didn't break his neck on a hidden log, the horse could just as easily crush him, but he damn sure wasn't going to die scalped or gutted like a hog.

He tried firing at Dead Knife again, but the Paterson that had served his father well fighting the Comanch a dozen years earlier, misfired. He threw the gun away from him and pushed Jacob to the limits of their lives and the banks of the Delaware river.

The animal saw the precipice 50 feet in front of him and like every other task he'd ever been given, he strained every sinew, every muscle to snapping in the effort. At the edge of the bank the horse somehow leapt a full 20 feet straight out and over the river.

For a moment in time, a moment the likes of which most men will never know, the earth and everything in her stood still and silent all around the rider. For that moment, when he and his Bay thoroughbred were laughing at gravity and the fates, he felt somehow free. Free and safe, hurtling through space with no screaming savages chasing him into hell, no river waiting to drown him. His body separated from the horse and his arms began to float up and away from his sides like a sparrow's wings caught in a powerful gust of wind.

Jacob's loyal, pounding heart burst in midair, the horse was dead before they both slammed into the water from 30 feet above. They were a tangled, thrashing mess of legs, saddle, horse and rider.

He heard the impact but felt nothing when he and the nearly thousand-pound animal crashed into the water like two flailing and doomed meteors. It sounded like the dynamite he had heard exploding at a rock quarry a year ago. But this was exploding on top of him.

After the explosion his world was silent. Even though his body mostly missed Jacob's at impact, the terrible force of the fall broke his jaw when he bit through his tongue, chipped two teeth and dislocated his right shoulder.

He didn't hear the gunfire coming from the opposite bank of the river as two men fired at the killers chasing him. The Paiutes had stopped short of the drop-off and were trying to ease down the bank to retrieve and murder their quarry. Someone was giving cover fire and Dead Knife and his brother-in-law, Catches Many Fish, had to retreat. There wouldn't be any scalping or gutting today.

He was already nearly unconscious but could think enough to hold his breath and kick to the surface. His head burst through the water and he attempted to swim towards the bank, but the searing pain in his shoulder caused him to black out completely.

His next sensation was being dragged like a ragdoll from the water. It felt like he was a 10-year-old child being tossed by his father in a game. Someone had him by his left arm and a leg and was pulling him out of the current and a dozen yards onto dry land, as if a few feet weren't enough. He was regaining his hearing and could hear their voices.

"Make sure them devils ain't crossing over someplace else."

"How many was there? I think there was two or three."

"I guess. I'll see if he's drowned, you get reloaded."

"Yep. Lord, you see how far that horse jumped? I thought they were gonna clear the whole river. Looked like they just fell out of the sky."

The boy was moving, trying to speak and sit up. He could barely move because of his shoulder and could hardly talk with his jaw broken and tongue bit to pieces.

"Who are… what are you… My shoulder…something's broke…"

"You damn right something's broke. Prob'ly your neck from that fall. Don't move too much. We ain't but a mile from the express station. You one of them riders, son?"

He grimaced and nodded his head, his eyes still tightly shut from the pain.

"You likely done with that outfit for a while. Your arm is hanging funny, I think you dislocated that shoulder. And your bleeding pretty bad from your mouth, son."

"I'm reloaded daddy. Is he alive?"

The half-crushed boy had opened his eyes and could see who had been talking and had jerked him out of the water.

"I'm Micah Turner. Some folk call me big Mike. This here is my boy Ed."

Micah Turner was a coal black giant. He stuck out his hand and the rider's hand nearly disappeared in the elder Turner's grasp when the two shook. It was no wonder he had thrown him from the river. He looked like he could hoist a half-grown cow over his head.

Micah's son Ed had walked closer and was smaller, but not by much.

"Howdy. Looks like you ain't drowned. Sorry about your horse. Looked like a thoroughbred, what little I seen of him. I never seen a horse jump that far."

"Me neither."

Micah spoke again.

"We'll get you to the Kickapoo stop over yonder, I believe they got a doc, might be a dentist that can help with whatever you broke. I don't know if we can get any of them letters back out of the water. What's your name, son?"

"Bill Hitt. I'm from Texas."

My Muse Lives There

Beneath the mountain
behind the clouds
somewhere out there
that's where she lives
she certainly doesn't live nearby
she will come when she is ready

She has come before
many times
but I can't remember the circumstances
I can't reproduce the situation
but I know I have shared her cookies
I have sipped her tea
and we have wandered together in the garden

You tell me you need her to visit
that you are stuck
and can't go on without her
she doesn't come on demand
you should know that
there is no need to call for her
to shout her name
to demand an audience
she only comes when she is ready

Shy and stubborn
she likes the shadows
where she feels safe
she hates being judged
judgments are like straight lines
and she is terrified of straight lines
neither does she respond to
confrontation or cross-examination
it will be on her terms or not at all
so check your impatience
do not wait in expectation
just do your work

That is why she likes the shadows
she can hide until you are working
or distracted or fully-absorbed
when she can sidle up close
peek over your shoulder
and if she decides,
leave a sprinkle of dust
or maybe even sit with
you at your table

And if she does visit, be warned
she may not stay long
she may bolt suddenly
and leave you stunned
wondering what has happened
leaving you with only faint hints
of your time together

What I do know is that
   she lives somewhere out there
beneath the mountains
behind the clouds
harvesting her magic garden
planning her next visits
so you must be ready
set her a table every day
do your work
   do not sit and wait
she will come when she is ready

~ Marv Himmel

Spring

For just a moment
I am the flowering trees
the butter-yellow daffodils
my molecules the fragrance
of newly mown grass
my heartbeat reflecting in birdsong.

Then I was a child skipping
along narrow, country roads.
Today, it is a swift stride
on a suburban sidewalk.

But oh
that sense of joy
and peace
and belonging
that urge to skip
that alive.

~ Susanne Twight-Alexander

The Shoeshine Man
By Dave Polhamus

I had pulled up into the elevated shoeshine chair. It felt comfortable, easy. The shine man began some chatter. He placed my feet on stands—metal risers. I was then reminded of the country/western song Johnny Cash sang about a shoeshine boy. I had folded and unfolded the boarding schedule several times, by now; would this indulgence be an inconvenience? Did I have enough time before my flight?

My teen-years mentor, Jack, came to mind. He had taught me to always have shiny shoes.

"People judge your character by your shoes—how neat and clean they are."

"Okay."

"Someday, have your shoes polished at a stand—by a professional. Give the man a big tip."

"Cause he'll do a good job, right?"

"Yeah, and you'll both be happy."

Today, was all that shoeshine man stuff overrated? Could it live up to its billing? Was it the same, 40-some years later?

As the man now tucked the loose ends and loops of my laces inside my shoes, he asked how I was. He pointed out that I needed to look good wherever I was going. I smiled, nodding.

In his tucking my laces out of the way, it reminded me of my barber throwing a cape 'round my shoulders prior to a haircut. It felt good—familiar. I was wearing black oxfords today. In applying various waxes and polishes, the man's hands seemed to caress, or work my feet—therapeutic. It reminded me of myself shining my shoes for Sunday School as a kid, years ago. His was an easy conversation, like talking with my barber. Time pressure had slipped my mind. I was relaxing. Several times, the man pulled up his buffing rag and snapped it tight, making a soft popping sound. At ease, I began taking a trip down memory lane.

I had an urge to tell the man I was here due to a former close friendship. Jack had been a father figure to me. He taught me the value of work. From time-to-time, he had talked of fighting in World War II.

"We battled the German troops. Later, we were assigned to be peace-keepers there after the war—the truce."

"Oh, okay. A change of efforts."

"Yeah, General Eisenhower said to not fraternize, but we did, some anyway."

At the time, that scenario was difficult for my teenage mind to accept—killing German people today, and wanting to have a relationship them tomorrow.

Way-back-when, Jack had effectively coached me through the procedure of changing gears in a truck without using the clutch—up and down the shifting pattern; pretty slick. I had practiced to a proficiency. In a remote central Oregon forest setting, he and I had used draft horses to skid logs to load onto a truck to a lumber mill. After work and dinner, we played cards—usually 5-card stud and using wooden stick matches for the pot ante. From time-to-time, we'd shoot illegal game meat—pretty much, living off the land. Other times, we ate chipped beef gravy on fried potatoes, or trout caught without a license.

Jack's attitude had piqued my mind about the shoeshine man—whoever he might be. That's why I was here, now.

Like all GIs in today's army, I'd brought my boots up to the "spit polish shine"—something I could see my reflection in. Even now I keep my shoes scuff-free. They weren't dull now, I'd just wanted them freshened up a bit.

This was the first time I'd had my oxfords done by a "professional." I'd used Greyhound Bus stations, my early years; and had traveled the rails 'til localized passenger service was no longer available. I'd been to other airports similar to this one—San Francisco, Salt Lake City, Denver, Portland, Chicago, Atlanta, DC, and several in Europe. These travel terminals all had shoeshine service available... I've never taken advantage of them before.

Perhaps it's the "plastic" service evident at airports now. Generic food, similarly uniformed airline personnel, and pre-recorded announcements; they give airline travel a one-size-fits-all feeling. Perhaps I'd wanted something personal in all this assembly-line business. The shoeshine man had given me 15 or 20 minutes of something I'd never had before, but had missed; if that makes sense. It made me smile—a warm feeling. Jack was right, it was the big deal. Stepping down off the elevated chair, I dug for my wallet. Back to reality—the here and now.

"That's great. I feel like a new man."

"Alright. Be cool. Have a good trip."

"Thank you, thank you."

I now had clean bright shoes. I also had a good memory of Jack, and a smile from a big tip to the shoeshine man. Why had I waited so many years? I had plenty of time to catch my flight, and the shoeshine man and I were both happy.

The Call of The Sea

The sea is calling out to me
Sitting on the sand in my chair
As the waves come on shore

I feel the breeze in the air and the blue skies
My toes curling in the sand
Sunlight shining bring

At the edge of the water
The splash
I try to stay upright

She says,
Welcome to the sea, my friend

Come on in, the water's fine!

~ Oswald Perez

Wild Children

Wild children,
We play in desert dust and dirt
In the trailer-court driveway.

Some of us are barefoot,
One has a runny nose,
Another a ragged dress.

A rattlesnake slithers up,
Coils, hisses,
Shakes its tail.

With one mind,
We form a circle,
Then each pick up a stone.

A volley of rocks
Slams the snake,
Crushing it flat and quiet.

Our circle
Grows smaller and smaller,
Until we stand silently together.

A dead snake
Lies in the center.
We smile in savage pleasure.

~ Rachel Rich

A Perfect Day

Singing with joy for the morn~
I am so happy I was born~

See the sun peeking through a cloud~
Makes me want to shout out loud~

Seeing the rainbow in the sky~
I wish for wings so I could fly~

To the wonders of this earth~
Where God's plan gave it birth~

Someday as it was foretold~
When we walk on the streets of gold.

~ Mildred "Millie" Thacker Graves

And Baby Makes Three
By Judy Dellar

It took some time to convince the labor nurses at Cedars Sinai Hospital that I was qualified to enter the hallowed halls of maternity land. It seemed that my girth was insufficient to convince them that I was indeed at full term and about to deliver with or without their permission. It only took twenty-seven hours of labor to prove my point to the skeptics.

Meanwhile, the angels of mercy demonstrated their mastery of the healing arts by abandoning me, contractions and all, in a bleak, freezing room. Occasionally one of them would wander in and half-heartedly perform an unpleasant intervention and then wordlessly leave. Twenty some hours later I delivered a beautiful and brilliant five-pound three-ounce baby girl who would remain in the hospital nursery until the pediatrician deemed her plump enough to be liberated. So it was that I departed the hospital holding a resentment against the doctor instead of holding my tiny baby.

When I returned home without Lauren, I had a busy schedule. I would awake at sunrise and begin my daily routine of ceaseless weeping. I eschewed food and coffee breaks in favor of a full menu of tears. One morning I stopped crying momentarily due to a shocking news bulletin from my husband. It seemed that my mother, in an uncharacteristically nurturing gesture, had offered to prepare dinner for us.

John had responded enthusiastically, as he was not receiving much sustenance from my lamentations. Before you could say "tuna casserole," the newly-minted grandmother arrived bearing a plucked chicken. She horrifyingly pointed out that we would be eating something that weighed more than Lauren. (If you look in the Guinness Book of World Records, you will see my name next to the entry for the fastest time ejecting an insensitive parent and her chicken).

After nearly a week, Lauren was freed and was soon ensconced in the cheerful red and white nursery we had prepared for her. Although her room was warm and welcoming, she may have longed to return to the safer precincts of Cedars after spending a few days with her anxious and klutzy new mother. During her first week in my care, I was so nervous that I pinned a diaper directly to her bottom and was so distraught by it that I accidently dropped her. Lauren survived the titanic disasters with no ill effects, but I took to my bed, traumatized by my fear of committing infanticide.

Miraculously, I managed not to wreak further havoc on her little self and she progressed to the stage of consuming pureed baby food. That Lauren Dellar was no fool! She rejected the little jars of unidentifiable mush in favor of a strict nutritional regimen of Cheerios and bacon. No other food substances were permitted past the barrier of her little pink gums. She made her position clear by emphatically shaking her head "NO!!!" and vehemently spitting out the offending baby fare. I felt that she had made an odd choice, but preferred it to the alternative of starvation. Visions of scurvy and beriberi danced in my head at her every so-called 'meal.'

Despite her gustatory peculiarities, Lauren was an irresistible little girl who had one wish in life: to have a "doggie" as her best friend. She was nearly three when we moved to a modest house in the suburbs with the best feature of all... a fenced backyard just made for a "doggie." So it was that Harry came into our previously peaceful lives.

Harry's pedigree didn't specify that he was certified to bounce off walls or spin madly around in circles, so his peripatetic antics came as a not so pleasant surprise. His specialty was welcoming visitors by leaping high into the air and depositing a generous splash of urine on their shoes to demonstrate his enthusiasm over their arrival.

Lauren provided a pragmatic solution to Harry's anti-social behaviors by rapping him smartly on his head with a metal potato masher that she stowed handily in her toy chest. Her disciplinary strategy caught Harry's attention and he became paranoid and wary of kitchen utensils. The blows he sustained may have contributed to a case of PTSD, as he took to nipping little girls, especially those who resembled Lauren.

As a result of his sociopathic behavior, Harry was sent into exile with an unsuspecting family and when last heard of he was entertaining their guests with his hydrating of the shoes welcoming ritual.

Despite her diminished birth weight and peculiar eating habits as a small child, Lauren endured and expanded her palate well beyond bacon and Cheerios and retained her love of doggies. Today you might find her strolling down the avenue munching an *escargot* while walking a canine beast named Cassie.

My Trip Out West

I started out young with tubing and cloth,
Planned, created and formed with much thought.
A new coat for the trip, fresh paint for good
  looks,
My very own engine and airframe logbooks.

Fifty-five was the year, September the month,
Compared to a cub, I was just a small runt.
Well, after I flew and passed my flight test,
I left Lock Haven, en route, headed west.

Veterans and citizens were flying about,
The G.I. Bill helped a few of them out.
Landed in Yakima, my new-found home,
With many admirers, not much time alone.

Two brothers flew me until fifty-eight,
Then on to Vancouver, a new home I'd take.

A doctor cared for me until sixty-one,
Sixty-two I was majored, fixed up to run.

In Richland I joined a pilots' flight club,
Surviving the sixties 'til seventy-one.
Lots of annuals and hundred-hour inspects,
Few minor incidents and no major wrecks.

Then on to Kennewick for a six-year stay,
Two owners later and twenty years of age.
Stylish aluminum aircraft was so popular now.
They called me the milkstool, meant for a cow.

At home in Lewiston, a new set of gear,
My nose wheel was gone; I sat low in the rear.
Thirty-foot wings, a bit stubby in length,
I'm prone to swap ends, taking pilots to the brink.

Drooped tips, a fresh cover and that's not all,
Just like brand new with a fresh overhaul.
My wings came off; I went into a shed,
I thought I would fly, but saw storage instead.

My owner went south for ten years and more,
No one to watch over, tend to or care for.
I stayed in this shed at Lewiston Airfield,
Alone in the dark for fourteen long years.

Covered with the dust of long elapsed time,
Loss of a medical, no way could I fly.
A rambler bought me and received my keys.
In ninety-five some pilots mounted my wings,

All A.D.'s caught up and a few new parts,
Old radios are gone; I've up-to-date smarts.
I'm actively flying Idaho State,
Guided by satellite each route that I take.

Out West in a hangar, I'm ready to go,
When weather permits and fields are clear of
  snow.
Forty years old, I'm now free to roam,
Exploring vast country from my new-found home.

~ Dana Graves

Benign: A Fantasy
By Michael Matchulat

The surgeon stood with bowed head and lifted hands. "I can't cut any closer, and this won't peel or tear loose." This time the talent was flown in from a nearby hospital to the sterile village operating room. All the tools to do the job were there, but nobody is ready for a surgical railroad of unplanned switchbacks and tissue types intersecting every reverse stitch of the blade. Eight hours passed in time since Michael was unconscious in the realm we all share as existence.

Michael was a piece of jellied meat. He was well-marbled with layers consistent with a childhood filled with vitamins and good food until his diet rings showed the branching of his habits. During his work years, he ate like a human raccoon-hybrid. His teeth showed how hard life can punch you straight in the kisser and you can still keep living. He'd lived in a small town his entire life, divided in thirds. The first third was with his parents, second with his lusts, and third with his real self he found along the way. Michael changed everything or, more appropriately, cancer changed everything for him because he had no opportunity do anything about it.

After a mentor died, Michael ate better. He exercised consistently and still he was lying on a table with his entire front open in a scar which would be called the Double Mercedes if he lived. Michael had become a rich man in his piles of wisdom and financial planning. He was the type of man who throws his wallet in the local fireman's boot expecting nothing back. Michael had devils and skeletons he carried around although nobody cared about them except when he told the real stories behind the closet doors. He was a master with spoken comforts and knew he was going to Heaven.

Still there he was, lying on the table. The team of eight experts above him were waiting for the next announcement from the chief surgeon in the hospital. There was no other case scheduled for the day. Michael was the most important person in the room and he was unconscious. He was unable to hear the slurping and clicking of machinery around him, each with its own incessant beeping modules. The experts beside the devices attached to Michael's cords knew the sounds better than their own babe's cry. Michael was a rock star and he didn't want anyone to ever tell him how much the concert would cost his insurance.

Michael remembered the words from his pre-operative meeting in his nightmares, "With tumors this size, it's extremely complicated. It will be mostly an experiment." The surgeon rambled too long, "But I suppose you're used to that sort of thinking?"

Michael had a gasping gulp-frog jumping out of his calm throat. He was prepared to die several times prior to this and was saved by miracles thrice. He was money ahead and down the road in a pink Cadillac with the loose ladies from the casino.

"Sounds good." He reached out for a handshake from the surgeon before he accepted a pen and signed the consent document. They were alone in the room. The light was faintly buzzing on a three-second interval which a mouse would have trouble hearing. Michael heard every sound wave as it floated past his still working ears. He couldn't hear well out of his left ear from an old nail gun accident. At times the chemotherapy regimens took his hearing by giving him such unbearable tinnitus he wanted to squeeze the grains of gooey sand he felt inside his brain in a special vice he imagined.

The surgeon paused. The pen and three-layered carbon document were set aside from the exam table. Due to current precautions, everyone had to wear gloves and a mask. Michael felt alone as the surgeon stood up and removed the mask and gloves exposing the reality of the moment. Before Michael knew how to react, there was an outstretched arm in his face. Both stood up, Michael also removed both his mask, and they shook hands. It was a true gentleman's bet how the rest of his life would go after this procedure. There were two weeks left to D-Day, and the bet included that Amberleigh would get to accompany Michael into surgery and be the first to hear news about a lab results or a biopsy.

Michael and Amberleigh were together since always. They met, fell in love, and were married forever right now with bumps along the way. Amberleigh might view life with Michael as a post Hollywood film minefield with the set lights off. Amberleigh would have waited still except Michael was so exciting. He also called her Amber.

Amber was mousy. She spent her days pleasing her own whimsy and still made time to bake cakes at night for her family. Amber knew every sound in her house because she was the nesting type and could keep track of everything in a regimented, social household. Amber was exceptionally smart and intellectual and she continually told Michael stories about friends in her life which he both could not fathom, and mostly couldn't follow along with.

The operating room was cold, like beef. The biopsy results were in. They came via phone at hour six just after the third hydration break. The team was exhausted due to the preparations they made for this surgery with special handling of tissues and samples for laboratory capture. The hospital was four hours from the nearest 'big' hospital for tissue examination and results. At the sixth hour, the team watched a dissection of a nerve and surrounding spinal columns. They watched a conductor delicately sushi chef a line of tumor tissues along Michael's spine. This was unexpected. The surgery was supposed to be lumpectomies in the mid-abdomen below the diaphragm. Branches of these tumors were embedded into his spine like roots seeking moisture. They ascended and descended from Michael's central nervous system's main

highway. The upper portion was dangerously close to the pericardial sack (the lung and heart 'vacuum bag' for the layman). If the tumors were touched farther below where was exposed, Michael certainly would not walk again because his spine would be dissected.

Nobody cared about the biopsy, anyway. Michael had adenocarcinoma, and it was chasing him through his body like a rabbit through a series of terrier-sized tunnels. Chemotherapy adapted his body to his new experience of normal, and his body's cancer cells adapted around the chemotherapy. Michael was failing, and Amber knew long before he did.

One of the surgical techs picked up the document from the operating room fax tray and set it down in a stack of papers to be organized later. The fax was only used for direct document transfer into the sterile operating room, and the sounds were lost among the harmony and plethora of machinery surrounding it. Nobody was cued into its tones. It was only for direct operating room documents and it didn't sound often. Michael's spidering tumors were now spectacularly inoperable without paralysis.

"Damn," was loudly whispered over the theater silence. Surgery was paused, waiting for the chess master to announce the next move.

"F...!" She screamed as the room skidded to a halt. A subordinate took over from the teacher to keep Michael alive. The expert had obviously been defeated.

Amberleigh, still in the room as promised, ripped off her bloodied sterile gloves and started organizing the room with her eyes. She saw the biopsy results at the top of the stack of papers on a tech cart. This paper looked different than the ones she'd seen before with the same pixilated font. The spacing was different and there were two independent results printed on the paper.

"Benign tissue." She said. "Benign tissue!" She exclaimed a second time.

All eyes were now on the headmaster of the room, Amberleigh. Normally unflappable, she grasped the document and her specialty robotic eyeglasses fogged with joy and emotion.

"Everyone stop!" she shouted. "Close him up, we're done." She could make that call after all her and Michael had been through. It was a miracle they let her in the operating room, let alone be the chief surgeon. Abdominal surgery was her primary specialty. She knew all the flavors of the surrounding tissue areas, but she couldn't be ready for any news as sweet as contained in this single Fax.

"And leave a big scar," Amberleigh joked. Michael's body and the chemotherapy he had taken to simply stay alive now came to a head in front of her during open surgery. She was about to give up on her soulmate, but she took one last glimpse around before committing to make a bad decision when she was ready to quit. Amber was as exhausted as she was talented. No one in the room understood her instructions. They were in the middle of open surgery and the surgeon told them to abandon ship. None of the experts understood why she was so joyfully excited. Amberleigh took four square breaths. She explained herself. She held up the fax from the Biopsy Lab.

"His journey ends here," she started. "The tumors and pathways we see here are benign tissue. We overlooked the lab results and only assumed these tumors were the same." The team started to understand her joy.

"I don't have to choose between cancer and paralyzing my husband." Amber sighed aloud. The room started to comprehend her excitement. All the other samples previously in Michael's body showed he was losing the battle. Now he had finally won the war, at least in Amber's mind, for now. The tumors may take his legs at some point but she wouldn't have to.

"Close him up well and get me when you're done." Everyone knew she was going to the equally comfortable and expensive massage recliner in the quiet room for a nap.

Michael and Amberleigh had a future of unknowns to investigate together after the surgical closing. For now she stood over Michael's good ear on his right side without a mask and whispered into his pale body, "Benign baby, benign."

The Chrysalis

The chrysalis encases me.
I sense the strands that hold me in place,
Sourced by the pandemic, the isolation, the
    distancing.
The strands hold me as I navigate my days.
I walk carefully, obeying their direction.

But deep within
I feel a churning, a transforming that is achingly
    slow.
Pushing on the strands.
I lack stamina now.
I contend with lethargy.
But the pushing continues.

A time of change seems inevitable.
Will the vaccines release me?
The inward working of an unfamiliar mixture
As in the butterfly's cocoon,
Seems to continue.
Fostering creative chaos as it
    churns inside me.

What will emerge?
Will I be me, but changed
Will I be renewed
Transformed,
A better self,
A lesser self?

I watch the images of a butterfly pushing aside
    the chrysalis,
Transformational indeed... unlike the liquid soup
    it wrestled from.
Now graceful, exuding beauty into the day.

What form will I take after the strands are
    removed, or lessened?
Certainly....a time of change.

~ Kathryn Fisher

At Day's End

at
day's end
a darkened sky
sprinkles starlight
on snowcapped mounts
reflected in cool alpine lakes
at day's end
the gentle winds
whisper softly through
ponderosa pine and aspen
the sweet lullaby of the gloaming
at day's end
when crickets chirp
a lone wolf call beckons
through snowcapped mounts
a darkened sky of sprinkled starlight

~ D.J. Barber
Groundwaters Vol 7 Iss 2 (2010)

The Morning of Our Love

The soft gentle promise of morning
caresses the day awake;
And brings new beginnings
the whisper of magic.
It fills our hearts with hope,
the joy of anticipation,
of new things to come
more mountains to climb.
The valleys of the past night
are forgotten with the sunrise;
as sun-kissed trees lift
branches to heaven.
Sweet scent of budding flowers
mingle with lilting songs of birds.
Our love becomes the morning.
Our hearts embrace.
God seems to be here waiting,
calling us to come.
Come taste the morning
Rejoice in the gift of love.

~Sherry Hunter
Groundwaters Vol 11 Iss 2 (2015)

The Train

The train moves swiftly
Through the dark tunnel
Lined with small soft lights
Increasing in speed as it goes.

And the little boy by the window is crying.

A small light appears and grows
Finally enveloping the speeding train
In sunlight.
Now visible are long, dusty country roads
Lined with wooden fence posts
Used as resting places for the crows,
Endless green pastures
Dotted with trees
And cows insensitive to the world
Around them.

And the little boy by the window is crying.

Soon suburban houses
In pastel colors appear.
The colors seem to run together
Like the paint on a painter's palet
As our speed increases further.

And the little boy by the window is crying.

A huge metropolis of skyscraping buildings
Now surrounds us,
But the train's speed is like
That of fire through a dry forest,
The bright city lights
Becoming a blur.

And the man by the window is crying.

~ Kelly Edwards
Groundwaters Vol 5 Iss 1 (2008)

wild geese

we light a score of candles
talk long into the night
the flames meet the darkness
like a brace of geese
flying into a storm.

~ Emily Hart
Groundwaters Vol 8 Iss 3 (2012)

Thankful Times on Thanksgiving Day

The New York Times shares happy times,
From poets all around
From Illinois, my childhood home,
To Oregon, where now I'm bound

Some with lines that even rhyme,
Some in just free-verse.
Some that catch my fancy,
Some that are kind o' worse

And as I took my morning jog
I mulled my blessings full
Thankful that I'm still alive
And lawnmower can push and pull

And that I have a yard of oak
And leaves to vacuum up
And wife and kids all happy,
Overflowing plate and cup.

I'm thankful too for neighbors,
Who wave and greet on walks,
And share their ups and downs
And pause for little talks.

And for my cousin's wife
Who lives on in nursing home,
In spite of Covid danger
In Wisconsin when I phone.

I'm thankful my carotid arteries
Are clear, my doctor says,
In spite of nurse's worry
From stethoscopic sounds' malaise.

And that the pain is over
From many needle stabs
In urologic prostate project
Research in the labs.

I'm grateful for my doctors
Who keep me well and kickin'.
In spite of 80 years and more
I dodge the road to sicken.

I'm thankful too for humor
And even corny jokes
That ease our elder burdens
Which we bear like thorny yokes:
What did one testicle say to the other?

"Why are we condemned as guilty, when
the slim guy did all the shootin'?"
(This from the urologist, while stabbing me
with research needles on Monday.)

Back to my poem, lest I roam
Too far from my intention,
Which is to thank you all, my friends,
For easing Covid detention.

You smile and wave, you nod and greet
When out for walks with dogs on street,
Reassure, that though we're apart six feet
Some month next year we again will meet,
To share a glass of wine,

To bemoan the Covid time,
To celebrate a street-found dime,
To enjoy a piece of pie, Key lime.
Happy Thanksgiving!

~ William McConochie

cleanup on aisle three

the day is...
looking so tired
and feeling uninspired
must be the pink shadow
of the setting moon
    covered...
    insulated...
    no bag full of joy

reflecting bonified shudders
of cleanup... cleanup...
cleanup on aisle three

I must remember
these are the remnants
of my life
got to get out
and do the things
that belong to only me

~ C. Steven Blue

Take a Hike
By Lee Boutell

In 1975, my girlfriend, Paige, and I worked at a Eugene natural foods restaurant and profit-sharing collective. She had hardly ever been out of Eugene and pined for adventure. She'd heard stories about beautiful Maui and its easy life. In mid-May, she flew to Maui—a brave move for an 18-year-old who didn't know anyone there.

Although I missed her, I understood her need for new experience. She wrote every day and mailed several letters a week. She seemed lonely and uncertain about leaving, writing:

I can't put into words how much you mean to me. There have been moments I've really hated myself for leaving you, but it was something that had to happen, another lesson we have to learn. My heart is yours. I miss you terribly, Babe. I love you.

Another letter said:

I dreamed about you last night. We were making love in the woods for hours. I woke up and expected you to be there. But I know you were there in spirit... I just read your letter. It was beautiful, caused a couple tears but mostly smiles. Bless you.

She called and begged me to visit. I said I'd finish my commitments and come soon. Her next letter said:

I can't wait until I can be with both you and Maui at the same time—the islands are meant for lovers. I feel like Sita waiting in paradise for Ram to fly on his golden chariot and rescue her. See you soon!

She advised me of the best day to arrive and to bring a small tent. I made arrangements and completed my work. I packed a swimsuit, pup tent, sleeping bag and a canteen in an aluminum-framed backpack. Paige said she'd pick me up at the Maui airport.

From my window seat, high above the island, I marveled at light blue waters, white beaches, rugged mountains and the huge volcanic crater, Haleakala. Maui looked magical.

Upon landing, as I grabbed my backpack, Paige arrived, kissed my cheek and placed over my head a lei of white Plumeria flowers so fragrant it felt unworldly, like I'd stepped through the doors of heaven.

I felt happy to see her, but she didn't seem to share my joy. She looked distracted somehow. Maybe my newcomer enthusiasm put her off, as she'd been there for six weeks and the newness was gone. I wondered what was wrong.

We rode in a borrowed car to a group house where she lived in Pukalani ("Hole in Heaven"). She lived with a couple of women and their boyfriends. They shared rent and lived cheaply, many on food stamps. Most were artists who sold their work at markets and festivals.

Asha introduced herself. With straight dark braided hair, a pretty face, dark mysterious eyes and a vaguely mid-eastern look, she crafted custom handbags and beautiful jewelry from shells, stones, beads and feathers. I found her warm, sincere, sweet smile endearing.

Keith painted airbrush murals and custom signs and showed me his portfolio—colorful tropical flowers, birds and island scenery. His artistry impressed me. Keith had long wavy ginger hair, reddish beard and blue eyes. He was friendly, confident and charismatic, undoubtedly good at selling his artistry to merchants wanting to dress up their shops.

Keith took me and Paige for dinner at a nearby cafe in the Makawao General Store, a hip place with natural foods and affordable lifestyle items like herbal creams, sunglasses and Hawaiian shirts. Over dinner, Keith talked, but Paige remained strangely quiet.

He talked about Maui and the fabled Hawaiian good life. After eating, he dropped a hammer—he and Paige were a couple. I would not be hanging out or sleeping with her.

What the...? She'd begged me to visit and this happens? After all those romantic letters? Apparently her feelings turned once Keith showed up. She avoided eye contact.

Guess I was late and she'd moved on. Now I was the lonely one. Betrayed and crushed, I felt like an intruder.

Now what? I still had two weeks before my return flight. I sat stunned, my eyes searching for anything. Thankfully Keith treated me with respect and Paige didn't show him overt signs of affection, which would have really hurt. I mumbled, "I don't know what to do."

Keith knew Maui and said I could go to the top of Haleakala to see the spectacular sunrise over the volcanic moonscape. I could hike into the crater and either hike back or out the other end and down to the beach. Then I could see the fabled red sand beach and ride back on the infamous narrow, winding "Road to Hana" with stunning viewpoints and waterfalls.

Now instead of Ram flying on his golden chariot to rescue Sita, I was just a tourist.

I decided to hike the crater the next morning. I grabbed supplies at the General Store—a Maui map, bags of figs and nuts, crackers and a couple oranges. I didn't especially want to hang with Paige and Keith, but I needed overnight lodging and they offered me the floor.

In the morning Asha prepared me coffee, fresh papaya and mango for breakfast. She knew what happened and felt bad for me. She talked about beautiful Maui and we had a nice conversation. I didn't see Paige or Keith that morning.

In the darkness I left "Hole in Heaven" with a hole in my heart. The house was right on the highway to Haleakala and I easily caught a ride with a young couple in a VW van, also going for the sunrise.

The red sky over Haleakala looked spectacular, with the distant rim of dark mountains outlined by the rising sun. Long shadows filled the crater with mystery. Sunshine slowly illuminated the giant hole in the earth, revealing a moonscape of scattered red and orange cinder cones that seemed to glow, hills of volcanic ash, and sandy expanses of emptiness. It appeared a formidable hike which I hoped would clear my head after my world got turned upside down. It started at over 10,000 feet elevation and descended to about 6000 feet.

I hiked a downward path of continuous switchbacks in sandy volcanic soil. Once down the rim, I began to notice spikey, globe-shaped, silver-colored shrubs called Silverswords, a threatened species that lives only in this crater. I felt a reverence for Haleakala, "The House of the Sun," and understand why Native Hawaiians worship it as a sacred place.

My hike on sliding sands went slowly in the dry, thin air as the July sun grew hotter. Ahead of me, white clouds flirted with crater mountains, slowly crawling over rim tops like puffy spiders of cotton. As I progressed east, the sandy moonscape gave way to a sagebrush landscape of scattered shrubs.

I hadn't seen one other person, which seemed spooky. After several hours without shade, I encountered a guest cabin. Nearby I saw two women hikers, one resting on her back. Feeling some reassurance, I found shade and took a break, eating figs and nuts. I'd already emptied much of my canteen.

Looking back to where I began, the trail had sloped downward the whole way, so hiking back would be a difficult trek on sliding sands and I might run out of water. Was this hike a mistake? Did Keith send me on a fool's mission? Is this why Paige said to bring a tent?

I checked the map. Further east a trail went up and out the crater through a gap much lower than the starting point, an easier climb plus it looked green and shaded. I decided to camp at the end of the crater. In the cool morning I would hike up the side, out the Kipahulu Gap and down to the coast where I could catch a ride back to civilization. I only had half a canteen of water, but at least I had a plan.

I reached the east end of Haleakala before sunset as it clouded over and set up my pup tent in a grassy spot surrounded by rocks and shrubs. As darkness arrived I crawled into my mummy bag and quickly drifted off.

In the middle of the night, forceful winds awakened me. Gusts blew stronger until the tent collapsed, falling on my face. Then it started raining. I crawled out into the storm to secure ropes that had slipped off rocks I'd tied them to. In those couple minutes I got really wet. After an hour, rain had soaked into my bag and my clothes. I couldn't sleep. Shivering, it got much colder than I expected as winds and rain continued.

By morning, a bright sky shined above, though my tent remained in shade. Exhausted, I lay until the sun shined on my tent. Emerging, I spread my clothes and sleeping bag on rocks to dry. I ate an orange and sunned.

After a couple hours, I ate the last crackers, packed and hiked up to the Kipahulu Gap. Gaining elevation, the landscape greened with flowers, shrubs and trees, which felt much friendlier and inviting than the moonscape below. Hopefully I could find some fruit or water. Luckily the forest provided shaded breaks from the sun.

Nearing the top of the rim as I anticipated the view, my heart raced. Catching my first glimpse, it took my breath away—endless deep blue Pacific blending into infinite sky. I sat down to absorb the view, took off my boots, snapped a photo and drank my last water. It didn't look that far to the coast, maybe four or five miles. I hoped I'd be there in a couple hours. I'd be okay without food, but I needed water.

Putting on my boots, I saw no road or signs of civilization down there. The map showed this part of Maui to be wilderness with no major road and no cities. How could I catch a ride back to town if there's no road? I hoped I could at least find water to drink.

As I started down the trail, the trees got taller but I found no fruit. After two or three hours, I ate my last orange. I was only about halfway down and was out of food and water. *Good planning, buddy.* My feet hurt and I was tired. At least it wasn't uphill, but hiking down is hard on my knees and feet so I took frequent rest breaks. It became late afternoon and I only had a couple hours left of daylight. I'd become horribly thirsty.

Finally, I made it to a humble gravel path of two ruts with grass in the middle, like a farmer's tractor path. I followed it toward the coast until it intersected a gravel road paralleling the beach. It seemed promising, but was so rough and rocky it had to be only a jeep and tractor road. Shadows grew longer in the early evening sun. I hadn't seen a soul since the two women at the cabin yesterday. I walked east toward Hana.

I spotted a rough gravel driveway leading to the ocean, and that's where I wanted to go. I soon approached a white building near the ocean—a simple white missionary church from the mid-1800's. It was just a box with gables and a bell tower on the roof. It looked neglected, but intact.

The church had a single door on the front and three windows on each side. Stone walls were a couple feet thick, but surface mortar had loosened, exposing rounded dark stones inside. It sat on a small, flat, grassy bluff overlooking the ocean—a gorgeous setting!

Suddenly over the ocean and outlining the church glowed a perfect rainbow. I gazed at it, mesmerized. I believed it to be a message I was safe now. I set up my camera and took a timed photo of me standing with a backpack at the church door, the rainbow shining above.

Not a soul was near. I opened the front door and entered the darkened sacred space. It had wooden pews and an altar, but it looked like nobody had used the church for years, as pews were out of place or damaged, and debris lay scattered around. I'd found my lodging for the night. I didn't want to set up that lousy pup tent again, anyway. I glanced above and gave thanks.

I still needed water. Outside the church stood a couple of coconut palms. A few brown coconuts lay on the ground. I shook one—no liquid. Overhead were big green coconuts, so I took off my boots and climbed the shortest palm tree. I dropped two big coconuts and jumped down.

With my trusty Swiss Army knife I cut off the thick green husk. Exposing the brown nut inside, I smashed it repeatedly on a pointed rock until it had a hole. I drank the coconut water. Ummmm, best drink ever. I gulped down the whole thing, then ate sweet chunks of coconut meat.

Time for a swim! Watching waves gently roll in, I stripped and jumped off a rock into warm blue Pacific waters, swimming out past the swirling currents near shore. I floated on my back and took in the amazing scenery around me. After my refreshing cool-down, the warm breeze dried my skin as long evening shadows grew into darkness.

Back in the church, I rolled out my sleeping bag on the floor near the altar, laid down and listened to the sound of waves dancing on the shoreline. All secure in my little abandoned church, I didn't worry about late night rains. I slept great.

In the morning, I drank more coconut water and ate sweet chunks. After a morning meditation and thankful prayer, I consulted the map and continued my hike east toward Hana. I needed a decent meal and to replenish supplies, but the rocky road had no traffic.

On sore feet, I walked for a couple miles and didn't see anyone. I was getting blisters and at this rate it would be an all-day hike to town. Behind me I heard a faint vehicle sound. I stopped and waited. After a minute I saw a yellow Volkswagen "thing"—an open Jeep-like vehicle slowly approaching with two gentlemen dressed in khaki clothing and safari hats. I waved and they stopped.

"G'day!" the driver said with a smile.

"Good morning!" I replied. "Could I catch a ride to town?"

"Hop in, mate." I took off my pack, tossed it into the back seat and climbed in.

"Thanks! Great to see you out here. I haven't seen anyone all day. We're pretty far from civilization!"

The middle aged Australians were topping off their holiday with a wilderness trek on the back roads of Maui. They'd certainly dressed for it. We had a pleasant cross-cultural conversation. They asked me to join them for lunch in Hana.

"Sure!" I said. I felt incredibly thankful, and so did my tired feet.

Silence to Create

Why do I like to drift and roam
And carry on this way alone

Remoteness brings much time to think
You test your mind, you can create

A backwoods retreat, a second home
A place to create my thoughts alone

A mountain pass, a peaceful creek
Look to the sky, the mind will speak

A place to escape is what I prefer
Remote and alone, a simple world

My mind wanders for something brand-new
A special verse created for you

And when it hits, it's such a surprise
Think of the words, where do they hide

Search for the meaning and share with a few
Lines you create from scratch to brand-new

Simple and sweet, the words that I find
A few off-beat, hard-hitting some time

When boredom and restless catch me alone
I search for silence and write a new poem

~ Dana Graves

Tossing Stones at Odie's Roof
By Dave Polhamus

"Hey, Odie, jump in," somebody said. "Ya." He slid into the open front door. We roared off.

"Odie, wha'cha' doing? What's going on?" Smiling, he was obviously glad to see us.

"Nuckin', nuckin.'"

It seemed I'd heard that scenario a thousand times. In reality, it was more like 30 or 40. As a couple of high school guys riding around that edge of town, we'd stop and pick up Odie on his way home. I don't remember us first giving rides, seems he was always there. He lived alone three or four miles out the end of a rutted dirt road. His house might have been white at one time. Walking to town and back, we thought, kept him skinny. He seemed real skinny.

Odie could be seen toting a wooden lettuce crate from the local grocery store containing shriveled veggies past ripe. Was that his food? Sometimes the crate contents were smelly—rotten? Sometimes it was half full or less.

Though he might have been 25 or 30 years older than us, Odie was always a fun guy. I don't know if we were much fun to him, though. We liked to visit—boredom? It was more entertaining than the Dairy Queen downtown and cost less. Odie always knew when we arrived. Just before we got to his home, we'd stop and bang road gravel off his corrugated metal roof. It always brought him out. We'd laugh.

"Hey, Odie, how are you?" we'd yell. "What you doing?"

"Nuckin', nuckin','" he'd say, smiling. Odie had only about five teeth in his head and was born somewhere other than the United States. Rumor was that he was Slavic, Bulgarian, or maybe German. His curly brown hair probably never saw a comb. On walks to town, Odie wore a suit—a dark Sunday-go-to-meetin' suit; it looked three sizes too big or he looked awfully skinny. We wondered if his habit of wearing a suit might be a hold-over from a European tradition? His English was hard to understand at times. He might have been "shell-shocked" during the war, some said. "Nuckin', nuckin'" was a stock answer to any question asked of him. Even when he was doing something, he always said he was doing "nuckin.'"

Though we hassled him some, Odie always seemed happy to see us.

"Hi, Odie. How you been?"

"Ya, ya," he smiled. Word was that his brother lived in town, but we never knew of him being at Odie's. We never saw anybody else there, either. Even when we play-wrestled with him, Odie smiled. When we rattled his bird cage in the living room, or when we pretended to axe down his old house, he became upset. When upset, he waved his arms and slurred, "I call Andy Nem. I call Andy Nem."

"Okay, okay, Odie," I said. "No more, I quit." Andy Nemecheck was the county sheriff, but we weren't too worried, because we knew Odie had no phone.

During winter, Odie wore a coat everywhere; it looked too big for him. Inside, his home smelled sour like a second-hand refrigerator. Winter or summer, his lights were seldom on. The wood pile was mostly a scattering of limbs and scrap lumber. When not being obnoxious, my buddy and I would split up a week's supply of firewood for him. Odie would nod and smile, lacking the English words for "thank you." He loved ice cream. We'd usually bring chocolate... his favorite. With mis-matched spoons, we'd eat right out of the carton. In a playful moment at the wobbly old table, we'd all three have a miniature sword fight with our spoons. Odie would throw his head back and laugh loudly, showing three brown teeth.

My buddy smoked and offered Odie some. Nope. He'd swear at Odie and Odie smiled back—not understanding a word. A favorite scenario would be us pretending to be The

Three Stooges—Curly, Moe, and Larry. Odie would receive the brunt of the slapstick humor. We didn't hurt him, but he didn't like it either. Curious, I talked with the lady at the post office once. "You know a guy named Odie?"

"Odie? Odie? What's his last name?"

Uh, I dunno'. Walks around with a box, a produce crate on his shoulder. Thin guy; looks like he's about to starve to death."

"Oh-h-h, I know who you're talking about. That's his name, Odie? Nope, he's never been here for mail—guess nobody writes him. Yeah, he IS skinny. Poor guy—carries that box, rain or shine. You think that's his food source—cast off veggies."

"Yeah, might be."

At the appointed date, I graduated and snagged acceptance to a college on the west coast—Linfield College in McMinnville, Oregon. I spent summers with my aunt and uncle near there, working at my uncle's hayfield. One season rolled into the next. Following four years of college was four years in the military.

After high school graduation, my buddy had left town to find a job in Denver. Never heard from him again. As a teen, I had not mentioned Odie much to my folks; they'd never informed me of when he died.

Today, I was back in southwest Wyoming visiting my parents for the first time in several years. I also had a need to be at the county courthouse. Heading out the front door one morning, I said, "Mom, I'm gone. I'll be at the courthouse—look at some tax statements. Be back in an hour, or so."

"Okay. You may want to stop by the cemetery, see your brother-in-law's gravestone. It looks nice," she said from the kitchen table.

"Okay. 'Bye."

At the courthouse, I met my former girlfriend's younger sister. She works there. We talked some. She told of Odie's passing. Methodius was his real given name, she informed me.

"Uh, let's see... some history. Methodius... Wasn't there a medieval Christian monk named Methodius?" I said. "His brother was Cyril?"

"I think you're right," she nodded, then went on... Nobody had claimed Odie's body, so the county had been stuck with the cost of burial and all. She said, however, that until death, Odie's brother had been receiving his disability checks. By way of power-of-attorney, he had been cashing them—spending minimal on Odie. She said that Odie was a Slav, and that he and his relatives had bitterly fought Hitler's Nazis at their homeland. She eventually explained where Odie was buried. The death certificate and newspaper had disclosed natural causes, but those more aware said he slowly starved— didn't have enough to eat. That had been my concern, my conflict; he always seemed skinny, too skinny. Leaving the courthouse, I felt sad, perplexed, and angry.

My brother-in-law had fallen ill four years ago. Cancer. He'd died six months after the diagnosis. Now at the cemetery, his internment plot was neat and well-cared for. Mom was right, it did look nice. I visited Odie, too. I had gotten flowers for him as well. First, I tidied up, pulled some offensive weeds; I was irritated at the unkempt condition. I felt I wanted to talk with him some. Maybe, say I was sorry for it all—sorry for hassling him; sorry he had such a hard life, sorry that his brother wasn't more caring, sorry he didn't have enough to eat.

After the graveyard, I drove to Odie's place at the end of the bumpy road. Out of my car, I looked around. The old house is gone. Nothing. Looking at the windblown grit and tumbleweeds, you'd swear there'd never been a home there at all. In a moment, I was flooded with memories. I sighed. I slowly shook my head. I sighed, heavily. I found a lump in my throat. I tried to keep it down—no use. I thought of him in his over-sized suit. I thought of his three-tooth smile and how happy he always seemed to see us. I thought of the lettuce crate on his shoulder. I thought of stones rattling on a tin roof and Odie saying, "Nuckin', Nuckin'." I had an urge to go buy some ice cream, a whole bunch of ice cream. Chocolate.

The Dreamer

An old blind man told me once
that he could see the wind,
I never paid him any mind
and went about my way.
Tonight as I reflect, I can hear his words again,
I wondered why I thought of him
and why it was today.
But that old man never fooled me
because I could see it too,
I saw leaves dance in the trees
every time it blew,
But those words stayed with me
and deep inside I knew.
Chance encounters come and go,
we'd never meet again,
Any fool can look at trees…
it takes a dreamer to see the wind.

~ Michael J. Barker
Groundwaters Vol 8 Iss 3 (2012)

The Shell

Gentle shuffling, tumbling,
currents flowing,
opening, closing, oozing,
knowing, bubbles floating,

soft insides trembling,
hard shell shielding.

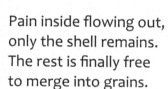

Stomp, stomp.
Crack the shell.
No more fortress,
all is not well!

Pain inside flowing out,
only the shell remains.
The rest is finally free
to merge into grains.

Carried then by waves
onto the sand, hard still,
but oh, so fragile;
I lie in your gentle hand,
waiting.

~ Joanne Sprott

My Spirit

The perfume of the starry night filled the air
Quiet, perfect, and still I could hear the breeze sing
   its sweet melody
As I lay, swarmed by wisps of grass and wild
   flowers,
The thoughts raided my mind.

The spirit of the sky shone down upon me, like a
   star-filled heaven
Now I know that I am trapped in this world for only
   a while,
And then I can escape to that heaven
Where I would truly know the value of humanity

That is when I will be wrenched back to this world,
Where I can only stay for a while.

~ Linsey Kau
Groundwaters Vol 5 Iss 2 (2008)

I Know You Are There

In this capricious universe
Of planet, moon and star,
And people by the millions,
I wonder where you are.
I look at others closely,
And now and then I see,
The eyes of my beloved
Smiling back at me.

~ Elizabeth Tyler Brown
Groundwaters Vol 7 Iss 4 (2011)

The Stinkbug

A marmorated stinkbug is lurking in my curtain
A decision IS required, that is Oh, so certain!

Shall I squash-it flat against the window pane?
But that would stink the room it's plain!

I think that I will look the other way
And come back ANOTHER DAY.

~ Frances Burns

The Needle
By Tom Oroyan

There has been talk that an oral version of the COVID vaccine be developed to be taken orally as soon as possible, but this won't happen until testing has been completed at the end of 2021 or later. Some medical experts say 'oral' is the way to go in order to expedite matters, especially in developing countries, as it is simpler and can be taken at home without the intervention of professional health personnel.

There are a lot of reasons some people may have for not taking the vaccine including health concerns, political motivation, religious beliefs, etc., but I believe one of the biggest ones is a phobia based on the vehicle that delivers the vaccine... the Needle.

Fighting the fear of the Needle varies from standing your ground, psyching yourself and looking away, to physically running away from extreme fear.

In my decades of life so far, I can cite a few personal experiences related to the Needle administered by both dental and medical doctors and their technicians, attesting to that fear.

My introduction to the Needle as a third grader, was not a good one. To give a little background... in Honolulu, in the early 1940s, grade school kids, en masse, were taken to a dental clinic for dental work and there were numerous dentists. The dentist assigned to me did not prepare me for such a new adventure in my young life. He hardly spoke while he examined me and never talked about what he was about to do, to ease me into the situation mentally, physically and psychologically. He didn't talk about the Needle that was filled with novocaine that would ease the pain of pulling a bad tooth.

This dentist had no bedside manner nor any sensitivity to the feelings of a young child. He looked young and, I suspect, was just out of dental school. As he prepared the Needle at a counter, though his back was to me, I saw him lift the Needle—that looked to be a foot long—to the light to check its content.

When he turned around, I asked, "What are you going to do?"

He said, "I'm going to pull your tooth!" as he came toward me.

I started crying and quickly yelled out "No, you're not!"

He put his hand in my mouth and clamped his fingers over my lower teeth and jaw. I bit down hard and, like a frightened pit bull, I wouldn't let go... and he yelped! That brought a fellow dentist running over to help.

Despite this nightmarish first encounter, I've developed more tolerance, brought on by more information and maturity, in accepting the dentist's needle. In fact, some of the dentists I've gone to over the years have developed kinder, gentler techniques when injecting the novacaine. They don't show you the needle until the moment they enter your mouth. They now wiggle the cheek near the tooth to be pulled prior to the injection which somehow temporarily numbs or prepares the gum area for the shot. They now also apply a swab of local anesthetic in the gum area to numb the bite of the needle.

In 1963, out of college and having landed my first career-related job with an architectural firm, I felt it was about time to catch up on my personal dental needs that had been generally neglected during the five years in college. One of my neighbors recommended Dr. Lum. "He just opened his business in Sacramento, and seems to know the latest in dental services! I like him," said Kathy.

I was fine with the dental work Dr. Lum performed on me... that is, until he said I needed a couple of wisdom teeth pulled. The dreaded Needle would be needed once again.

Dr. Lum practically did gymnastics in pulling the well-embedded teeth. He practically had to stand on my chest to yank the teeth out. He had to really work on chiseling the side gums that naturally adhered to the teeth and in the midst of it all, even sought some quick advice from another dental surgeon. With all the fuss in doing the wisdom work, it should have signaled me of further things to come.

That late afternoon, when I left the dentist's office after what seemed like hours of dental surgery, I was numb and groggy, but not in real pain. After I got home, I could hardly eat dinner, so I went to bed early. Then it happened! The excruciating pain came on; I couldn't sleep; I was moaning, whimpering and, to some extent, crying like a baby. I called in sick the next day and called Dr. Lum.

I faulted Dr. Lum for not insisting I get some pain pills, explaining that I would later feel 'after effects' of the dental work. I faulted the novocaine for giving me the false impression that everything would be "ok." It masked the pain which was to come. And boy! did it come... big time!

In 1958, I joined the Hawaii Army National Guard Unit. Seventeen of us guys, ranging from 18 to 20 years of age, from Waimanalo Town, joined the Guard, lured by a guardsman/recruiter who lived in the town. He did a great 'sell job' that warranted the bonuses and credits he was getting. His pitch about serving your country at home while not getting drafted in the Regular Army was interesting (As we now know, the Guard and Reserves were also called to join the fight up front in recent wars). But, the recruiter was inviting and made joining the Guard at the same time with fellow friends from the same town sound fun. Guys who were out of work, or were students attending college, liked the lure of being 'Weekend Warriors' because we got paid something for our service.

Upon joining the Guard, one had to complete physicals which not only meant being examined, but we were required to get shots and vaccinations, as well.

I was hesitant at first as we—all naked as jaybirds—lined up to be examined by army medical personnel. Like some, I couldn't help feeling inadequate as some of my fellow guardsmen were well-built and some the size of football tacklers.

However, I had my chest out when I took my required shots, for I could not help noticing that some of those 'well-built' guys were copping out of line and some even fainted when given a shot. Fear of the Needle was a real thing.

It got more real in later years, when in 1986, upon returning from the dentist, I began telling the staff in my office of my experiences and anxiety about needles. Before I could say another word, one of our draftsmen ran out of the office, puked in the restroom, told the receptionist he was sick, and hurriedly left for home. He later confessed he gets squeamish just hearing the word "needle" or seeing photos of it.

In April and May of 2021, when I received my COVID shots, I did not feel a needle prick and had no after-effects as some did. However, my wife gael jumped each time she was injected... possibly due to built-up anxiety from the scare stories told to her by relatives about the bad side effects from the shots that they had experienced.

Reflecting from my own past experiences, I wonder how many have not taken the shots for fear of "the Needle."

I researched, on-line, the technical term for this needle phobia. It's called 'Trypanophobia' and is defined as the fear of syringes, needles and injections.

"The Needle" phobia is real as hell! Definitely the oral COVID vaccine must be developed soon.

To Crash or Not to Crash
By Mary Lee Radka

My airline career started when was living in Salt Lake City. It was 1966, and I was in my last semester at the University of Utah, going for a major in business and a minor in skiing the wonderful powder at Alta, Utah.

I took some friends out to the airport in my funky International Metro Mite van, and met a tall, redheaded stewardess. Her name was Nancy Soucup, and we didn't particularly like each other. She was referred to as "Tall Red," later I was "Petite Red." My impetuous thought was, Gee! If she could be a stewardess, then I surely could be one day, too. Two weeks later, I was driving my van and towing my old "bathtub," 356 B Porsche, behind it, on my way to Seattle, Washington.

Luckily, some seasoned stewardess' clued me in on carrying four-plus pounds of quarters under my loose-fitting blouse, which literally saved my job on future monthly weigh-ins. If you gained more than three pounds in a month, you were off the line without pay for one whole month. There were lots of requirements back then. You had to be single, have some college time, wear a girdle, and you signed an agreement that you would retire at the ripe old age of 32.

The first plane that I worked on the most was a DC-3, also known as a C-47 in the military, and a "gooney bird" and the "workhorse" airplane during World War II. She was a tail-dragger on the ground. With the required "high heels," it was easy walking while in the air, but on the ground, it wasn't so much fun. After a few months as being the solo stewardess on the DC-3, I graduated to the F-27's prop-jets. The Fairchild had Rolls Royce engines, and she resembled a flying grasshopper with her wings above the fuselage. Again I was the solo worker in the back with 23 passengers.

A lot of pilot's suffered major hearing loss because of those screamingly loud engines on the F-27. They usually shut down the starboard engine in order to keep deplaning passengers out of harm's way if they turned right instead of going straight into the terminal. There wasn't as much extra security for passengers getting on or off, or wandering around on the tarmac like there is today. One time my sister-in-law, Cathy, brought her three young daughter's out on the tarmac and, as I was boarding the plane, coached them to say to me, "Mommy, Mommy, please don't leave us again." Luckily, I was able to tell the pilots that it was a joke, and my very nosey supervisor wasn't around to fire me.

By the time I was working on the jet planes—namely the DC-9—there were at least two of us in the back for 99 passengers. The pilots had also worked their way up from the DC-3 to the DC-9. The instrumentation was a big shift for them.

So, one time, as we were approaching Yakima on final approach, I was walking down the aisle giving my, "Are your seatbelts fastened and your tray tables returned to their original positions?" speech, when the plane flipped over!

The overhead bins had no closing doors on them and were open for me for fly right up into one. Nancy Soucuop (Big Red) was in the seat below me and she literally pulled me out of the bin and buckled me into the seat next to her. We held hands and said if we lived through it, we would do something fun on land, snow, or water once a month. I had broken a rib and had several nasty bruises. Both engines had gone out, and the pilots were able to restart them while upside down, and flip us back over. Turns out that the autopilot on the DC-9 was a whole lot more sensitive to touch and turning than on the F-27's. We learned later that the wings were only inches off the ground when the plane was righted.

The pilots had made the decision to fly over Yakima and on to Spokane, which was our final destination that day. When we landed in Spokane, there was cheering and clapping in the back. The pilots both looked white as sheets and they didn't wait for the passengers to deplane before they got off first.

Nancy and I did have our play dates once a month until I took the first maternity leave offered to a Continental flight attendant, and my daughter Shanda was born, August 3, 1970.

Once a Lifetime

Above a mountain reservoir
one chilly morning late in May
a scene unfolded most bizarre
still widely disbelieved today.

So, time it is to bury doubt
and validate the story shared.
'Tis good as gold, this true account.
I know 'cause I was fishing there!

While trolling for our catch that day
an Osprey circling in the sky
beguiled us with its raptor play...
a carnival for earthbound eyes.

Then suddenly the creature dived
and hijacked something from the lake,
then goal attained and lunch in mind
departed with the morning's take.

But cruising soon across the sky
above the fruitful fishery,
it seemed to scorn a threat nearby
intending airborne piracy.

Though steward of the captive prey--
a bass or trout of decent size--
yet like a child absorbed in play,
it paid no mind to hostile eyes.

The eagle opted not for war;
but neither did it hesitate
to activate a fancy for
appropriated fish fillet.

In time, the space between the two
no longer was discernable,

and when the smaller bird withdrew,
the outcome was predictable.

With head and tail of purest white
and wings of brown from tip to tip
the Baldy's dogged, pesky strikes
unlocked the Osprey's iron grip.

Completed then the forced exchange,
the Baldy, with a fish to tend,
hostilities would reengage,
the pilfered treasure to defend.

Deception not a strategy
a new invader joined the game,
a bird of royal majesty
the fish maligned about to claim.

The Golden Eagle soon caught up
and tracked the Baldy close behind;
then, like a Poodle to her pups
appeared to speak its eagle-mind.

The Baldy's choice to up the pace
was nothing more than try-and-fail.
The Golden, focused on fillet
maintained position nose to tail.

Then as the two passed out of sight
'twas clear just one fulfilled a wish:
The Baldy turned and quit the fight;
the Golden clutched the tortured fish.

Yes, wingspan makes a difference
for those contending in the air;
and when computing recompense
the smaller bird had best beware.

But combat in the sky aside,
this story's not about control.
Like oceans sailed and mountains climbed
inspire it does the heart and soul.

Since rare it is, that scene sublime,
and seldom viewed by human eyes,
enthralled I am a pair were mine
that day when magic filled the sky!

~ *Wayne Westfall*

It's a Red Letter Day

By Mildred "Millie" Thacker Graves

This is a sweet recollection of a very dear friend of mine. Her name was Alta Harness Tweedy, but she went by the nickname of Tweedy. She was born in Missouri and had many of the country expressions learned in her youth. She was 20 years older than I, but we were like sisters. She was joyful and found enjoyment in most of her activities. She had a strong faith and a great sense of humor. She loved to travel, even on short trips in her car. She referred to herself as Granny Go Go! I, as her sidekick, was often included in her plans. I liked to be with her because she made me laugh. She loved her family and her friends.

Tweedy struggled throughout most of her life with a weight problem and her body reflected her fondness for eating in restaurants. She had a sort of shelf that stuck out along her bustline. She was fastidious in her dress, but as she aged, when we went out to eat, quite often some food would end up caught on her clothing—the shelf. She tried to be very careful, but often after inspecting the front of her clothing, she would find that she had failed. The food never was to be found lower than the upper part of her garment, since the shelf caught it all. Upon completing a meal, she would inspect herself and if she found no food spots, she would raise her arms in the air over her head and say, "It's a Red Letter Day"—sometimes a little too loudly—in celebration of her success.

One day, we had finished eating lunch at McGrath's, a seafood restaurant in Eugene, Oregon, and Tweedy did her inspection and found nothing foreign on her clothing, so she did her little celebration. The next thing we knew, a group of employees arrived at our table with a cupcake with a candle, singing "Happy Birthday." They placed the fish hat on top of her head—sort of ruffling her hairdo—and feathers, as well, because she was very particular about having her hair carefully styled all the time.

The person holding the fish hat said, "What day is your birthday?" For the first time ever, I saw Tweedy at a loss for words. I told them that actually, it was a belated birthday and I went on to explain that we had tried to celebrate several times before and hadn't managed to accomplish it until today. I held my breath after that, hoping they wouldn't pursue the exact date of her birth. Later we had many laughs over the whole incident.

Tweedy is no longer a part of this world and I am in my 80s. In her honor, I find myself doing an inspection of my clothing, just like Tweedy did, and if I find nothing foreign there—I quietly comment on it being a red letter day, but I never say it very loudly!

When Both Sides of Me Meet

I close my eyes
And find myself back in Barcelona

As I look out to the skyline from Parc Guell
A stranger named Joy appears

"Bom Dia!"
He is me from October 2016

We catch the Bus Turistic
The sights all bring back memories of the first time in the city

Of a different person filled with joy
Our last stop... La Barceloneta

As the sun sets over the Mediterranean Sea
He tells me, "this is what joy feels like!"

I stay behind and look out to the sea

~ Oswald Perez

Mara: Gattara
By Virginia Landgreen

The last time Bridget and Bruno had seen Mara was a year and a half ago, when they had spent a month living next door to her in Assisi. They had planned that trip to fall during Easter, since Bridget loved the church pageantry. There were dozens of candles, a single drum beating, and the statue of Jesus taken from the wooden cross and carried in a procession of clergy from various churches. The line of people flowed from the top of the hill town of Assisi at San Rufino (the old church. where St. Francis had worshiped) to the Basilica di San Francesco at the bottom.

During their month there, friends and family from the U.S. visited and joined them in celebratory meals and outings. Bruno's stepdaughter, Rosaria, and her travel mate, Salvo, were among the visitors, and Angela and Marco visited after his residence at Rome's American Academy, where Marco had a studio for painting and Angela soaked up art and culture. Warming weather and the dappled light of spring cheered them day by day. The birdsong in Umbria seemed to Bridget to be a hymn to all creation.

Mara had always been unusual. Growing up in rural Pennsylvania, she developed a passion for Italian Opera that she shared with her father. She spent her high school years humming arias and writing down librettos. As a grown woman, she developed her own style of dress. She would often wear a knit head covering with a hole cut out for the face and another hat on top of that. She was medium-to-small build, and since she had come to Italy, she had thrown off her knee and back braces and no longer had joint pain. She had required them in Eugene and took them to Italy and attributed her cure to all the climbing she did in the hills of her adopted hometown.

Mara had short brown hair, and lively blue eyes. Her hands, though small, were the hands of a baker, which Mara had been for many years with notable success. Bridget had met Mara in the early '80s and they clicked. Mara had given her great advice about men and life in general. Bridget might have given up hope of finding a mate if Mara, who had a twenty-year career as a marriage and family counselor, hadn't convinced her to keep her heart open. Soon after Bridget met Bruno.

Mara was a notoriously good cook, too. Bridget had eaten dozens of great vitamin-filled meals, prepared by Mara. When Jan, Bridget's son, was fourteen, he fell in love with Mara when they all shared a camping trip and Mara performed miracles with food over the campfire, proving that "the way to a man's heart is through his stomach." Bruno met Mara not long after he met Bridget, twenty years ago. He enjoyed Mara's friendship and they shared a love of Italy. Bridget was pleased that Bruno also cherished her eccentric friend.

A trip to Italy would never be complete for them without visiting Mara; this would be their ninth reunion.

On Bridget's first trip to Italy with Bruno, Mara had marched them immediately upon their arrival to the Mercado Centrale in Florence for a boiled beef panini. Never mind visual art—Italy was all about food for Mara. On various different trips, the three of them had met together for a few days in Bologna, in Gubbio, and in Spoleto. On some of these adventures, Lu, Mara's ex-husband and still-fast-friend, was with them. Then on one trip, Mara had simply remained in Assisi instead of returning to Eugene and had been there ever since—which, in part, explained the ex-husband. She managed to obtain her permesso (papers for ex-patriots enabling them to stay in Italy permanently and receive health benefits) using the same passion that she applied to other areas of her life: cooking, baking, being a counselor, an Italophile, and a Gattara extraordinaire.

A Gattara is a woman who feeds and cares for cats, both the strays and the opportunists. Mara rises every morning at 5:00 a.m. to join forces with another Gattara. The women travel from the top of Assisi to the bottom, often performing first aid or getting a cat to the vet if necessary. Occasionally a male friend—another Gattaro—joins them. They raise money through a cat organization to have wild cats spayed or neutered. Through every kind of weather, Mara joyfully ministers to her four-pawed friends.

Now, a misty morning in October, Bridget and Bruno boarded the bus that would take them to the train to Passignano by Lago de Trasimeno, where they would meet Mara. They had met in this same way six years earlier. It was an easy bus and train connection through farm country for Mara (from Assisi) to Italy's fourth- largest lake.

As soon as Bridget and Bruno got off the train, they found a bench where they could wait for Mara's train to arrive. When it did, moments later, Bridget's heart rose to her throat as she watched Mara step down from the train. What a sight for sore eyes, she thought, as Mara trudged toward them, bundled up in spite of the mild day and wearing a back pack with provisions and items like extra shoes and sweaters in case the need would arise in the next four hours.

Mara looked good. Bridget believed she was aging backwards. Mara would agree and say it was from all of the olive oil, cheese, salami and wine of Italy. Mara looked a bit like Helen Mirren, if Helen were playing the role of a pensioner and Gattara.

The three friends embraced, kissing two cheeks all around. Then they made their way through the small tourist town to the lake. Mara seemed distracted by her tale of Cleopatra's feline revolution in the neighborhood.

Mara had nearly missed the bus to the train because she had to wrest command

from the black temptress to allow the other cats to get to the food outside Mara's gate. The cat tales continued as they walked through a pleasant neighborhood with fenced courtyards, geraniums and inviting doorways. Mara stopped in her tracks in great surprise to announce, "Why don't I come here more often? I love it here!"

By then they were near the lake and could hear it gently lapping the shore. Small boats and pedal water floats dotted the edge. "And Rosito…" Mara continued, filling Bruno and Bridget in with the latest news of her most favorite cat of all.

They found their special restaurant, which was empty, but the owner was happy to serve them lunch. Bruno gave Mara the rechargeable batteries he had bought that would work in Mara's charger, and Bridget presented the plastic lids for cat food cans that Mara had also requested. She always had a request for things she simply couldn't find in Assisi and was overjoyed when they arrived. Earlier year's gifts had included four jars of peanut butter, and shoes with special soles that did not slip on the vertical stone paths that she walked early in the morning.

They ordered wine and an antipasto with fresh fish, scampi, clams and carpaccio (raw, thinly sliced fish). When the generous platter arrived, they toasted their good fortune and friendship. Soon Mara disappeared under the table. Bridget and Bruno could hear her chatting in Italian with a cat. They looked at each other and read each other's minds. There had been no "How have you been? How is the trip going? How is the family?"… No, Mara stayed beneath the table. Clearly she had reached a new level of preoccupation with cats.

When she did manage to bring herself up, Mara explained to her friends that the cats around the restaurant were probably sick of fish from the lake. She had prepared for the visit by getting the extra good cuts of meat from the butcher who helps feed some of her favorite cats, and bringing it to the cats she knew she would encounter by the lake. From the sounds coming from under the table, they clearly appreciated it.

She popped her head up again, soon after, to order. They would all have freshly-made pasta with sole. Indeed, it was a feast. As they ate, the three friends did get a chance to visit and share stories. The meal lasted two hours. Mara was always full of good insights about politics and human nature.

At the end of the meal, when Bruno and Bridget looked at the bill, they saw that a huge discount had been deducted from the total, the word GATARRA had been written at the bottom. They thanked the proprietor in their best Italian. Mara had remembered the bond she and the owner had formed over cats on a previous visit. Most Italians appreciated the Gattaras, although Mara told tales of the exceptions, of those who went so far as to poison cats.

They all crowded their faces into Bridget's small camera's frame for a selfie photo, then walked to the train station in a mellow mood. Bridget reminded Mara to come back to the lake. The weather was perfect. Mara hadn't needed the extra rain gear that she had packed after all.

At the station they sat on a bench. Bridget felt sad to say goodbye so quickly after hello. She wondered if she would ever see Mara again. Mara had vowed never to come back to the U.S. Bridget had pledged to Bruno not to plan any more trips out of the country until he could catch up on his glass work at home. He had work to finish that required long periods of concentration, so Bridget refrained from her habit of setting the wheels in motion for the next trip before the current trip was even complete.

As her eyes welled up with tears, she held in her heart the picture of them waving goodbye while boarding their separate trains.

The Creation of Me

I am from conglomeration – how rocks are made – little pieces of one thing and another hardened and patched together with the sands of time.

I am from farmers, people of arts and letters, loggers of forests, fiddle players, eccentric rulers in foreign lands, cattle drivers and forbidden ghost dancers.

I am from things made with our hands, fine laces and beaded buckskins, smooth butter and crunchy chitlins, fine furniture and cracking bullwhips.

I am from Saturday night musicians, preachers of hell-fire and brimstone, and users of the sweat lodge.

I am from men who were clean shaven and uncomplicated, who gave handshakes not contracts, who were always there for their neighbors.

I am from men who drank heavily of white lightning, who sang and danced and created their own wild stories with large and extended families.

I am from women of honesty and honor who wore dresses whether they plowed a field or made delicate embroidery stitches, they cooked without recipes and catered to their men.

I am from women who gave up their dreams in exchange for marital servitude, frustration, and bitterness.

I am from restrictions of what could be spoken, of artistic endeavor, of what could be worn and what could be consumed.

I am from freedom to roam and explore forested mountains scattered with numerous wild creatures, mysterious caves, and splashy giggling waters.

I am from violence and pain, whispered secrets and hidden bruises, addictions and illnesses of the brain.

I am from the storms that erode, little bits and pieces scatter, some are lost, some are added to one thing or another, hardened and patched together as the sands of time move on.

~ Wanda Edwards
Groundwaters, Vol 5 Iss 4 (2009)

About the Cover Photos

"Checkermallow Access"
front cover photo taken by Jennifer Chambers

"Driftwood Shores Visit
back cover photo taken by Jim Burnett

This photo was a lucky shot that I saw on a walk with my family in the fall of 2021. We are more careful than most with our pandemic activities, due to my autoimmune disease. This walk is in West Eugene at the poetically named "Checkermallow Access" point and bike/walking path off Greenhill Road. Part of the extensive bike path system in Eugene, the path is the perfect pandemic (or any time) walk because you can cover as much distance as you'd like, and walk the wide, level paths, safely distanced. At one point in the pandemic, we walked there twice a week! The path overlooks the West Eugene wildlife refuge. Often, we count how many varieties of birds we see there. I was so pleased to get this heron photo and its reflection to commemorate the way my family took good care of our physical and mental health as best as we could during this time. Give the path a try and see if it brings you peace.

In 2003, Pat Edwards' sister, Barbara Isborn, her brother, Jim Burnett, Pat and their spouses, took their 88-year old mother, Ruth Kinsman Ward, and her husband Chuck, to Driftwood Shores in Florence for a weekend outing. Since she wasn't able to navigate the sand trails down to the beach, one of Ruth's favorite things to do was feed the seagulls by hand from the second floor balcony. They would circle around and fly close enough to take food from her fingers. They never pecked her or scared her in any way. I don't remember what she was feeding them, but it was something that we all knew would not hurt them in any way.

"She thoroughly enjoyed that trip, and we have so many good memories of that special weekend. Mama lived to the age of 96 and I miss her still.

I came across this picture, which my brother took, in a folder on my computer of photos to possibly use on a future cover of *Groundwaters*. I forgot that it was there, but when I saw how well it complimented Jen's photo, I decided that this year was the time to use it."

Pat

A Letter to Groundwaters
By Mildred "Millie" Thacker Graves

From the time I was a little girl, I always wrote things. I wrote them; I read them. I felt they were of no value, so I wadded the papers up, and added them to the other items of no value in the wastepaper basket. Later they were burned in our wood-burning stove, giving me the proof that my writing was no good. It was only when I saw it in print that, finally, I could see that if someone believes it is good enough to print, and others are good enough to read it, maybe—just maybe—it is good. Seeing it in print gave me the courage to continue to write—if not necessarily for anyone else—but for my own feeling of accomplishment. The *Groundwaters* magazine and, later, the anthologies, gave that to me. A huge gift! Your staff, and Judy Hays-Eberts who began *Groundwaters* magazine many years ago, were the fires that lit the flame!

I am, and will ever be, grateful to each of you for giving me a voice—bad or good! I am also indebted to you all for giving my children confidence that they could do it, too. My son, Dana, who was a jock, interested in only sports in school, saw my poetry in *Groundwaters* and, at 27 years of age, child-like, said to himself, "If my Mom can write poetry, so can I—it's in my genes." And, so it began. His talent now far surpasses mine!

Now, at 86 years of age, I feel that writing is a bit of a legacy that I'll leave behind and *Groundwaters* made it happen! It has been wonderful, amazing, and somewhat mind-boggling to see the results of how the latter generations have been drawn into it. It's the gift that has kept on giving.

Thank you very much.

FROM THE BOOKSHELF

Pacifica Rising
by Jerry Brule

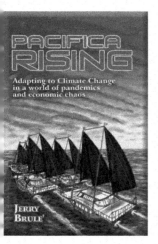

Pacifica Rising is a speculative fiction novel that takes place about 25 years in the future. Around that time there will be over 250 million people displaced from their homes by increasing wars, famine, floods, extreme weather, droughts, desertification, and heat zones that will be unlivable because of Climate Change. At the same time the population will increase by over two billion people. The earth is already too crowded, resources are running out, the rivers and aquifers are drying up, the farmland is becoming infertile, and the oceans are dying. Where will climate refugees go and what will they eat? 72% of the earth's surface is covered by oceans that are essentially unpopulated. Why not make it possible to live on the seas? *Pacifica Rising* explores how people can live and prosper on the oceans, and begin the healing of the earth and seas. *https://www.pacifica-rising.com*

Shoulder to Shoulder
by Evelyn Searle Hess

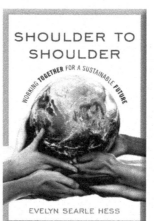

An antidote to despair about climate and social issues, *Shoulder to Shoulder* shows a path forward, telling real-life stories of people-power. Groups working together for the health of the world and each other find camaraderie and hope as they make a positive difference.
https://rowman.com/ISBN/9781538144398/Shoulder-to-Shoulder-Working-Together-for-a-Sustainable-Future discount until Dec. 31 use CODE RLFANDF30

Shakespeare's Money Talks
by Alexandra Mason

In this long-awaited revised and expanded second edition of "Econolingua," now entitled "Shakespeare's Money Talks," Alexandra Mason offers an easily-accessible classic reference work to all lovers of Shakespeare and his dramatic times. Shakespeare's world and his characters come to life in this study of metaphor as they self-consciously test the limits of words and their exchange function in establishing social hierarchy, social status and value. Each glossed term conveniently gives the phrase of its usage in the entry, both the literal and the metaphorical for full illumination. Introductory and supplemental essays catalogue dramatic usage of econolingua (terms related to coins, money and value) and discuss "Usury and the Right Uses of Wealth" and "Shakespeare's Economics," the impact of a changing system of social value on the structures of his plays.

Happy Christmas Miss Lawrence
by Jeanette-Marie Mirich

Set in England at Christmas time, this romantic mystery takes the reader on a merry ride. Amateur Steeplechase Jockey, Robin Huntington is confused then suspicious when he's asked to aid an innocent appearing young woman in a legal tangle. Finding a missionary in the slammer isn't Robin's only problem, his family is involved in Alexandra Lawrence's arrest. Lies, jealousy, and greed are what is served at a family gathering...

You Promised Me Paris
by Jeanette-Marie Mirich

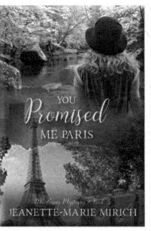

This is the third mystery in the D.B. Burns mystery series.

Discovering a young man with a knife in his chest was not exactly what Delilah Burns Morgan planned for her honeymoon.

Delilah did not have a dream wedding. In fact, after their vows, she and Lyle raced for a court appearance which revealed decades of secrets in their small Kentucky town...

As they unwrap the wonders of their newfound love while trying to uncover the secrets of a murder, a suspicious real estate agent, and a shady new neighbor, will Lyle and Delilah learn to work as a team?

We Are Akan
by Dorothy Brown Soper

Our People and Our Kingdom in the Rainforest - Ghana, 1807

In a richly illustrated story middle grade readers join Kwame, Kwaku, and Baako, two royals and a slave, who strive to become leaders in the Akan culture of the Asante Kingdom. Adventures abound at home, in the capital city, and on a mission to the coast where two boys are kidnapped and threatened with sale to the Atlantic slave trade. Visit the author at *http://www.dorothybrownsoper.com* to see the illustrations in downloadable format, hear recordings of the Akan language, and find links to buy the book.

Index

Groundwaters Publishing, LLC
P.O. Box 50, Lorane, OR 97451
http://groundwaterspublishing.com